# THE LAW AND THE LAWYERS

BY
M. K. GANDHI

Compiled and Edited by
S. B. KHER

NAVAJIVAN PUBLISHING HOUSE
AHMEDABAD-380 014

**Rupees Forty**

© Navajivan Trust, 1962

First Edition, October 1962
Revised Edition, January 1999
New Revised Edition, 2,000 Copies, May 2004
Third Reprint, 3,000 Copies, May 2009
Total : 41,000 Copies

ISBN 81-7229-051-9

Printed and Published by
Jitendra T. Desai
Navajivan Publishing House
Ahmedabad-380 014
( INDIA )

Phone : 079 – 27540635, 27542634
Fax : 079 – 27541329
E-mail : jtndrnavajivan@hotmail.com
Website : www.navajivantrust.org

# INTRODUCTION

1. Mahatma Gandhi sailed for England on 4th September, 1888 to study law and become a barrister. He kept terms at the Inner Temple and after nine months' intensive study he took all his subjects in one examination which he passed. He was called to the Bar on 10th June, 1891 and was enrolled in the High Court of England the next day. A day later, he sailed home. After his return to India he started practice as a lawyer at first in the High Court at Bombay and a little later in Rajkot but did not make much headway in the profession. It was only when the hand of destiny guided his steps to South Africa that he soon made his mark there as a lawyer and as a public worker. Gandhiji practised as a lawyer for over twenty years before he gave up the practice of the profession in order to devote all his time and energy to public service. The valuable experience and skill that he acquired in the course of his large and lucrative practice stood him in good stead in fighting his battles with the South African and British governments for securing political, economic and social justice for his fellow-countrymen. Gandhiji was not a visionary but a practical idealist. As Sir Stafford Cripps has remarked : "He was no simple mystic; combined with his religious outlook was his lawyer-trained mind, quick and apt in reasoning. He was a formidable opponent in argument."[1]

2. Gandhiji went to South Africa in April 1893 and stayed for a whole year in Pretoria in connection with the case of Sheth Dada Abdulla who was involved in a civil suit with his near relative Sheth Tyeb Haji Khan Mahammad who also stayed in Pretoria. The year's

---

1. M. K. Gandhi, *Homage to the Departed*, p. 146

stay in Pretoria proved to be a most valuable
experience in Gandhiji's life. Here it was that he had
opportunities of learning public work and acquired
some measure of his capacity for it. Here it was that
the religious spirit within him became a living force. It
was here too that he acquired a true knowledge of legal
practice and learnt the things that a junior barrister
learns in a senior barrister's chamber and also gained
confidence that he would not after all fail as a lawyer.
It was likewise here that he learnt the secret of success
as a lawyer.[2] Dada Abdulla's was no small or ordinary
case. The suit which he had filed against Tyeb Sheth
who was his near relative claiming £ 40,000/- arose out
of business transactions and was full of intricacies of
accounts. The claim was based partly on promissory
notes and partly on the specific performance of promise
to deliver promissory notes. The defence was that the
promissory notes had been fraudulently obtained and
lacked sufficient consideration[3]. There were numerous
points of fact and law in this intricate case and both
sides had engaged the best attorneys and counsel.[4] The
preparation of the plaintiff's case involved much patient
industry and close study of facts. Furthermore it
needed clear thinking and judgment.[5] Gandhiji took the
keenest interest in the case and threw himself heart
and soul into it.[6] He gained the complete confidence of

---

2. M K. Gandhi, *An Autobiography,* De Luxe Edition
Vol. I (1968), p. 195

3. *Ibid,* p. 195

4. *Ibid,* p. 195

5. Pyarelal, *Mahatma Gandhi — The Early Phase,*
Vol. 1, p. 313

6. M. K. Gandhi, *An Autobiography,* De Luxe Edition
Vol.1 (1968), p. 196

both the parties and persuaded them to submit the suit to an arbitrator of their choice instead of continuing with expensive, prolonged, and bitter litigation. The arbitrator ruled in Dada Abdulla Sheth's favour, and awarded him £37,000/- and costs. It was however impossible for Tyeb Sheth to pay down the whole of the awarded amount. Gandhiji then managed to persuade Dada Abdulla to let Tyeb Sheth pay him the money in moderate instalments spread over a long period of years, rather than ruin him by insisting on an immediate settlement.[7] Gandhiji was overjoyed at the success of his first case in South Africa and concluded that the whole duty of an advocate was not to exploit legal and adversary advantages but to promote compromise and reconciliation.[8]

3. It was Dada Abdulla's case which enabled Gandhiji to realize early in his career the paramount importance of facts. As he observes in his autobiography "facts mean truth and once we adhere to truth, the law comes to our aid naturally".[9] Facts according to Gandhiji constituted three-fourths of the law and if we took care of the facts of a case the law would take care of itself. As a result of this realization of the paramount importance of facts in Dada Abdulla's case, Gandhiji was never known afterwards to brush aside or slur over a fact however inconvenient or prejudicial it might seem. Strict adherence to this principle enabled him more than once in a crisis to find

---

7. Ved Mehta, *Mahatma Gandhi and His Apostles,* Penguin Books (1983), pp. 100, 101

8. Ved Mehta, *Mahatma Gandhi and His Apostles,* Penguin Books (1983), p. 101

9. M. K. Gandhi, *An Autobiography* De Luxe Edition, Vol. I (1968), pp. 196, 197

a way out of what to all intents and purposes looked like an impenetrable ring of steel.[10] From this and several similar experiences Gandhiji learnt to regard law not as an intellectual legerdemain to make black appear white and white black, but as "codified ethics". The profession of law became to him the means to enthrone justice, not "entangle justice" in the net of law.[11]

4. From 1893 till 1913 Gandhiji practised in South Africa. Early in his practice he realized that "the true function of a lawyer was to unite parties riven asunder". "This lesson", he writes, "was so indelibly burnt into me that a large part of my time during the twenty years of my practice as a lawyer was occupied in bringing about private compromises of hundreds of cases."[12]

5. If there was one characteristic more than another that stamped Gandhi as a man amongst men, it was his extraordinary love of truth. The Mahatma was an ardent and inveterate votary of truth. Truth, like nonviolence, was the first article of his faith and the last article of his creed. It was therefore no wonder that in his practice of the law, he maintained the highest traditions of the profession and did not swerve by a hair's breadth from the path of rectitude and integrity. He was always valiant for truth, bold in asserting it in scorn of all consequence, and never sold the truth to serve the interests of his clients. He never forgot "that if he was the advocate of an individual, and *retained* and remunerated, often inadequately, for his

10. Pyarelal, *Mahatma Gandhi ~ The Early Phase,* Vol. I, p. 313

11. *Ibid*, p. 313

12. M. K. Gandhi, *An Autobiography* (1959), p. 97

valuable services, yet he had a prior and perpetual *retainer* on behalf of truth and justice." It may truly be said of him that he practised law without compromising truth. As he observes, "My principle was put to the test many a time in South Africa. Often I knew that my opponents had tutored their witnesses, and if I only encouraged my client or his witnesses to lie, we could win the case. But I always resisted the temptation. . . . In my heart of hearts I always wished that I should win only if my client's case was right. . . . I warned every new client at the outset that he should not expect me to take up a false case or to coach the witnesses, with the result that I built up such a reputation that no false cases used to come to me. Indeed some of my clients would keep their clean cases for me, and take the doubtful ones elsewhere."[13]

Thorough-going and meticulous as a matter of habit, he took extraordinary pains to study every case. He earned the esteem of his colleagues as much as that of the magistrates and judges who had come to respect him for clarity of thought and expression, legal acumen and intellectual vigour.[14] The way he argued his cases before the judges was typical of him. Free from heat and passion, he scrupulously avoided aggressive advocacy and relied entirely on facts and reasoning. It was his habit not to hide any flaw in his brief. In presenting the case he liked to reveal the whole truth. The frankness with which he would admit a weak point gave him added strength to put things in their proper perspective and to focus attention on the critical issues

---

13. M. K. Gandhi, *An Autobiography* (1959), p. 267

14. *Gandhi Ordained in South Africa* by J. U. Uppal p. 87, Publications Division, Minsitry of Information and Broadcasting, Government of India, 1995.

which generally determined the outcome of a legal dispute.[15] Truth was the only touchstone by which he judged his duty toward his client and the court. According to him the greatest wrong a lawyer could commit in the process of law was to be a party to the miscarriage of justice.[16]

He had the reputation, among both professional colleagues and his clients, of being a very sound lawyer and was held in the highest esteem by the courts. They all recognized his complete integrity and uprightness.[17] Magistrates and judges alike paid careful attention to any case that he advocated realizing that it had intrinsic merits or that he sincerely believed that it had. An expert cross-examiner, he seldom failed to break down a dishonest witness.[18] Gandhiji was, however, equally strict with his own clients. He had been known to retire from a case in open court, and in the middle of the hearing, having realized that his client had deceived him. He made it a practice to inform his client before accepting his brief that if, at any stage of litigation, he was satisfied that he was being deceived, he would be at liberty to hand back his brief, for, as an officer of the Court, he could not knowingly deceive it.[19] During his professional work it was Gandhiji's habit never to conceal his ignorance

---

15. *Gandhi Ordained in South Africa* by J. U. Uppal p. 88, Publications Division, Ministry of Information and Broadcasting, Government of India, 1995.

16. *Ibid* p. 87

17 Polak, Brailsford and Lord Pethick-Lawrence, *Mahatma Gandhi*, p. 49

18. D. G. Tendulkar, *Mahatma*, Vol. I, p. 84

19. Polak, Brailsford and Lord Pethick-Lawrence, *Mahatma Gandhi*, p. 49

from his clients or his colleagues. Wherever he felt himself at sea, he would advise his client to consult some other counsel, or if he preferred to stick to Gandhiji, he would ask his client to let him seek the assistance of senior counsel. This frankness earned Gandhiji the unbounded affection and trust *of* his clients who were always willing to pay the fee whenever consultation with senior counsel was necessary.[20] As far as possible, Gandhiji advised his clients to settle with their opponents out of Court. A large part of his legal practice was in the interest of public work, for which he charged nothing beyond out-of-pocket expenses, and these too he sometimes met himself.[21] Where poor people were concerned he charged them very low fees, or did not charge at all. In fixing his fees, he never made them conditional on his winning the case. Whether his client won or lost, he expected nothing more nor less than his fees.[22] At the same time, he never issued a notice of demand against a client who committed a default in payment of fees due to him, threatening legal proceedings if the debt was not speedily liquidated, and steadfastly refused to invoke the law to secure payment of his fees, for he held that his client, if an honest man, would pay when he could, and if a dishonest man, would not be made the more honest by the use of legal compulsion.[23] Indeed, in his every action, the Mahatma vindicated his hostility to the doctrine of force and his abiding faith in that of love as a rule of life.

---

20 M. K. Gandhi, *An Autobiography*, (1959), pp. 269-270

21 *Ibid*, p. 266.

22. *Ibid*

23. Polak, Brailsford and Lord Pethick-Lawrence, *Mahatma Gandhi*, p. 50

6. Practice as a lawyer, however, was and always remained for Gandhiji a subordinate occupation. A considerable part of his time during active practice was devoted to public service which was almost a passion with him. As his Satyagraha campaigns against the South African Government for its racial and discriminatory policies, based on colour prejudice, against Indians and Negroes, gathered momentum and spread throughout the length and breadth of South Africa, the compulsion of political events made it increasingly difficult for him to attend to the needs of his clients. Besides he also felt that in the Satyagraha struggle, only devoted Satyagrahis could be relied upon, since in no circumstances would they surrender to temptation or to fear of the consequences. Furthermore, as his views about truth and non-violence crystallized and matured, he came to the conclusion that to earn one's livelihood from a profession, which finally made an appeal to the policeman or the jailer to enforce the decrees of the courts, and thus derived its ultimate sanction from physical force, was a denial of Ahimsa.[24] Accordingly, in 1910 Gandhiji entirely abandoned the practice of law and henceforth devoted his entire time and energy to the service of the community. Thereafter, in the remaining years of his earthly sojourn, whether in South Africa or in India, Gandhiji, as a Satyagrahi, was very often engaged in breaking laws rather than in expounding or interpreting them in the courts of the land. It may here be recalled that when, after his imprisonment in 1922, during his first civil disobedience movement in India, he was disbarred by his Inn, he would not apply thereafter for reinstatement, as he regarded himself as a farmer and

---

24. Polak, Brailsford and Lord Pethick Lawrence, *Mahatma Gandhi*, p. 78

a handicraftsman, who had renounced the profession of law deliberately many years before in South Africa.

7. It may interest the reader to know that the Inner Temple which had disbarred Gandhiji in 1922 after his imprisonment during his first civil disobedience movement in India has since not only restored his name on its rolls but honoured his immortal memory by unveiling in 1984 his special portrait in the library of the Inner Temple.[25]

Furthermore, Gandhiji's bust now adorns the coffee room of the Inner Temple and his statue has been installed in its lawns.[26]

8. Gandhiji's role as a lawyer in society has been very forcefully described by the American author Mr. James Cavanagh who in a warm and moving tribute to his work observed :

There is a famous non-lawyer of recent history, who comes close to being, like Lincoln, a transfigured lawyer, a lawyer who has simply grown beyond the usual confines rather than grown away from them, who has enlarged the scope of the lawyer's functions rather than changed them, who has kept the virtues of the lawyer and only deepened them. He loved his country and its people; he respected civil authority even while opposing it; his weapons were non-violence and passive resistance; his aims were moderate and realistic; he was willing to negotiate and to advance step by step; he was humble in manner and took as his symbols the simple handicrafts of his people. And true to the negative leadership the lawyer exercises, he became a martyr to his country's liberty. He was an Indian lawyer

---

25. See Appendix VII, letter to the Editor by Lord Denning dated 15-12-1984.

26. See column entitled 'Out of Court' *Times of India*, 28-10-2001 by Soli S. Sorabjee.

named Gandhi.[27]

9. Parts I and II of the book deal with Gandhiji as a law student and as a practising barrister. The Editor craves the indulgence of the reader for including in these parts, some portions of Gandhiji's *Autobiography* which, strictly speaking, have no bearing on the subject of this book. This however was unavoidable and had to be done in order to maintain the thread of continuity in the narrative, and to make it clear, coherent and consistent.

10. Part III of the book contains the political trials of Gandhiji in South Africa and in India. Here Gandhiji appears in the role of a Satyagrahi, as a civil resister of unjust laws. The trial of Gandhiji at Ahmedabad in 1922 on the charge of sedition will for ever remain one of the most momentous and memorable events of modern times. The trial aroused considerable interest not only in India, but also in Europe and America. In many respects it was a most remarkable trial. Never before was such a prisoner arraigned before a British court of justice. Never before were the laws of an all—powerful government so defiantly, yet with such humility, challenged. Men of all shades of political opinion, indeed all who had stood aloof from the movement and had condemned it in no uncertain terms, marvelled at the wisdom, compassion and heroism of the thin spare figure in a loin cloth thundering his anathemas against the Government. And yet none could be gentler nor more sweet-tempered than the prisoner at the bar with a smile and a nod of thanks and recognition for every one including his prosecutors.[28] The unique personality of the principal

---

27. James J. Cavanagh, *The Lawyer in Society*
28. *Speeches and Writings of Mahatma Gandhi,* 3rd ed.. Natesan, Madras, p. 62

accused before the Court, his international reputation as a saint and patriot, the offence with which he was charged, the political situation then prevailing in the country and the probable consequences of his conviction on the political future of India, all these combined, made the occasion momentous and invested the trial with a historic significance. The trial being on so ennobling a plane brought forth the best that could conceivably be expected from the one who judged and the one who was judged. The trial indeed was noteworthy, both for the dignity of the prisoner at the bar, and also for the noble utterance of the judge who delivered the sentence. Much of the bitterness at the time was taken away from men's minds owing to the judge's speech.[29] The late Mrs. Sarojini Naidu, a close associate of the Mahatma in the freedom struggle, who was present at the trial, has with her usual felicity of expression given a very vivid and moving account of the trial which will interest the reader. She wrote :

A convict and a criminal in the eyes of the law : Nevertheless the entire Court rose in an act of spontaneous homage when Mahatma Gandhi entered — a frail, serene, indomitable figure in a coarse and scanty loin cloth, accompanied by his devoted disciple and fellow-prisoner, Shankarlal Banker.

'So you are seated near me to give me your support in case I break down,' he jested, with that happy laugh of his which seems to hold all the undimmed radiance of the world's childhood in its depths. And looking round at the hosts of familiar faces of men and women who had travelled far to offer him a token of their love, he added, 'This is like a family gathering and not a Law Court.'

---

29. *Mahatma Gandhiji's Ideas* by C. F. Andrews, pp. 290, 291

A thrill of mingled fear, pride, hope and anguish ran through the crowded hall when the judge took his seat — an admirable judge deserving of our praise alike for his brave and resolute sense of duty, his flawless courtesy, his just perception of a unique occasion and his fine tribute to a unique personality.

The strange trial proceeded and as I listened to the immortal words that flowed with prophetic fervour from the lips of my beloved master, my thoughts sped across the centuries to a different land and a different age, when a similar drama was enacted and another divine and gentle teacher was crucified, for spreading a kindred gospel with a kindred courage. I realized anew that the lowly Jesus of Nazareth cradled in a manger furnished the only true parallel in history to this sweet, invincible apostle of Indian liberty who has loved humanity with surpassing compassion and to use his own beautiful phrase, 'approached the poor with the mind of the poor'.

The pent-up emotion of the people burst in a storm of sorrow as a long, slow procession moved towards him in a mournful pilgrimage of farewell, clinging to the hands that had toiled so incessantly, bowing over the feet that had overruled so continuously, in the service of his country.

In the midst of this poignant scene of many-voiced and myriad-hearted grief he stood untroubled in all his transcendent simplicity, the embodied symbol of the Indian Nation, its living sacrifice and sacrament in one.[30]

The whole trial lasted one hundred minutes, each minute enacting a page in the history of the battle of India's freedom.[31]

---

30. *Speeches and Writings of Mahatma Gandhi*, 3rd ed., Natesan, Madras, Appendix II, p. 45

31. Chief Justice Shelat's introduction to the *Trial of Gandhi*, p.XXXV, Gujarat High Court Publication, 1965

The three articles written and published by Gandhiji in his weekly paper *Young India* for which he was tried on the charge of sedition have been reproduced in Appendix I at pp. 246-53

11. The trial which took place on March 18, 1922 in the small crowded court-room in Ahmedabad before the District and Sessions Judge Robert Broomfield, was so calm, so orderly, so lacking in contentiousness and anger, that it assumed the character of a quiet confrontation between two men who had known and studied each other for a long time. The judge was mild-mannered and apologetic. He gave the impression of a man who was performing a distasteful task with courtesy and good sense. Gandhiji was quietly content and would sometimes break out in smiles. [32] The judge was the son of a lawyer and he had a long experience of the law. He came to India as a junior barrister attached to the Indian Civil Service in 1905, and had spent all his active life within the Bombay Presidency. He generally liked the Indians and had a considerable respect amounting almost to affection for Gandhiji.[33] The tone of the trial was set by the judge when he took his seat, bowing gravely to the distinguished prisoner. Gandhiji returned the bow.[34] The trial which was listed as "Sessions Case No. 45, Imperator V. (1) Mr. M. K. Gandhi, (2) Mr. S. C. Banker," was concerned to punish the author of three seditious and inflammatory articles which had appeared in *Young India* at intervals during the previous year 1921.

12. The trial came to be known as "the great trial",

---

32. *The Life and Death of Mahatma Gandhi* by Robert Payne, Rupa & Co., Mumbai 1997 p. 361.

33. Ibid p. 363

34. Ibid p. 368

because both the judge and the prisoner behaved with uncommon courtesy and because Gandhiji had stated the case for India's freedom with fairness and precision.[35]

13. Sir Thomas Strangman who as the Advocate-General of Bombay conducted the prosecution of Gandhiji on behalf of the State was deeply moved by the prevailing atmosphere of the trial. In his interesting account of the trial he observed :

The trial took place at Ahmedabad on the 18th March 1922. I went up from Bombay to conduct the prosecution. On arrival I was at once struck by the magnetic influence exercised by Gandhi upon the officials. The prevailing note was one of sadness. It was realized, of course, that Gandhi had been conducting the most dangerous campaign, that that campaign had resulted in considerable bloodshed and disorder, and that one course and one only was possible, viz., the course which had been adopted. None the less, the thought uppermost in the minds of the officials was the extreme pity of it all — pity that it should be necessary to prosecute so charming a personality. As illustrative of the prevailing atmosphere: The Collector who had come up to the station to meet me left me to see that various Indian ladies, supporters of Gandhi, who had come up from Bombay by the same train in order to attend the trial, should obtain proper conveyances to their destinations.

Gandhi had prepared a written statement. Before reading it he dealt orally with what I had said. . . . Gandhi then proceeded to read the written statement in which he set out at length how he had come to lose faith in the British Government and stated that he saw no course open to him but that which he had adopted. Whilst Gandhi was

---

35. *The Life and Death of Mahatma Gandhi* by Robert Payne, Rupa & Co., Mumbai 1997, p. 361.

reading the statement an incident occurred which exemplified the atmosphere of the trial. He referred to some incident as having taken place in a particular year. The District Superintendent of Police interposed in the most friendly way. He said : "I think you have made a mistake, surely it took place in the following year?" Gandhi thanked him for his assistance and made the necessary correction in the statement.. So ended the trial. I confess that I myself was not wholly unaffected by the atmosphere of the trial.[36]

14. Gandhiji's speech at the trial pleading guilty to the offence of sedition with which he had been charged and inviting Judge Broomfield to inflict on him the severest penalty has now become a part of English Literature and finds a place of honour in the great legal classic *The Law as Literature*[37] which contains an anthology of great writing about and in the law such as essays, accounts, letters, opinions, pleas and transcripts from Plato to the present times.

15. Barring the trial of Socrates there is perhaps no trial in the history of mankind, comparable to that of Gandhiji, which stimulated so much interest and whose influence on the life of humanity has been so profound. Involving as it did the issue of morality versus law, it is but natural that the trial of Gandhiji must immediately bring to mind that kindred trial involving kindred issue. Meletus, the prosecutor of Socrates, indicted the accused of two charges : one of not worshipping the gods whom the state of Athens worshipped and the other of introducing novel religious

---

36. Sir Thomas Strangman, *Indian Courts and Characters,* William Heinemann Ltd., London (1931), pp. 136-143

37. See *The Law as Literature,* edited by Ephraim, London (1970), pp. 459-466

practices and of corrupting the young by his teachings. He demanded the penalty of death. The similarity of attitude adopted by Socrates and Gandhiji towards the Tribunals which tried them is at once manifest, for each placed Truth above law and sought the punishment which the breach of the law warranted.[38]

16. Why has the trial of Gandhiji been universally acknowledged to be a great historic trial out-shadowing all similar trials of leaders and patriots? Surely, not merely because of the personality of the accused, nor because of his extra-ordinary sway over India's teeming millions whom he treated as his own, nor because of its consequences on the political future of India. There is no doubt that these were all contributory factors which invested the trial with a historic significance. However the chief and most important factor which made the trial historic was the profound issue involved in it, namely, that of obedience to law as against obedience to moral duty. It was that issue which elevated the trial to the highest plane and the characters too who played their part in it. The issue raised by Gandhiji in the trial was not an isolated, sporadic issue arising from the breach of Section 124A of the Penal Code though it apparently was made to appear so. It was the perennial issue of Law versus Conscience, an issue of abiding interest to all civilized people of all times. It invoked the inalienable moral right and duty to resist a system of governance whose only claim to loyalty and obedience was superior physical might. The trial is of profound and momentous significance in that Gandhiji during the trial sought to establish beyond doubt the superiority of soul force over

---

38. See Chief Justice Shelat's introduction to *The Trial of Gandhi. p.* III, Gujarat High Court Publication, 1965.

sheer brute force, born out of the gospel of self-suffering and the doctrine of wilful yet holy withdrawal from all that is foul, base and unholy in human behaviour, a conclusion which will have an abiding purpose and a meaning until humanity survives.[39]

17. Part IV of the book discusses the role of lawyers in the Satyagraha struggle. It also gives an account of the farcical political trials held in the Punjab in 1919 during the Martial Law regime, when several innocent persons were sentenced by special courts to death or life-imprisonment on the flimsiest of evidence. These trials indeed furnish a sad commentary on the administration of justice in Punjab during that period of great storm and stress. Part V deals with Gandhiji's views on sundry and miscellaneous topics having some bearing on the subject of this book. Appendix II contains select thoughts of Gandhiji on the law and the lawyers. Appendix III contains the text of the speech of the late B. N. Gokhale, ex-judge of the Bombay High Court at the symposium organized by the Bombay Branch of the Gandhi Smarak Nidhi on 1-7-1963 in which he dealt with Gandhiji's legal philosophy. Appendix IV contains Gandhiji's application dated 16-11-1891 for enrolment as an advocate of the Bombay High Court. Appendix V contains Gandhiji's certificate of being called to the Bar by Inner Temple. Appendix VI contains the certificate from Mr. W. D. Edwards, author and practising barrister in the Supreme Court of Judicature in England recommending Gandhiji's name for admission as an advocate of the High Court of Bombay. Appendix VII contains the order issued by the Benchers of Inner Temple on 10th November 1922

---

39. See Chief Justice Shelat's introduction to the *Trial of Gandhi,* p. XXXVI

disbarring Gandhiji and removing his name from the
roll of barristers on his conviction and sentence to six
years' imprisonment on 18th March 1922 by the Court
of the Sessions Judge, Ahmedabad. Appendix VIII is a
letter from the eminent judge and jurist Lord Denning
to the Editor informing him that the Inner Temple
which had disbarred Gandhiji in 1922 after his
imprisonment during his first civil disobedience
movement in India and had restored his name on its
rolls shortly after India attained freedom had honoured
Gandhiji's memory by unveiling in 1984 his special
portrait in the library of the Inner Temple. Last is the
glossary of Indian terms used in the book with their
English translation.

18. Many people regard the law as something of a
mystery, and there is a considerable amount of
prejudice against the lawyers which exists in the minds
of many members of the public. The lawyer's profession
is regarded by many people as a liar's profession. It
seems strange and indeed wrong to the ordinary
citizen, that a man of honour and integrity should
defend a man that he must know in his heart to be
guilty of the crime with which he is charged and be
paid for doing so. 'How is it possible', men say, 'for an
advocate to resist an argument that appears to be
founded on truth, and to seek to make the worse
appear the better reason?' For, put quite starkly, the
charge against the advocate is that he cannot possibly
be sincere or indeed honest in the conduct of his
profession. For the ordinary citizen only espouses some
particular cause because he believes in it, but the
advocate espouses a cause because he is paid to do so,
whether he believes in it or not.[40] This is the perennial

---

40. Lord Birkett, *Six Great Advocates,* p. 98

ethical indictment against the profession and it was put into its most deadly form by the strange and erratic genius, Dean Swift, *in Gulliver's Travels,* when he said of the Bar that 'they were a society of men bred up from their youth in the art of proving by words multiplied for the purpose, that white is black and black is white according as they are paid.' This charge is effectively answered by the Mahatma who believed in spiritualizing not only public life but also the practice of the legal profession. Says he, "And there is another thing I would like to warn you against. In England, in South Africa, almost everywhere I have found that in the practice of their profession lawyers are consciously or unconsciously led into untruth for the sake of their clients. An eminent English lawyer has gone so far as to say that it may even be the duty of a lawyer to defend a client whom he knows to be guilty. There I disagree. The duty of a lawyer is always to place before the judges, and to help them to arrive at, the truth, never to prove the guilty as innocent."[41]

19. Year by year, the enlightened opinion of the world enshrines Gandhi in a noble place in the hearts of mankind. The life and example of the Mahatma who ennobled the legal profession, who remained faithful to its highest traditions, and who showed the heights to which it can be raised ought to form part of the teaching and training of every law student. At a time when the legal and professional standards among both judges and lawyers have fallen woefully, it behoves the legal fraternity to bestir itself and infuse a moral tone into the profession by pledging itself with renewed vigour and deep devotion to the ideals and the precepts of Gandhiji and presenting him to the profession as a

---

41. *Young India,* 22-12-1927, p. 42

model truly worthy of the closest emulation.

18. This book will have more than served its purpose if it inspires the reader, be he a lawyer or a layman, with the belief that the vocation of the lawyer is an honourable vocation requiring the highest standards of rectitude, integrity and uprightness, and that its practice is in no way inconsistent with the pursuit of truth.

Bombay, 2nd October, 1962

Sunit B. Kher

# ACKNOWLEDGEMENTS

Acknowledgements with thanks are due to G. A. Natesan & Co. for quoting some extracts from the book, *Speeches and Writings of Mahatma Gandhi,* (3rd edition), and to Khadi Gramodyog for reproducing the speech of the late B. N. Gokhale, ex-judge of the Bombay High Court dealing with Gandhiji's legal philosophy.

# PREFACE TO THE FOURTH EDITION

This book was published in 1962. The sale of the book received a great fillip when the Gujarat and the Saurashtra Universities prescribed the book as a text book for the paper on professional conduct, advocacy and drafting in the third LL.B. examination. The second edition was published in 1975. It is a matter of great satisfaction that the third edition which was published in 1981 was sold out within two years.

The year 1983 will above all be remembered as the year of the screening of the epic movie 'Gandhi'. The film despite certain historical and chronological inaccuracies revived memories of the greatest man of this century, received universal acclaim and recognition, was adjudged the best film of the year, won several international awards and Oscars, and made a deep and abiding impact on audiences at home and abroad. The film also revived public interest in the Gandhian literature and as a result several copies of this book were sold throughout the country as also abroad.

While preparing the fourth edition, I came across some further useful material on the subject which has been referred to in the Introduction and incorporated in the book. I earnestly hope that the law students not only of Gujarat and Saurashtra but also of other Universities in the country will find the book useful and derive inspiration from it in the practice of their profession. As Gandhiji has rightly observed 'a true lawyer is one who places truth and service in the first place and the emoluments of the profession in the next place only.'

HIGH COURT,                                    SUNIT B. KHER
BOMBAY, March 19, 1984

# CONTENTS

## Section I : Gandhiji as a Law Student

## Section II : Gandhiji as a Lawyer

## Section III : The Trials of Gandhiji

## Section IV : Lawyers and Satyagraha

## Section V : Miscellaneous

## Appendices

# THE LAW AND THE LAWYERS

# TO THE READER

I would like to say to the diligent reader of my writings and to others who are interested in them that I am not at all concerned with appearing to be consistent. In my search after Truth I have discarded many ideas and learnt many new things. Old as I am in age, I have no feeling that I have ceased to grow inwardly or that my growth will stop at the dissolution of the flesh. What I am concerned with is my readiness to obey the call of Truth, my God, from moment to moment, and, therefore, when anybody finds any inconsistency between any two writings of mine, if he has still faith in my sanity, he would do well to choose the later of the two on the same subject.

M. K. Gandhi

*Harijan*, 29-4-1933 p. 2

# SECTION I
## GANDHIJI AS A LAW STUDENT

### 1
### PREPARATION FOR ENGLAND

I passed the matriculation examination in 1887. It then used to be held at two centres, Ahmedabad and Bombay. The general poverty of the country naturally led Kathiawad students to prefer the nearer and the cheaper centre. The poverty of my family likewise dictated to me the same choice. This was my first journey from Rajkot to Ahmedabad and that too without a companion.

My elders wanted me to pursue my studies at college after the matriculation. There was a college in Bhavnagar as well as in Bombay, and as the former was cheaper, I decided to go there and join the Samaldas College. I went, but found myself entirely at sea. Everything was difficult. I could not follow, let alone taking interest in, the professors' lectures. It was no fault of theirs. The professors in that college were regarded as first-rate. But I was so raw. At the end of the first term, I returned home.

We had in Mavji Dave, who was a shrewd and learned Brahman, an old friend and adviser of the family. He had kept up his connection with the family even after my father's death. He happened to visit us during my vacation. In conversation with my mother and elder brother, he inquired about my studies. Learning that I was at Samaldas College, he said: 'The times are changed. And none of you can expect to succeed to your father's *gadi* without having had a proper education. Now as this boy is still pursuing his studies, you should all look to him to keep the *gadi*. It will take him four or five years to get his B.A. degree, which will at best qualify him for a sixty rupees' post, not for a Diwanship. If like my son he went in for law, it would take him still longer, by which time there would be a host of lawyers aspiring for a Diwan's post. I would far rather that you sent him to England. My son Kevalram says it is very easy to become a barrister. In three years' time he will return. Also expenses will not exceed four to five thousand rupees. Think of that barrister who has just come back from England. How stylishly he lives! He could get the Diwanship for the asking. I would strongly advise you to send Mohandas to England this very year. Kevalram has numerous friends in England. He will give notes of introduction to them, and Mohandas will have an easy time of it there.'

Joshiji—that is how we used to call old Mavji Dave—turned to me with complete assurance, and asked: 'Would you not rather go to England than study here?' Nothing could have been more welcome to me. I was fighting shy of my difficult studies. So I jumped at the proposal and said that the sooner I was sent the better. It was no easy business to pass examinations quickly. Could I not be sent to qualify for the medical profession?

My brother interrupted me: 'Father never liked it. He had you in mind when he said that we Vaishnavas should have nothing to do with dissection of dead bodies. Father intended you for the bar.'

Joshiji chimed in : 'I am not opposed to the medical profession as was Gandhiji. Our Shastras are not against it. But a medical degree will not make a Diwan of you, and I want you to be Diwan, or if possible something better. Only in that way could you take under your protecting care your large family. The times are fast changing and getting harder every day. It is the wisest thing therefore to become a barrister. Turning to my mother he said: 'Now, I must leave. Pray ponder over what I have said. When I come here next I shall expect to hear of preparations for England. Be sure to let me know if I can assist in any way.'

Joshiji went away, and I began building castles in the air.

My elder brother was greatly exercised in his mind. How was he to find the wherewithal to send me? And was it proper to trust a young man like me to go abroad alone?

My mother was sorely perplexed. She did not like the idea of parting with me. This is how she tried to put me off: 'Uncle,' she said, 'is now the eldest member of the family. He should first be consulted. If he consents we will consider the matter.'

My brother had another idea. He said to me: 'We have a certain claim on the Porbandar State. Mr. Lely is the Administrator. He thinks highly of our family and uncle is in his good books. It is just possible that he might recommend you for some State help for your education in England.'

I liked all this and got ready to start off for Porbandar. There was no railway in those days. It was a five days' bullock-cart journey. I have already said that I was a coward. But at that moment my cowardice vanished before the desire to go to England, which completely possessed me. I hired a bullock-cart as far as Dhoraji, and from Dhoraji I took a camel in order to get to Porbandar a day quicker. This was my first camel ride.

I arrived at last, did obeisance to my uncle, and told him everything. He thought it over and said: 'I am not sure whether it is possible for one to stay in England without prejudice to one's own religion. From all I have heard, I have my doubts. When I meet these big barristers, I see no difference between their life and that of Europeans. They know no scruples regarding food. Cigars are never out of their mouths. They dress as shamelessly as Englishmen. All that would not be in keeping with our family tradition. I am shortly going on a pilgrimage and have not many years to live. At the threshold of death, how dare I give you permission to go to England, to cross the seas? But I will not stand in your way. It is your mother's permission which really matters. If she permits you, then godspeed! Tell her I will not interfere. You will go with my blessings.'

'I could expect nothing more from you,' said I. 'I shall now try to win mother over. But would you not recommend me to Mr. Lely?'

'How can I do that?' said he. 'But he is a good man. You ask for an appointment telling him how you are connected. He will certainly give you one and may even help you.'

I cannot say why my uncle did not give me a note of recommendation. I have a faint idea that he hesitated to co-operate directly in my going to England, which was, in his opinion, an irreligious act.

I wrote to Mr. Lely, who asked me to see him at his residence. He saw me as he was ascending the staircase; and saying curtly, 'Pass your B.A. first and then see me. No help can be given you now,' he hurried upstairs. I had made elaborate preparations to meet him. I had carefully learnt up a few sentences and had bowed low and saluted him with both hands. But all to no purpose!

I thought of my wife's ornaments. I thought of my elder brother, in whom I had the utmost faith. He was generous to a fault, and he loved me as his son.

I returned to Rajkot from Porbandar and reported all that had happened. I consulted Joshiji, who of course advised even incurring a debt if necessary. I suggested the disposal of my wife's ornaments, which could fetch about two to three thousand rupees. My brother promised to find the money somehow.

My mother, however, was still unwilling. She had begun making minute inquiries. Someone had told her that young men got lost in England. Someone else had said that they took to meat; and yet another that they could not live there without liquor. 'How about all this?' she asked me. I said : 'Will you not trust me? I shall not lie to you. I swear that I shall not touch any of those things. If there were any such danger, would Joshiji let me go?'

'I can trust you', she said. 'But how can I trust you in a distant land? I am dazed and know not what to do. I will ask Becharji Swami.'

Becharji Swami was originally a Modh Bania, but had now become a Jain monk. He too was a family adviser like Joshiji. He came to my help, and said: "I shall get the boy solemnly to take the three vows, and then he can be allowed to go.' He administered the oath and I vowed not to touch wine, woman and meat. This done, my mother gave her permission.

*An Autobiography*, (1959), pp. 26-28

## 2

# PREPARATION FOR THE BAR

[ Editor's Note : As the Bar examinations did not require much study, Gandhiji did not feel pressed for time. He therefore thought that he should not only be called to the Bar, but have some literary degree as well. He inquired about the Oxford and Cambridge University courses but gave up the idea of going to either of these places as it would have meant greater expense and a much longer stay in England than he was prepared for. Ultimately he decided to study for the London Matriculation. It appears, however, that from 1888 to 1889, Gandhiji had enrolled himself as a student in the University College, London, for recently the University College, London has proudly claimed Gandhiji as one of its 18th Century distinguished alumni. The alumni department of the college dug back its archives and found an old card index box containing a small yellowing index card in which is handwritten Gandhiji's name and dates of attendances. It is now established that Gandhiji from 1888 to 1889 was enrolled as a student in the University College, London for courses in Indian law and jurisprudence.[1] ]

I knew that Bar examinations did not require much study, and I therefore did not feel pressed for time. My weak English was a perpetual worry to me. Mr. (afterwards Sir Frederic) Lely's words, 'Graduate first and then come to me,' still rang in my ears. I should, I thought, not only be called to the Bar, but have some literary degree as well. I inquired about the

---

1. See column entitled 'out of court', Times of India, 28-10-2001 by Soli S. Sorabjee.

Oxford and Cambridge University courses, consulted a few friends, and found that, if I elected to go to either of these places, that would mean greater expense and a much longer stay in England than I was prepared for. A friend suggested that, if I really wanted to have the satisfaction of taking a difficult examination, I should pass the London Matriculation. It meant a good deal of labour and much addition to my stock of general knowledge, without any extra expense worth the name. I welcomed the suggestion. But the syllabus frightened me. Latin and a modern language were compulsory! How was I to manage Latin? But the friend entered a strong plea for it:

'Latin is very valuable to lawyers. Knowledge of Latin is very useful in understanding law-books. And one paper in Roman Law is entirely in Latin. Besides a knowledge of Latin means greater command over the English language.' It went home and I decided to learn Latin, no matter how difficult it might be. French I had already begun, so I thought that should be the modern language. I joined a private Matriculation class. Examinations were held every six months and I had only five months at my disposal. It was an almost impossible task for me. But the aspirant after being an English gentleman chose to convert himself into a serious student. I framed my own time-table to the minute; but neither my intelligence nor memory promised to enable me to tackle Latin and French besides other subjects within the given period. The result was that I was ploughed in Latin. I was sorry but did not lose heart. I had acquired a taste for Latin, also I thought my French would be all the better for another trial and I would select a new subject in the science group. Chemistry which was my subject in science had no attraction for want of experiments, whereas it ought to have been a deeply interesting study. It was one of the compulsory subjects in India and so I had selected it for the London Matriculation. This time, however, I chose Heat and Light instead, of Chemistry. It was said to be easy and I found it to be so. . . .This was also a period of intensive study. Plain living saved me plenty of time and I passed my examination.

*An Autobiography*, (1959), pp. 38-39

3

## 'CALLED'—BUT THEN ?

I have deferred saying anything up to now about the purpose for which I went to England, viz. being called to the bar. It is time to advert to it briefly.

There were two conditions which had to be fulfilled before a student was formally called to the bar : 'keeping terms,' twelve terms equivalent to about three years; and passing examinations. 'Keeping terms' meant eating one's terms, i.e. attending at least six out of about twenty-four dinners in a term. Eating did not mean actually partaking of the dinner, it meant reporting oneself at the fixed hours and remaining present throughout the dinner. Usually of course every one ate and drank the good commons and choice wines provided. A dinner cost from two and six to three and six, that is from two to three rupees. This was considered moderate, inasmuch as one had to pay that same amount for wines alone if one dine at a hotel. To us in India it is a matter for surprise, if we are not 'civilized', that the cost of drink should exceed the cost of food. The first revelation gave me a great shock, and

I wondered how people had the heart to throw away so much money on drink. Later I came to understand. I often ate nothing at these dinners, for the things that I might eat were only bread, boiled potato and cabbage. In the beginning I did not eat these, as I did not like them; and later, when I began to relish them, I also gained the courage to ask for other dishes.

The dinner provided for the benchers used to be better than that for the students. A Parsi student, who was also a vegetarian, and I applied, in the interests of vegetarianism, for the vegetarian courses which were served to the benchers. The application was granted, and we began to get fruits and other vegetables from the benchers' table.

Two bottles of wine were allowed to each group of four, and as I did not touch them, I was ever in demand to form a quarter, so that three might empty two bottles. And there was a 'grand night' in each term when extra wines, like champagne, in addition to port and sherry, were served. I was therefore specially requested to attend and was in great demand on that 'grand night'.

I could not see then, nor have I seen since, how these dinners qualified the students better for the bar. There was once a time when only a few students used to attend these dinners and thus there were opportunities for talks between them and the benchers, and speeches were also made. These occasions helped to give them knowledge of the world with a sort of polish and refinement, and also improved their power of speaking. No such thing was possible in my time, as the benchers had a table all to themselves. The institution had gradually lost all its meaning but conservative England retained it nevertheless.

The curriculum of study was easy, barristers being

humorously known as 'dinner barristers'. Everyone knew that the 'examinations had practically no value. In my time there were two, one in Roman Law and the other in Common Law. There were regular text-books prescribed for these examinations which could be taken in compartments, but scarcely any one read them. I have known many to pass the Roman Law examination by scrambling through notes on Roman Law in a couple of weeks, and the Common Law examination by reading notes on the subject in two or three months. Question papers were easy and examiners were generous. The percentage of passes in the Roman Law examination used to be 95 to 99 and of those in the final examination 75 or even more. There was thus little fear of being plucked, and examinations were held not once but four times in the year. They could not be felt as a difficulty.

But I succeeded in turning them into one. I felt that I should read all the text-books. It was a fraud, I thought, not to read these books. I invested much money in them. I decided to read Roman Law in Latin. The Latin which I had acquired in the London Matriculation stood me in good stead. And all this reading was not without its value later on in South Africa, where Roman Dutch is the common law. The reading of Justinian, therefore, helped me a great deal in understanding the South African law.

It took me nine months of fairly hard labour to read through the Common Law of England. For Broom's *Common Law*, a big but interesting volume, took up a good deal of time. Snell's *Equity* was full of interest, but a bit hard to understand. White and Tudor's *Leading Cases*, from which certain cases were prescribed, was full of interest and instruction. I read also with interest Williams' and Edwards' *Real Property* and Goodeve's *Personal Property*. Williams' book read like a novel. The one book I remember to have read on my return to India, with the same unflagging interest, was Mayne's *Hindu Law*. But it is out of place to talk here of Indian law-books.

I passed my examinations, was called to the bar on the 10th of June 1891, and enrolled in the High Court on the 11th. On the 12th I sailed for home.

But notwithstanding my study there was no end to my helplessness and fear. I did not feel myself qualified to practise law.

## My Helplessness

It was easy to be called but it was difficult to practise at the bar. I had read the laws, but not learnt how to practise law. I had read with interest 'Legal Maxims', but did not know how to apply them in my profession. ' *Sic utere tuo ut alienum non laedas* (Use your property in such a way as not to damage that of others) was one of them, but I was at a loss to know how one could employ this maxim for the benefit of one's client. I had read all the leading cases on this maxim, but they gave me no confidence in the application of it in the practice of law.

Besides, I had learnt nothing at all of Indian law. I had not the slightest idea of Hindu and Mahommedan Law. I had not even learnt how to draft a plaint, and felt completely at sea. I had heard of Sir Pherozeshah Mehta as one who roared like a lion in law courts. How, I wondered, could he have learnt the art in England? It was out of the question for me ever to acquire his legal acumen, but I had serious misgivings as to whether I should be able even to earn a living by the profession.

I was torn with these doubts and anxieties whilst

I was studying law. I confided my difficulties to some of my friends. One of them suggested that I should seek Dadabhai Naoroji's advice. I have already said that, when I went to England, I possessed a note of introduction to Dadabhai. I availed myself of it very late. I thought I had no right to trouble such a great man for an interview. Whenever an address by him was announced, I would attend it, listen to him from a corner of the hall, and go away after having feasted my eyes and ears. In order to come in close touch with the students he had founded an association. I used to attend its meetings and rejoiced at Dadabhai's solicitude for the students, and the latter's respect for him. In course of time I mustered up courage to present to him the note of introduction. He said : 'You can come and have my advice whenever you like." But I never availed myself of his offer. I thought it wrong to trouble him without the most pressing necessity. Therefore I dared not venture to accept my friend's advice to submit my difficulties to Dadabhai at that time. I forget now whether it was the same friend or someone else who recommended me to meet Mr. Frederick Pincutt. He was a Conservative, but his affection for Indian students was pure and unselfish. Many students sought his advice and I also applied to him for an appointment, which he granted. I can never forget that interview. He greeted me as a friend. He laughed away my pessimism. 'Do you think,' he said, 'that everyone must be a Pherozeshah Mehta ? Pherozeshahs and Badruddins are rare. Rest assured it takes no unusual skill to be an ordinary lawyer. Common honesty and industry are enough to enable him to make a living. All cases are not complicated. Well, let me know the extent of your general reading.'

When I acquainted him with my little stock of

reading, he was, as I could see, rather disappointed. But it was only for a moment. Soon his face beamed with a pleasing smile and he said, 'I undrestand your trouble. Your general reading is meagre. You have no knowledge of the world, a sine qua non for a vakil. You have not even read the history of India. A vakil should know human nature. He could be able to read a man's character from his face. And every Indian ought to know Indian history. This has no connection with the practice of law, but you ought to have that knowledge. I see that you have not even read Kaye and Malleson's history of the Mutiny of 1857. Get hold of that at once and also read two more books to understand human nature.' These were Lavator's and Shemmelpennick's books on physiognomy.

I was extremely grateful to this venerable friend. In his presence I found all my fear gone, but as soon as I left him I began to worry again. 'To know a man from his face' was the question that haunted me, as I thought of the two books on my way home. The next day I purchased Lavator's book. Shemmelpennick's was not available at the shop. I read Lavator's book and found it more difficult than Snell's *Equity*, and scarcely interesting. I studied Shakespeare's physiognomy, but did not acquire the knack of finding out the Shakespeares walking up and down the streets of London.

Lavator's book did not add to my knowledge. Mr. Pincutt's advice did me very little direct service, but his kindliness stood me in good stead. His smiling open face stayed in my memory, and I trusted his advice that Pherozeshah Mehta's acumen, memory and ability were not essential to the making of a successful lawyer; honesty and industry were enough. And as I had a fair share of these last I felt somewhat reassured.

I could not read Kaye and Malleson's volumes in England, but I did so in South Africa as 1 had made a point of reading them at the first opportunity.

Thus with just a little leaven of hope mixed with my despair, I landed at Bombay from s. s. *Assam*. The sea was rough in the harbour, and I. had to reach the quay in a launch.

*An Autobiography*, (1959), pp. 56-59

# SECTION II
## GANDHIJI AS A LAWYER

### 4
### HOW I BEGAN LIFE

I said in the last chapter that the sea was rough in Bombay harbour, not an unusual thing in the Arabain Sea in June and July. It had been choppy all the way from Aden. Almost every passenger was sick; I alone was in perfect form staying on deck to see the stormy surge, and enjoying the splash of the waves. At breakfast there would be just one or two people besides myself, eating their oatmeal porridge from plates carefully held in their laps, lest the porridge itself find its place there.

The outer storm was to me a symbol of the inner. But even as the former left me unperturbed, I think I can say the same thing about the latter. There was the trouble with the caste that was to confront me. I have already adverted to my helplessness in starting on my profession. And then, as I was a reformer, I was taxing myself as to how best to begin certain reforms. But there was even more in store for me than I knew.

My elder brother had come to meet me at the dock. He had already made the acquaintance of Dr. Mehta and his elder brother, and as Dr. Mehta insisted on putting me up at his house, we went there. Thus the acquaintance begun in England continued in India and ripened into a permanent friendship between the two families.

My elder brother had built high hopes on me. The desire for wealth and name and fame was great in him. He had a big heart, generous to a fault. This combined with his simple nature, had attracted to him many friends, and through them he expected to get me briefs. He had also assumed that I should have a swinging practice and had, in that expectation, allowed the household expenses to become top-heavy. He had also left no stone unturned in preparing the field for my practice.

The storm in my caste over my foreign voyage was still brewing. It had divided the caste into two camps, one of which immediately readmitted me, while the other was bent on keeping me out. To please the former my brother took me to Nasik before going to Rajkot, gave me a bath in the sacred river and on reaching Rajkot, gave a caste dinner. I did not like all this. But my brother's love for me was boundless, and my devotion to him was in proportion to it, and so I mechanically acted as he wished, taking his will to be law. The trouble about re-admission to the caste was thus practically over.

I had planned reform in the education of children. My brother had children, and my own child which I had left at home when I went to England was now a boy of nearly four. It was my desire to teach these little ones physical exercise and make them hardy, and also to give them the benefit of my personal guidance. In this I had my brother's support and I succeeded in my efforts more or less. I very much liked the company of children, and the habit of playing and joking with them has stayed with me till today. I have ever since thought that 1 should make a good teacher of children.

The necessity for food 'reform' was obvious. Tea and coffee had already found their place in the house. My brother had thought it fit to keep some sort of English atmosphere ready for me on my return and to that end, crockery and such other things, which used to be kept in the house only for special occasions, were now in general use. My 'reforms' put the finishing touch. I introduced oatmeal porridge, and cocoa was to replace tea and coffee. But in truth it became an addition to tea and coffee. Boots and shoes were already there, I completed the Europeanization by adding the European dress.

Expenses thus went up. New things were added every day. We had succeeded in tying a white elephant at our door. But how was the wherewithal to be found? To start practice in Rajkot would have meant sure ridicule. I had hardly the knowledge of a qualified vakil and yet I expected to be paid ten times his fee! No client would be fool enough to engage me. And even if such a one was to be found, should I add arrogance and fraud to my ignorance, and increase the burden of debt I owed to the world?

Friends advised me to go to Bombay for some time in order to gain experience of the High Court, to study Indian law and to try and get what briefs I could. I took up the suggestion and went. In Bombay I started a household (at Girgaum).

But it was impossible for me to get along in Bombay for more than four or five months, there being no income to square with the ever-increasing expenditure.

This was how I began life. I found the barrister's profession a bad job—much show and little knowledge. I felt a crushing sense of my responsibility.

*An Autobiography*, (1959), pp. 63-67

# 5

# THE FIRST CASE

Whilst in Bombay, I began, on the one hand, my study of Indian law and, on the other, my experiments in dietetics in which Virchand Gandhi, a friend, joined me. My brother, for his part, was trying his best to get me briefs.

The study of Indian law was a tedious business. The Civil Procedure Code I could in no way get on with. Not so, however, with the Evidence Act. Virchand Gandhi was reading for the Solicitor's Examination and would tell me all sorts of stories about barristers and vakils. 'Sir Pherozeshah's ability,' he would say, 'lies in his profound knowledge of law. He has the Evidence Act by heart and knows all the cases on the thirty-second section. Badruddin Tyabji's wonderful power of argument inspires the judges with awe.'

The stories of stalwarts such as these would unnerve me.

'It is not unusual', he would add, 'for a barrister to vegetate for five or seven years. That's why I have signed the articles for solicitorship. You should count yourself lucky if you can paddle your own canoe in three years' time'

Expenses were mounting up every month. To have a barrister's board outside the house, whilst still preparing for the barrister's profession inside, was a thing to which I could not reconcile myself. Hence I could not give undivided attention to my studies. I developed some liking for the Evidence Act and read Mayne's Hindu Law with deep interest, but I had not the courage to conduct a case. I was helpless beyond words, even as the bride come fresh to her father-in-law's house!

About this time, I took up the case of one Mamibai. It was a 'small cause'. 'You will have to pay some commission to the tout,' I was told. I emphatically declined.

'But even that great criminal lawyer Mr. so-and-so, who makes three to four thousand a month, pays commission!'

'I do not need to emulate him', I rejoined. 'I should be content with Rs. 300/- a month. Father did not get more.'

'But those days are gone. Expenses in Bombay have gone up frightfully. You must be businesslike.'

I was adamant. I gave no commission, but got Mamibai's case all the same. It was an easy case. I charged Rs. 30/- for my fees. The case was not likely to last longer than a day.

This was my *debut* in the Small Causes Court. I appeared for the defendant and had thus to cross-examine the plaintiff's witnesses. I stood up, but my heart sank into my boots. My head was reeling and I felt as though the whole court was doing likewise. I could think of no question to ask. The judge must have laughed, and the vakils no doubt enjoyed the spectacle. But I was past seeing anything. I sat down and told the agent that I could not conduct the case, that he had better engage Patel and have the fee back from me. Mr. Patel was duly engaged for Rs. 51. To him of course, the case was child's play.

I hastened from the court, not knowing whether my client won or lost her case, but I was ashamed of myself, and decided not to take up any more cases until I had courage enough to conduct them. Indeed I did not

go to court again until I went to South Africa. There
was no virtue in my decision. I had simply made a
virtue of necessity. There would be no one so foolish as
to entrust his case to me, only to lose it!

But there *was* another case in store for me at
Bombay. It was a memorial to be drafted. A poor
Mussalman's land was confiscated in Porbandar. He
approached me as the worthy son of a worthy father.
His case appeared to be weak, but I consented to draft
a memorial for him, the cost of printing to be borne by
him. I drafted it and read it out to friends. They
approved of it, and that to some extent made me feel
confident that I was qualified enough to draft a
memorial, as indeed I really was.

My business could flourish if I drafted memorials
without any fees. But that would bring no grist to the
mill. So I thought I might take up a teacher's job. My
knowledge of English was good enough, and I should
have loved to teach English to Matriculation boys in
some school. In this way I could have met part at least
of the expenses. I came across an advertisement in the
papers : 'Wanted, an English teacher to teach one hour
daily. Salary Rs. 75.' The advertisement was from a
famous high school. I applied for the post and was
called for an interview. I went there in high spirits, but
when the principal found that I was not a graduate, he
regretfully refused me.

'But I have passed the London Matriculation with
Latin as my second language.'

'True, but we want a graduate.'

There was no help for it. I wrung my hands in
despair. My brother also felt much worried. We both
came to the conclusion that it was no use spending
more time in Bombay. I should settle in Rajkot where
my brother, himself a petty pleader, could give me some

work in the shape of drafting applications and memorials. And then as there was already a household at Rajkot, the breaking up of the one at Bombay meant a considerable saving. I liked the suggestion. My little establishment was thus closed after a stay of six months in Bombay.

I used to attend High Court daily whilst in Bombay, but I cannot say that I learnt anything there. I had not sufficient knowledge to learn much. Often I could not follow the cases and dozed off. There were others also who kept me company in this, and thus lightened my load of shame. After a time, I even lost the sense of shame, as I learnt to think that it was fashionable to doze in the High Court.

If the present generation has also its briefless barristers like me in Bombay, I would commend them a little practical precept about living. Although I lived in Girgaum I hardly ever took a carriage or a tramcar. I had made it a rule to walk to the High Court. It took me quite forty-five minutes, and of course, I invariably returned home on foot. I had inured myself of the heat of the sun. This walk to and from the court saved a fair amount of money, and when many of my friends in Bombay used to fall ill, I do not remember having once had an illness. Even when I began to earn money, I kept up the practice of walking to and from the office, and I am still reaping the benefits of that practice.

*An Autobiography*, (1959), pp. 67-69

# 6

# THE FIRST SHOCK

Disappointed, I left Bombay and went to Rajkot where I set up my own office. Here I got along moderately well. Drafting applications and memorials brought me in, on an average, Rs. 300 a month. For this work I had to thank influence rather than my own ability, for my brother's partner had a settled practice. All applications etc., which were, really or to his mind of an important character, he sent to big barristers. To my lot fell the applications to be drafted on behalf of his poor clients.

I must confess that here I had to compromise the principle of giving no commission, which in Bombay I had so scrupulously observed. I was told that conditions in the two cases were different; that whilst in Bombay commissions had to be paid to touts, here they had to be paid to vakils who briefed you; and that here as in Bombay all barristers, without exception, paid a percentage of their fees as commission. The argument of my brother was, for me, unanswerable. 'You see,' said he, 'that I am in partnership with another vakil. I shall always be inclined to make over to you all our cases with which you can possibly deal, and if you refuse to pay a commission to my partner, you are sure to embarrass me. As you and I have a joint establishment, your fee comes to our common purse, and I automatically get a share. But what about my partner? Supposing he gave the same case to some other barrister, he would certainly get his commission from him.' I was taken in by this plea, and felt that, if I was to practise as a barrister, I could not press my principle regarding commissions in such cases. That is how I argued with myself, or to put it bluntly, how I deceived myself. Let me add, however, that I do not remember ever to have given a commission in respect of any other case.

Though I thus began to make both ends meet, I got the first shock of my life about this time. I had heard what a British Officer was like, but up to now had never been face to face with one.

My brother had been secretary and adviser to the late Ranasaheb of Porbandar before he was installed on his *gadi*, and hanging over his head at this time was the charge of having given wrong advice when in that office. The matter had gone to the Political Agent who was prejudiced against my brother. Now I had known this officer when in England, and he may be said to have been fairly friendly to me. My brother thought that I should avail myself of the friendship and, putting in a good word on his behalf, try to disabuse the Political Agent of his prejudice. I did not at all like this idea. I should not, I thought, try to take advantage of a trifling acquaintance in England. If my brother was really at fault, what use was my recommendation? If he was innocent, he should submit a petition in the proper course and, confident of his innocence, face the result. My brother did not relish this advice. 'You do not know Kathiawad,' he said, ' and you have yet to know the world. Only influence counts here. It is not proper for you, a brother, to shirk your duty, when you can clearly put in a good word about me to an officer you know.'

I could not refuse him, so I went to the officer much against my will. I knew I had no right to approach him and was fully conscious that I was compromising my self-respect. But I sought an appointment and got it. I reminded him of the old acquaintance, but I immediately saw that Kathiawad was different from England; that an officer on leave was not the same as an officer on duty. The Political Agent owned the acquaintance, but the reminder seemed to stiffen him. 'Surely you have not come here to abuse that acquaintance, have you?' appeared to be the meaning of that stiffness, and seemed to be written on his brow. Nevertheless I opened my case. The *sahib* was impatient. 'Your brother is an intriguer. I want to hear nothing more from you. I have no time. If your brother has anything to say, let him apply through the proper channel.' The answer was enough, was perhaps deserved. But selfishness is blind. I went on with my story. The *sahib* got up and said : 'You must go now.'

'But please hear me out,' said I. That made him more angry. He called his peon and ordered him to show me the door. I was still hesitating when the peon came in, placed his hands on my shoulders and put me out of the room.

The *sahib* went away as also the peon, and I departed fretting and fuming. I at once wrote out and sent over a note to this effect : 'You have insulted me. You have assaulted me through your peon. If you make no amends, I shall have to proceed against you'.

Quick came the answer through his *sowar* :

'You were rude to me. I asked you to go and you would not. I had no option but to order my peon to show you the door. Even after he asked you to leave the office, you did not do so. He therefore had to use just enough force to send you out. You are at liberty to proceed as you wish.'

With this answer in my pocket, I came home crestfallen and told my brother all that had happened. He was grieved, but was at a loss as to how to console me. He spoke to his vakil friends. For I did not know how to proceed against the *sahib*. Sir Pherozeshah Mehta happened to be in Rajkot at this time, having come down from Bombay for some case. But how could a junior barrister like me dare to see him ? So I sent him the papers of my case, through the vakil who had engaged him, and begged for his advice. 'Tell Gandhi,' he said, 'such things are the common experience of many vakils and barristers. He is still fresh from England, and hot-blooded. He does not know British officers. If he would earn something and have an easy time here, let him tear up the note and pocket the insult. He will gain nothing by proceeding against the *sahib*, and on the contrary will very likely ruin himself. Tell him he has yet to know life.'

The advice was as bitter as poison to me, but I had to swallow it. I pocketed the insult, but also profited by it. 'Never again shall I place myself in such a false position, never again shall I try to exploit friendship in this way,' said I to myself, and since then I have never been guilty of a breach of that determination. This shock changed the course of my life.

*An Autobiography*, (1959), pp. 70-72

# 7

# PREPARING FOR SOUTH AFRICA

I was no doubt at fault in having gone to that officer. But his impatience and overbearing anger were out of all proportion to my mistake. It did not warrant expulsion. I can scarcely have taken up more than five minutes of his time. But he simply could not endure my talking. He could have politely asked me to go, but power had intoxicated him to an inordinate extent. Later I came to know that patience was not one of the virtues of this officer. It was usual for him to insult his visitors. The slightest unpleasantness was sure to put the *sahib* out.

Now most of my work would naturally be in his court. It was beyond me to conciliate him. I had no desire to curry favour with him. Indeed, having once threatened to proceed against him, I did not like to remain silent.

Meanwhile I began to learn something of the petty politics of the country. Kathiawad, being a conglomeration of small States, naturally had its rich crop of politicals. Petty intrigues between States, and intrigues of officers for power were the order of the day. Princes were always at the mercy of others and ready to lend their ears to sycophants. Even the *sahib*'s peon had to be cajoled, and the *sahib*'s *shirastedar* was more than his master, as he was his eyes, his ears and his interpreter. The *shirastedar's* will was law, and his income was always reputed to be more than the *sahib*'s. This may have been an exaggeration, but he certainly lived beyond his salary.

This atmosphere appeared to me to be poisonous, and how to remain unscathed was a perpetual problem for me.

I was thoroughly depressed and my brother clearly saw it. We both felt that, if I could secure some job, I should be free from this atmosphere of intrigue. But without intrigue a ministership or judgeship was out of the question. And the quarrel with the *sahib* stood in the way of my practice.

Porbandar was then under administration, and I had some work here in the shape of securing more powers for the prince. Also I had to see the Administrator in respect of the heavy *vighoti* (land rent) exacted from the Mers. The officer, though an Indian, was, I found, one better than the *sahib* in arrogance. He was able, but the ryots, appeared to me to be none the better off for his ability. I succeeded in securing a few more powers for the Rana, but hardly any relief for the Mers. It struck me that their cause was not even carefully gone into.

So even in this mission I was comparatively disappointed. I thought justice was not done to my clients, but I had not the means to secure it. At the most I could have appealed to the Political Agent or to the Governor who would have dismissed the appeal saying, 'We decline to interfere'. If there had been any rule or regulation governing such decisions, it would have been something, but here the *sahib*'s will was law.

I was exasperated.

In the meantime a Meman firm from Porbandar wrote to my brother making the following offer : 'We have business in South Africa. Ours is a big firm, and we have a big case there in the court, our claim being £40,000. It has been going on for a long time. We have engaged the services of the best vakils and barristers. If you sent your brother there, he would be useful to us and also to himself. He would be able to instruct our counsel better than ourselves. And he would have the advantage of seeing a new part of the world and of making new acquaintances.'

My brother discussed the proposition with me. I could not clearly make out whether I had simply to instruct the counsel or to appear in court. But I was tempted.

My brother introduced me to the late Sheth Abdul Karim Jhaveri, a partner of Dada Abdulla and Co., the firm in question. 'It won't be a difficult job,' the Sheth assured me, 'we have big Europeans as our friends, whose acquaintance you will make. You can be useful to us in our shop. Much of our correspondence is in English and you can help us with that too. You will, of course, be our guest and hence will have no expense whatever.'

'How long do you require my services?' I asked. 'And what will be the payment?'

'Not more than a year. We will pay you a first class return fare and a sum of £105, all found.'

This was hardly going there as a barrister. It was going as a servant of the firm. But I wanted somehow to leave India. There was also the tempting opportunity of seeing a new country, and of having new experience. Also I could send £105 to my brother and help in the expenses of the household. I closed with the offer without any higgling and got ready to go to South Africa.

*An Autobiography*, (1959), pp. 72-73

# 8

# ARRIVAL IN NATAL

When starting for South Africa I did not feel the wrench of separation which I had experienced when leaving for England. My mother was now no more. I had gained some knowledge of the world and of travel abroad, and going from Rajkot to Bombay was no unusual affair.

This time I only felt the pang of parting with my wife. Another baby had been born to us since my return from England. Our love could not yet be called free from lust, but it was getting gradually purer. Since my return from Europe, we had lived very little together; and as I had now become her teacher, however indifferent, and helped her to make certain reforms, we both felt the necessity of being more together, if only to continue the reforms. But the attraction of South Africa rendered the separation bearable. 'We are bound to meet again in a year,' I said to her, by way of consolation, and left Rajkot for Bombay.

Here I was to get my passage through the agent

of Dada Abdulla and Company. But no berth was available on the boat, and if I did not sail then, I should be stranded in Bombay. 'We have tried our best,' said the agent, 'to secure a first class passage, but in vain—unless you are prepared to go on deck. Your meals can be arranged for in the saloon.' These were the days of my first class travelling, and how could a barrister travel as a deck passenger? So I refused the offer. I suspected the agent's veracity, for I could not believe that a first class passage was not available. With the agent's consent I set about securing it myself. I went on board the boat and met the chief officer. He said to me quite frankly, 'We do not usually have such a rush. But as the Governor-General of Mozambique is going by this boat, all the berths are engaged.'

'Could you not possibly squeeze me in?' I asked.

He surveyed me from top to toe and smiled, 'There is just one way,' he said. 'There is an extra berth in my cabin, which is usually not available for passengers. But I am prepared to give it to you.' I thanked him and got the agent to purchase the passage. In April 1893 I set forth full of zest to try my luck in South Africa.

The first port of call was Lamu which we reached in about thirteen days. The Captain and I had become great friends by this time. He was fond of playing chess, but as he was quite a novice, he wanted one still more of a beginner for his partner, and so he invited me. I had heard a lot about the game but had never tried my hand at it. Players used to say that this was a game in which there was plenty of scope for the exercise of one's intelligence. The Captain offered to give me lessons, and he found me a good pupil as I had unlimited patience. Every time I was the loser, and that made him all the more eager to teach me. I liked the game, but never carried my liking beyond the boat or my knowledge beyond the moves of the pieces.

At Lamu the ship remained at anchor for some three to four hours, and I landed to see the port. After Lamu the next port was Mombasa and then Zanzibar. The halt here was a long one—eight or ten days — and we then changed to another boat. As we had to remain in this port for a week, I took rooms in the town and saw a good deal by wandering about the neighbourhood. Only Malabar can give any idea of the luxuriant vegetation of Zanzibar. I was amazed at the gigantic trees and the size of the fruits. The next call was at Mozambique and thence we reached Natal towards the close of May.

*An Autobiography*, (1959), pp. 74-76

# 9

# SOME EXPERIENCES

The port of Natal is Durban also known as Port Natal. Abdulla Sheth was there to receive me. As the ship arrived at the quay and I watched the people coming on board to meet their friends, I observed that the Indians were not held in much respect. I could not fail to notice a sort of snobbishness about the manner in which those who knew Abdulla Sheth behaved towards him, and it stung me. Abdulla Sheth had got used to it. Those who looked at me did so with a certain amount of curiosity. My dress marked me out from other Indians. I had a frock-coat and a turban, an imitation of the Bengal *pugree*.

I was taken to the firm's quarters and shown into the room set apart for me, next to Abdulla Sheth's. He did not understand me. I could not understand him. He read the papers his brother had sent through me, and felt more puzzled. He thought his brother had sent him a white elephant. My style of dress and living struck him as being expensive like that of the Europeans. There was no particular work then which could be given me. Their case was going on in the Transvaal. There was no meaning in sending me there immediately. And how far could he trust my ability and honesty? He would not be in Pretoria to watch me. The defendants were in Pretoria, and for aught he knew they might bring undue influence to bear on me. And if work in connection with the case in question was not to be entrusted to me, what work could I be given to do as all other work could be done much better by his clerks ? The clerks could be brought to book, if they did wrong. Could I be, if I also happened to err? So if no work in connection with the case could be given me, I should have to be kept for nothing.

Abdulla Sheth was practically unlettered, but he had a rich fund of experience. He had an acute intellect and was conscious of it. By practice he had picked up just sufficient English for conversational purposes, but that served him for carrying on all his business, whether it was dealing with Bank Managers and European merchants or explaining his case to his counsel. The Indians held him in very high esteem. His firm was then the biggest, or at any rate one of the biggest, of the Indian firms. With all these advantages he had one disadvantage — he was by nature suspicious.

He was proud of Islam and loved to discourse of Islamic philosophy. Though he did not know Arabic his acquaintance with the Holy Koran and Islamic literature in general was fairly good. Illustrations he had in plenty, always ready at hand. Contact with him gave me a fair amount of practical knowledge of Islam.

When we came closer to each other, we had long discussions on religious topics.

On the second or third day of my arrival, he took me to see the Durban court. There he introduced me to several people and seated me next to his attorney. The Magistrate kept staring at me and finally asked me to take off my turban. This I refused to do and left the court.

So here too there was fighting in store for me.

Abdulla Sheth explained to me why some Indians were required to take off their turbans. Those wearing the Mussalman costume might, he said, keep their turbans on, but the other Indians on entering a court had to take theirs off as a rule.

I must enter into some details to make this nice distinction intelligible. In the course of these two or three days I could see that the Indians were divided into different groups. One was that of Mussalman merchants, who would call themselves 'Arabs'. Another was that of Hindu, and yet another of Parsi, clerks. The Hindu clerks were neither here nor there, unless they cast in their lot with the 'Arabs'. The Parsi clerks would call themselves Persians. These three classes had some social relations with one another. ' But by far the largest class was that composed of Tamil, Telugu and North Indian indentured and freed labourers. The indentured labourers were those who went to Natal on an agreement to serve for five years, and came to be known there as *girmitiyas* from *girmit*, which was the corrupt form of the English word 'agreement'. The other three classes had none but business relations with this class. Englishmen called them 'coolies', and as the majority of Indians belonged to the labouring class, all Indians were called 'coolies', or 'samis'. 'Sami' is a Tamil suffix occurring after many Tamil names, and it is nothing else than the Sanskrit *swami*, meaning a master. Whenever, therefore, an Indian resented being addressed as a sami and had enough wit in him, he would try to return the compliment in this wise: 'You may call me *sami*, but you forget that *sami* means a master. I am not your master !' Some Englishmen would wince at this, while others would get angry, swear at the Indian and, if there was a chance, would even belabour him; for *sami* to him was nothing better than a term of contempt. To interpret it to mean a master amounted to an insult!

I was hence known as a 'coolie barrister'. The merchants were known as 'coolie merchants'. The original meaning of the word 'coolie' was thus forgotten, and it became a common appellation for all Indians. The Mussalman merchant would resent this and say: 'I am not a coolie, I am an Arab,' or 'I am a merchant,' and the Englishman, if courteous, would apologize to him.

The question of wearing the turban had a great importance in this state of things. Being obliged to take off one's Indian turban would be pocketing an insult. So I thought I had better bid good-bye to the Indian turban and begin wearing an English hat, which would save me from the insult and the unpleasant controversy.

But Abdulla Sheth disapproved of the idea. He said, 'If you do anything of the kind, it will have a very bad effect. You will compromise those insisting on wearing Indian turbans. And an Indian turban sits well on your head. If you wear an English hat, you will pass for a waiter.'

There was practical wisdom, patriotism and a little bit of narrowness in this advice. The wisdom was apparent, and he would not have insisted on the Indian turban except out of patriotism; the slighting reference to the waiter betrayed a kind of narrowness. Amongst the indentured Indians there were three classes — Hindus, Mussalmans and Christians. The last were the children of indentured Indians who became converts to Christianity. Even in 1893 their number was large. They wore the English costume, and the majority of them earned their living by service as waiters in hotels. Abdulla Sheth's criticism of the English hat was with reference to this class. It was considered degrading to serve as a waiter in a hotel. The belief persists even today among many.

On the whole I liked Abdulla Sheth's advice. I wrote to the press about the incident and defended the wearing of my turban in the court. The question was very much discussed in the papers, which described me as an 'unwelcome visitor'. Thus the incident gave me an unexpected advertisement in South Africa within a few days of my arrival there. Some supported me while others severely criticized my temerity.

My turban stayed with me practically until the end of my stay in South Africa. When and why I left off wearing any head-dress at all in South Africa, we shall see later.

*An Autobiography*, (1959), pp. 76-78

# 10

# ON THE WAY TO PRETORIA

I soon came in contact with the Christian Indians living in Durban. The Court Interpreter, Mr. Paul, was a Roman Catholic. I made his acquaintance, as also that of the late Mr. Subhan Godfrey, then a teacher under the Protestant Mission, and father of Mr. James

Godfrey, who, as a member of the South African Deputation, visited India in 1924. I likewise met the late Parsi Rustomji and the late Adamji Miyakhan about the same time. All these friends who up to then had never met one another except on business, came ultimately into close contact as we shall see later.

Whilst I was thus widening the circle of my acquaintance, the firm received a letter from their lawyer saying that preparations should be made for the case, and that Abdulla Sheth should go to Pretoria himself or send a representative.

Abdulla Sheth gave me this letter to read, and asked me if I would go to Pretoria. 'I can only say after I have understood the case from you,' said I. 'At present I am at a loss to know what I have to do there.' He thereupon asked his clerks to explain the case to me.

As I began to study the case, I felt as though I ought to begin from the A B C of the subject. During the few days I had had at Zanzibar, I had been to the court to see the work there. A Parsi lawyer was examining a witness and asking him questions regarding credit and debit entries in account books. It was all Greek to me. Book-keeping I had learnt neither at school nor during my stay in England. And the case for which I had come to South Africa was mainly about accounts. Only one who knew accounts could understand and explain it. The clerk went on talking about this debited and that credited, and I felt more and more confused. I did not know what a P. Note meant. I failed to find the word in the dictionary. I revealed my ignorance to the clerk, and learnt from him that a P. Note meant a promissory note. I purchased a book on book-keeping and studied it. That gave me some confidence. I understood the case. I saw that Abdulla Sheth, who did not know how to keep accounts, had so much practical knowledge that he could quickly solve intricacies of book-keeping. I told him that I was prepared to go to Pretoria.

'Where will you put up?' asked the Sheth.

'Wherever you want me to,' said I.

'Then I shall write to our lawyer. He will arrange for your lodgings. I shall also write to my Memon friends there, but I would not advise you to stay with them. The other party has great influence in Pretoria. Should any one of them manage to read our private correspondence, it might do us much harm. The more you avoid familiarity with them, the better for us.'

'I shall stay where your lawyer puts me up, or I shall find out independent lodgings. Pray don't worry. Not a soul shall know anything that is confidential between us. But I do intend cultivating the acquaintance of the other party. I should like to be friends with them. I would try, if possible, to settle the case out of court. After all Tyeb Sheth is a relative of yours.'

Sheth Tyeb Haji Khan Muhammad was a near relative of Abdulla Sheth.

The mention of a probable settlement somewhat startled the Sheth, I could see. But I had already been six or seven days in Durban, and we now knew and understood each other. I was no longer a 'white elephant'. So he said:

'Y....es, I see. There would be nothing better than a settlement out of court. But we are all relatives and know one another very well indeed. Tyeb Sheth is not a man to consent to a settlement easily. With the slightest unwariness on our part, he would screw all sorts of things out of us, and do us down in the end. So please think twice before you do anything.'

'Don't be anxious about that,' said I."I need not

talk to Tyeb Sheth, or for that matter to anyone else, about the case. I would only suggest to him to come to understanding, and so save a lot of unnecessary litigation.'

On the seventh or eighth day after my arrival, I left Durban (for Pretoria).

*An Autobiography*, (1959), pp. 79-80

# 11

# FIRST DAY IN PRETORIA

I had expected someone on behalf of Dada Abdulla's attorney to meet me at Pretoria station. I knew that no Indian would be there to receive me, since I had particularly promised not to put up at an Indian house. But the attorney had sent no one. I understood later that, as I had arrived on a Sunday, he could not have sent anyone without inconvenience. I was perplexed and wondered where to go, as I feared that no hotel would accept me.

Pretoria station in 1893 was quite different from what it was in 1914. The lights were burning dimly. The travellers were few. I let all the other passengers go and thought that, as soon as the ticket collector was fairly free, I would hand him my ticket and ask him if he could direct me to some small hotel or any other such place where I might go; otherwise I would spend the night at the station. I must confess I shrank from asking him even this, for I was afraid of being insulted.

The station became clear of all passengers. I gave my ticket to the ticket collector and began my inquiries. He replied to me courteously, but I saw that he could not be of any considerable help. But an American Negro who was standing near by broke into the conversation.

'I see,' said he, 'that you are an utter stranger here, without any friends. If you will come with me, I will take you to a small hotel, of which the proprietor is an American who is very well known to me. I think he will accept you.'

I had my own doubts about the offer, but I thanked him and accepted his suggestion. He took me to Johnston's Family Hotel. He drew Mr. Johnston aside to speak to him, and the latter agreed to accommodate me for the night, on condition that I should have my dinner served in my room.

'I assure you,' said he, 'that I have no colour prejudice. But I have only European custom, and, if I allowed you to eat in the dining-room, my guests might be offended and even go away.'

'Thank you,' said I, 'even for accommodating me for the night. I am now more or less acquainted with the conditions here, and I understand your difficulty. I do not mind your serving the dinner in my room. I hope to be able to make some other arrangement tomorrow.'

I was shown into a room, where I now sat waiting for the dinner, and musing, as I was quite alone. There were not many guests in the hotel, and I had expected the waiter to come very shortly with the dinner. Instead Mr. Johnston appeared. He said: ' I was ashamed of having asked you to have your dinner here. So I spoke to the other guests about you, and asked them if they would mind your having your dinner in the dining-room. They said they had no objection, and that they did not mind your staying here as long as you liked. Please, therefore, come to the dining-room, if you will, and stay here as long as you wish.'

I thanked him again, went to the dining-room and had a hearty dinner.

Next morning I called on the attorney, Mr. A. W.

Baker. Abdulla Sheth had given me some description of him, so his cordial reception did not surprise me. He received me very warmly and made kind inquiries. I explained all about myself. Thereupon he said, 'We have no work for you here as barrister, for we have engaged the best counsel. The case is a prolonged and complicated one, so I shall take your assistance only to the extent of getting necessary information. And of course you will make communication with my client easy for me, as I shall now ask for all the information I want from him through you. That is certainly an advantage. I have not yet found rooms for you. I thought I had better do so after having seen you. There is a fearful amount of colour prejudice here, and therefore it is not easy to find lodgings for such as you. But I know a poor woman. She is the wife of a baker. I think she will take you and thus add to her income at the same time. Come, let us go to her place.'

So he took me to her house. He spoke with her privately about me, and she agreed to accept me as a boarder at 35 shillings a week.

I went to Mr. Johnston, paid the bill and removed to the new lodgings, where I had my lunch. The landlady was a good woman. She had cooked a vegetarian meal for me. It was not long before I made myself quite at home with the family.

I next went to see the friend to whom Dada Abdulla had given me a note. From him I learnt more about the hardships of Indians in South Africa. He insisted that I should stay with him. I thanked him, and told him that I had already made arrangements. He urged me not to hesitate to ask for anything I needed.

It was now dark. I returned home, had my dinner, went to my room and lay there absorbed in deep thought. There was not any immediate work for me. I informed Abdulla Sheth of it.

*An Autobiography,* (1959), pp. 85-87

## 12

## PREPARATION FOR THE CASE

The year's stay in Pertoria was a most valuable experience in my life. Here it was that I had opportunities of learning public work and acquired some measure of my capacity for it. Here it was that the religious spirit within me became a living force, and here too I acquired a true knowledge of legal practice. Here I learnt the things that a junior barrister learns in a senior barrister's chamber, and here I also gained confidence that I should not after all fail as a lawyer. It was likewise here that I learnt the secret of success as a lawyer.

Dada Abdulla's was no small case. The suit was for £40,000. Arising out of business transactions, it was full of intricacies of accounts. Part of the claim was based on promissory notes, and part on the specific performance of promise to deliver promissory notes. The defence was that the promissory notes were fraudulently taken and lacked sufficient consideration. There were numerous points of fact and law in this intricate case.

Both parties had engaged the best attorneys and counsel. I thus had a fine opportunity of studying their work. The preparation of the plaintiff's case for the attorney and the sifting of facts in support of his case had been entrusted to me. It was an education to see how much the attorney accepted, and how much he rejected from my preparation, as also to see how much use the counsel made of the brief prepared by the attorney. I saw that this preparation for the case would give me a fair measure of my powers of comprehension and my capacity for marshalling evidence.

I took the keenest interest in the case. Indeed I threw myself into it. I read all the papers pertaining to the transactions. My client was a man of great ability and reposed absolute confidence in me, and this rendered my work easy. I made a fair study of book-keeping. My capacity for translation was improved by having to translate the correspondence, which was for the most part in Gujarati.

Although, as I have said before, I took a keen interest in religious communion and in public work and always gave some of my time to them, they were not then my primary interest. The preparation of the case was my primary interest. Reading of law and looking up law cases, when necessary, had always a prior claim on my time. As a result, I acquired such a grasp of the facts of the case as perhaps was not possessed even by the parties themselves, in as much as I had with me the papers of both the parties.

I recalled the late Mr. Pincutt's advice — facts are three-fourths of the law. At a later date it was amply borne out by that famous barrister of South Africa, the late Mr. Leonard. In a certain case in my charge I saw that, though justice was on the side of my client, the law seemed to be against him. In despair I approached Mr. Leonard for help. He also felt that the facts of the case were very strong. He exclaimed, 'Gandhi, I have learnt one thing, and it is this, that if we take care of the facts of a case, the law will take care of itself. Let us dive deeper into the facts of this case.' With these words he asked me to study the case further and then see him again. On a re-examination of the facts I saw them in an entirely new light, and I also hit upon an old South African case bearing on the point. I was delighted and went to Mr. Leonard and told him everything. 'Right,' he said, 'we shall win the case. Only we must bear in mind which of the judges takes it.'

When I was making preparation for Dada Abdulla's case, I had not fully realized this paramount importance of facts. Facts mean truth, and once we adhere to truth, the law comes to our aid naturally. I saw that the facts of Dada Abdulla's case made it very strong indeed, and that the law was bound to be on his side. But I also saw that the litigation, if it were persisted in, would ruin the plaintiff and the defendant who were relatives and both belonged to the same city. No one knew how long the case might go on. Should it be allowed to continue to be fought out in court, it might go on indefinitely and to no advantage of either party. Both, therefore, desired an immediate termination of the case, if possible.

I approached Tyeb Sheth and requested and advised him to go to arbitration. I recommended him to see his counsel. I suggested to him that if an arbitrator commanding the confidence of both parties could be appointed, the case would be quickly finished. The lawyer's fees were so rapidly mounting up that they were enough to devour all the resources of the clients, big merchants as they were. The case occupied so much of their attention that they had no time left for any other work. In the meantime mutual ill-will was steadily increasing. I became disgusted with the profession. As lawyers, the counsel on both sides were bound to rake up points of law in support of their own clients. I also saw for the first time that the winning party never recovers all the costs incurred. Under the Court Fees Regulation there was a fixed scale of costs to be allotted as between party and party, the actual costs as between attorney and client being very much higher. This was more than I could bear. I felt that my duty was to befriend both parties and bring them together. I strained every nerve to bring about a compromise.

At last Tyeb Sheth agreed. An arbitrator was appointed, the case was argued before him, and Dada Abdulla won.

But that did not satisfy me. If my client were to seek immediate execution of the award, it would be impossible for Tyeb Sheth to meet the whole of the awarded amount, and there was an unwritten law among the Porbandar Memans living in South Africa that death should be preferred to bankruptcy. It was impossible for Tyeb Sheth to pay down the whole sum of about £ 37,000 and costs. He meant to pay not a pie less than the amount, and he did not want to be declared bankrupt. There was only one way. Dada Abdulla should allow him to pay in moderate instalments. He was equal to the occasion and granted Tyeb Sheth instalments spread over a very long period. It was more difficult for me to secure this concession of payment by instalments than to get the parties to agree to arbitration. But both were happy over the result, and both rose in the public estimation. My joy was boundless. I had learnt the true practice of law. I had learnt to find out the better side of human nature and to enter men's hearts. I realized that the true function of a lawyer was to unite parties riven asunder. The lesson was so indelibly burnt into me, that a large part of my time during the twenty years of my practice as a lawyer was occupied in bringing about private compromises of hundreds of cases. I lost nothing "thereby — not even money, certainly not my soul.

*An Autobiography,* (1959), pp. 95-97

# 13

# MAN PROPOSES, GOD DISPOSES

The case having been concluded, I had no reason for staying in Pretoria. So I went back to Durban and began to make preparations for my return home. But Abdulla Sheth was not the man to let me sail without a send-off. He gave a farewell party in my honour at Sydenham.

It was proposed to spend the whole day there. Whilst I was turning over the sheets of some of the newspapers I found there, I chanced to see a paragraph in a corner of one of them under the caption 'Indian Franchise'. It was with reference to the Bill then before the House of Legislature, which sought to deprive the Indians of their right to elect members of the Natal Legislative Assembly. I was ignorant of the Bill, and so were the rest of the guests who had assembled there.

I inquired of Abdulla Sheth about it. He said : 'What can we understand in these matters? We can only understand things that affect our trade. As you know all our trade in the Orange Free State has been swept away. We agitated about it, but in vain. We are after all lame men, being unlettered. We generally take in newspapers simply to ascertain the daily market rates, etc. What can we know of legislation? Our eyes and ears are the European attorneys here.'

'But' said I, 'there are so many young Indians born and educated here. Do they not help you?'

'They!' exclaimed Abdulla Sheth in despair. 'They never care to come to us, and to tell you the truth, we care less to recognize them. Being Christians, they are under the thumb of the white clergymen, who in their turn are subject to the Government.'

This opened my eyes. I felt that this class should be claimed as our own. Was this the meaning of Christianity? Did they cease to be Indians because they had become Christians?

But I was on the point of returning home and hesitated to express what was passing through my mind in this matter. I simply said to Abdulla Sheth: 'This Bill, if it passes into law, will make our lot extremely difficult. It is the first nail into our coffin. It strikes at the root of our self-respect.'

'It may,' echoed Sheth Abdulla. 'I will tell you the genesis of the franchise question. We knew nothing about it. But Mr. Escombe, one of our best attorneys, whom you know, put the idea into our heads. It happened thus. He is a great fighter, and there being no love lost between him and the Wharf Engineer, he feared that the Engineer might deprive him of his votes and defeat him at the election. So he acquainted us with our position, and at his instance we all registered ourselves as voters, and voted for him. You will now see how the franchise has not for us the value that you attach to it. But we understand what you say. Well, then, what is your advice?'

The other guests were listening to this conversation with attention. One of them said: 'Shall I tell you what should be done ? You cancel your passage by this boat, stay here a month longer, and we will fight as you direct us.'

All the others chimed in: 'Indeed, indeed. Abdulla Sheth, you must detain Gandhibhai.'

The Sheth was a shrewd man. He said: 'I may not detain him now. Or rather, you have as much right as I to do so. But you are quite right. Let us all persuade him to stay on. But you should remember that he is a barrister. What about his fees?'

The mention of fees pained me, and I broke in: 'Abdulla Sheth, fees are out of the question. There can be no fees for public work. I can stay, if at all, as a servant. And as you know, I am not acquainted with all these friends. But if you believe that they will co-operate, I am prepared to stay a month longer. There is one thing, however. Though you need not pay me anything, work of the nature we contemplate cannot be done without some funds to start with. Thus we may have to send telegrams, we may have to print some literature, some touring may have to be done, the local attorneys may have to be consulted, and as I am ignorant of your laws, I may need some law-books for reference. All this cannot be done without money. And it is clear that one man is not enough for this work. Many must come forward to help him.'

And a chorus of voices was heard: 'Allah is great and merciful. Money will come in. Men there are, as many as you may need. You please consent to stay, and all will be well.'

The farewell party was thus turned into a working committee. I suggested finishing dinner etc. quickly and getting back home. I worked out in my own mind an outline of the campaign. I ascertained the names of those who were on the list of voters, and made up my mind to stay on for a month.

Thus God laid the foundations of my life in South Africa and sowed the seed of the fight for national self-respect.

*An Autobiography,* (1959), pp. 100-01

# 14

## SETTLED IN NATAL

Sheth Haji Muhammad Haji Dada was regarded as the foremost leader of the Indian community in Natal in 1893. Financially Sheth Abdulla Haji Adam was the chief among them, but he and others always gave the first place to Sheth Haji Muhammad in public affairs. A meeting was, therefore, held under his presidentship at the house of Abdulla Sheth, at which it was resolved to offer opposition to the Franchise Bill.

Volunteers were enrolled. Natal-born Indians, that is, mostly Christian Indian youths, had been invited to attend this meeting. Mr. Paul, the Durban Court Interpreter, and Mr. Subhan Godfrey, Headmaster of a mission school, were present, and it was they who were responsible for bringing together at the meeting a good number of Christian youths. All these enrolled themselves as volunteers.

Many of the local merchants were of course enrolled, noteworthy among them being Sheths Dawud Muhammad, Muhammad Kasam Kamruddin, Adamji Miyakhan, A. Kolandavellu Pillai, C. Lachhiram, Rangasami Padiachi, and Amad Jiva, Parsi Rustomji was of course there. From among clerks were Messrs. Manekji, Joshi, Narsinhram and others, employees of Dada Abdulla & Co. and other big firms. They were all agreeably surprised to find themselves taking a share in public work. To be invited thus to take part was a new experience in their lives. In face of the calamity that had overtaken the community, all distinctions such as high and low, small and great, master and servant,

Hindus, Mussalmans, Parsis, Christians, Gujaratis, Madrasis, Sindhis, etc. were forgotten. All were alike the children and servants of the motherland.

The Bill had already passed, or was about to pass, its second reading. In the speeches on the occasion the fact that Indians had expressed no opposition to the stringent Bill, was urged as proof of their unfitness for the franchise.

I explained the situation to the meeting. The first thing we did was to despatch a telegram to the Speaker of the Assembly requesting him to postpone further discussion of the Bill. A similar telegram was sent to the Premier, Sir John Robinson, and another to Mr. Escombe, as a friend of Dada Abdulla's. The Speaker promptly replied that discussion of the Bill would be postponed for two days. This gladdened our hearts.

The petition to be presented to the Legislative Assembly was drawn up. Three copies had to be prepared and one extra was needed for the press. It was also proposed to obtain as many signatures to it as possible, and all this work had to be done in the course of a night. The volunteers with a knowledge of English and several others sat up the whole night. Mr. Arthur, an old man, who was known for his calligraphy, wrote the principal copy. The rest were written by others to someone's dictation. Five copies were thus got ready simultaneously. Merchant volunteers went out in their own carriages, or carriages whose hire they had paid, to obtain signatures to the petition. This was accomplished in quick time and the petition was despatched. The newspapers published it with favourable comments. It likewise created an impression on the Assembly. It was discussed in the House. Partisans of the Bill offered a defence, an admittedly lame one, in reply to the arguments advanced in the petition. The Bill, however, was passed.

We all knew that this was a foregone conclusion, but the agitation had infused new life into the community and had brought home to them the conviction that the community was one and indivisible, and that it was as much their duty to fight for its political rights as for its trading rights.

Lord Ripon was at this time Secretary of State for the Colonies. It was decided to submit to him a monster petition. This was no small task and could not be done in a day. Volunteers were enlisted, and all did their due share of the work.

I took considerable pains over drawing up this petition. I read all the literature available on the subject. My argument centered round a principle and an expedience. I argued that we had a right to the franchise in Natal, as we had a kind of franchise in India. I urged that it was expedient to retain it, as the Indian population capable of using the franchise was very small.

Ten thousand signatures were obtained in the course of a fortnight. To secure this number of signatures from the whole of the province was no light task, especially when we consider that the men were perfect strangers to the work. Specially competent volunteers had to be selected for the work, as it had been decided not to take a single signature without the signatory fully understanding the petition. The villages were scattered at long distances. The work could be done promptly only if a number of workers put their whole heart into it. And this they did. All carried out their allotted task with enthusiasm. But as I am writing these lines, the figures of Sheth Dawud Muhammad, Rustomji, Adamji Miyakhan and Amod Jiva rise clearly before my mind. They brought in the largest number of signatures. Dawud Sheth kept going about in his carriage the whole day. And it was all a labour of love, not one of them asking for even his out-of-pocket expenses. Dada Abdulla's house became at once a caravansarai and a public office. A number of educated friends who helped me and many others had their food there. Thus every helper was put to considerable expense.

The petition was at last submitted. A thousand copies had been printed for circulation and distribution. It acquainted the Indian public for the first time with conditions in Natal. I sent copies to all the newspapers and publicists I knew.

*The Times of India,* in a leading article on the petition, strongly supported the Indian demands. Copies were sent to journals and publishers in England representing different parties. The London *Times* supported our aims, and we began to entertain hope of the Bill being vetoed.

It was now impossible for me to leave Natal. The Indian friends surrounded me on all sides and importuned me to remain there permanently. I expressed my difficulties. I had made up my mind not to stay at public expense. I felt it necessary to set up an independent household. I thought that the house should be good and situated in a good locality. I also had the idea that I could not add to the credit of the community, unless I lived in a style usual for barristers. And it seemed to me to be impossible to run such a household with anything less than £300 a year. I therefore decided that I could stay only if the members of the community guaranteed legal work to the extent of that minimum, and I communicated my decision to them.

'But,' said they, 'we should like you to draw that

amount for public work, and we can easily collect it. Of course this is apart from the fees you must charge for private legal work.'

'No, I could not thus charge you for public work,' said I. 'The work would not involve the exercise on my part of much skill as barrister. My work would be mainly to make you all work. And how could I charge you for that? And when I should have to appeal to you frequently for funds for the work, and if I were to draw my maintenance from you, I should find myself at a disadvantage in making an appeal for large amounts, and we should ultimately find ourselves at a standstill. Besides, I want the community to find more than £300 annually for public work.'

'But we have now known you for some time, and are sure you would not draw anything you do not need. And if we wanted you to stay here, should we not find your expenses ?'

'It is your love and present enthusiasm that make you talk like this. How can we be sure that this love and enthusiasm will endure for ever ? And as your friend and servant, I should occasionally have to say hard things to you. Heaven only knows whether I should then retain your affection. But the fact is that I must not accept any salary for public work. It is enough for me that you should all agree to entrust me with your legal work. Even that may be hard for you. For one thing I am not a white barrister. How can I be sure that the court will respond to me? Nor can I be sure how I shall fare as a lawyer. So even in giving me retainers you may be running some risk. I should regard even the fact of your giving them to me as the reward of my public work.'

The upshot of this discussion was that about twenty merchants gave me retainers for one year for

their legal work. Besides this, Dada Abdulla purchased
me the necessary furniture in lieu of a purse he had
intended to give me on my departure.

Thus I settled in Natal.

*An Autobiography,* (1959), pp. 102-05


# 15

# COLOUR BAR

The symbol of a court of justice is a pair of scales
held evenly by an impartial and blind but sagacious
woman. Fate has purposely made her blind, in order
that she may not judge a person from his exterior but
from his intrinsic worth. But the Law Society of Natal
set out to persuade the Supreme Court to act in
contravention of this principle and to belie its symbol.

I applied for admission as an adovcate of the
Supreme Court. I held a certificate of admission from
the Bombay High Court. The English certificate I had
to deposit with the Bombay High Court when I enrolled
there. It was necessary to attach two certificates of
character to the application for admission, and thinking
that these would carry more weight if given by
Europeans, I secured them from two well-known
European merchants whom I knew through Sheth
Abdulla. The application had to be presented through
a member of the bar, and as a rule the Attorney
General presented such applications without fees. Mr.
Escombe, who, as we have seen, was legal adviser to
Messrs. Dada Abdulla and Co., was the Attorney
General. I called on him, and he willingly consented to
present my application.

The Law Society now sprang a surprise on me by
serving me with a notice opposing my application for

admission. One of their objections was that the original Englsih certificate was not attached to my application. But the main objection was, that when the regulations regarding admission of advocates were made, the possibility of a coloured man applying could not have been contemplated. Natal owed its growth to European enterprise, and therefore it was necessary that the European element should predominate in the bar. If coloured people were admitted, they might gradually outnumber the Europeans, and the bulwark of their protection would break down.

The Law Society had engaged a distinguished lawyer to support their opposition. As he too was connected with Dada Abdulla and Co., he sent me word through Sheth Abdulla to go and see him. He talked with me quite frankly, and inquired about my antecedents, which I gave. Then he said :

'I have nothing to say against you. I was only afraid lest you should be some colonial born adventurer. And the fact that your application was unaccompanied by the original certificate supported my suspicion. There have been men who have made use of diploma which did not belong to them. The certificates of character from European traders you have submitted have no value for me. What do they know about you ? What can be the extent of their acquaintance with you?'

'But,' said I, 'everyone here is a stranger to me. Even Sheth Abdulla first came to know me here.'

'But then you say he belongs to the same place as you? If your father was Prime Minister there, Sheth Abdulla is bound to know your family. If you were to produce his affidavit, I should have absolutely no objection. I would then gladly communicate to the Law Society my inability to oppose your application.'

This talk enraged me, but I restrained my feelings.

'If I had attached Dada Abdulla's certificate,' said I to myself, 'it would have been rejected, and they would have asked for Europeans' certificates. And what has my admission as advocate to do with my birth and my antecedents? How could my birth, whether humble or objectionable, be used against me?' But I contained myself and quietly replied:

'Though I do not admit that the Law Society has any authority to require all these details, I am quite prepared to present the affidavit you desire.'

Sheth Abdulla's affidavit was prepared and duly submitted to the counsel for the Law Society. It opposed my application before the Supreme Court, which ruled out the opposition without even calling upon Mr. Escombe to reply. The Chief Justice said in effect :

'The objection that the applicant has not attached the original certificate has no substance. If he has made a false affidavit, he can be prosecuted, and his name can then be struck off the roll, if he is proved guilty. The law makes no distinction between white and coloured people. The court has therefore no authority to prevent Mr. Gandhi from being enrolled as an advocate. We admit his application. Mr. Gandhi, you can now take the oath.'

I stood up and took the oath before the Registrar. As soon as I was sworn in, the Chief Justice, addressing me said:

'You must now take off your turban, Mr. Gandhi. You must submit to the rules of the Court with regard to the dress to be worn by practising barristers.'

I saw my limitations. The turban that I had insisted on wearing in the District Magistrate's Court I took off in obedience to the order of the Supreme Court. Not that, if I had resisted the order, the resistance could not have been justified. But I wanted to reserve my strength for fighting bigger battles. I should not exhaust my skill as a fighter in insisting on retaining my turban. It was worthy of a better cause.

Sheth Abdulla and other friends did not like my submission (or was it weakness?). They felt that I should have stood by my right to wear the turban while practising in the court. I tried to reason with them. I tried to press home to them the truth of the maxim, 'When at Rome do as the Romans do.' 'It would be right,' I said, 'to refuse to obey, if in India an English officer or judge ordered you to take off your turban; but as an officer of the court, it would have ill become me to disregard a custom of the court in the province of Natal.'

I pacified the friends somewhat with these and similar arguments, but I do not think I convinced them completely, in this instance, of the applicability of the principle of looking at a thing from a different standpoint in different circumstances. But all my life through, the very insistence on truth has taught me to appreciate the beauty of compromise. I saw in later life that this spirit was an essential part of Satyagraha. It has often meant endangering my life and incurring the displeasure of friends. But truth is hard as adamant and tender as a blossom.

The opposition of the Law Society gave me another advertisement in South Africa. Most of the newspapers condemned the opposition and accused the Law Society of jealousy. The advertisement, to some extent, simplified my work.

*An Autobiography,* (1959), pp. 105-07

# 16

# SETTLED IN BOMBAY ?

[Editor's Note: In the year 1901 Gandhiji returned to India with the intention of permanently settling down here. On Shri Gokhale's advice he decided to settle down in Bombay, practise at the bar and help him in public work. Within a short time, however, he had to give up practice and return to South Africa to carry on his public work there.]

Gokhale was very anxious that I should settle down in Bombay, practise at the bar and help him in public work. Public work in those days meant Congress work, and the chief work of the institution which he had assisted to found was carrying on the Congress administration.

I liked Gokhale's advice, but I was not overconfident of success as a barrister. The unpleasant memories of past failure were yet with me, and I still hated as poison the use of flattery for getting briefs.

I therefore decided to start work first at Rajkot. Kevalram Mavji Dave, my old well-wisher, who had induced me to go to England, was there, and he started me straightaway with three briefs. Two of them were appeals before the Judicial Assistant to the Political Agent in Kathiawad and one was an original case in Jamnagar. This last was rather important. On my saying that I could not trust myself to do justice, Kevalram Dave exclaimed : 'Winning or losing is no concern of yours. You will simply try your best, and I am of course there to assist you.'

The counsel on the other side was the late Sjt. Samarth. I was fairly well prepared. Not that I knew much of Indian law, but Kevalram Dave had instructed me very thoroughly. I had heard friends say, before I went out to South Africa, that Sir Pherozeshah Mehta had the Law of Evidence at his finger-tips and that that was the secret of his success. I had borne this in mind, and during the voyage had carefully studied the Indian Evidence Act with commentaries thereon. There was of course also the advantage of my legal experience in South Africa.

I won the case and gained some confidence. I had no fear about the appeals, which were successful. All this inspired a hope in me that after all I might not fail even in Bombay.

But before I set forth the circumstances in which I decided to go to Bombay, I shall narrate my experience of the inconsiderateness and ignorance of English officials. The Judicial Assistant's court was peripatetic. He was constantly touring, and vakils and their clients had to follow him wherever he moved his camp. The vakils would charge more whenever they had to go out of headquarters and so the clients had naturally to incur double the expenses. The inconvenience was no concern to the judge.

The appeal of which I am talking was to be heard at Veraval where plague was raging. 1 have a recollection that there were as many as fifty cases daily in the place with a population of 5,500. It was practically deserted, and I put up in a deserted *dharmashala* at some distance from the town. But where were the clients to stay? If they were poor, they had simply to trust themselves to God's mercy.

A friend who also had cases before the court had wired that I should put in an application for the camp to be moved to some other station because of the plague at Veraval. On my submitting the application, the *sahib* asked me: 'Are you afraid?'

I answered: 'It is not a question of my being afraid. I think I can shift for myself, but what about the clients?'

'The plague has come to stay in India,' replied the *sahib*. 'Why fear it? The climate of Veraval is lovely. [The *sahib* lived far away from the town in a palatial tent pitched on the seashore.] Surely people must learn to live thus in the open.'

It was no use arguing against this philosophy. The *sahib* told his *shirastedar:* 'Make note of what Mr. Gandhi says, and let me know if it is very inconvenient for the vakils or the clients!'

The *sahib* of course had honestly done what he thought was the right thing. But how could the man have an idea of the hardships of poor India ? How was he to understand the needs, idiosyncrasies and customs of the people? How was one, accustomed to measure things in gold sovereigns, all at once to make calculations in tiny bits of copper? As the elephant is powerless to think in the terms of the ant, in spite of the best intentions in the world, even so is the Englishman powerless to think in the terms of, or legislate for, the Indian.

But to resume the thread of the story. In spite of my successes, I had been thinking of staying on in Rajkot for some time longer, when one day Kevalram Dave came to me and said: 'Gandhi, we will not suffer you to vegetate here. You must settle in Bombay.'

'But who will find work for me there?' I asked. 'Will you find the expenses?'

'Yes, yes, I will,' said he. 'We shall bring you down here sometimes as a big barrister from Bombay and drafting work we shall send you there. It lies with us vakils to make or mar a barrister. You have proved your worth in Jamnagar and Veraval, and I have therefore not the least anxiety about you. You are destined to do public work, and we will not allow you to be buried in Kathiawad. So tell me, then, when you will go to Bombay.'

'I am expecting a remittance from Natal. As soon as I get it I will go,' I replied.

The money came in about two weeks, and I went to Bombay. I took chambers in Payne, Gilbert and Sayani's offices, and it looked as though I had settled down.

Though I had hired chambers in the Fort and a house in Girgaum, God would not let me settle down. Scarcely had I moved into my new house when my second son Manilal, who had already been through an acute attack of smallpox some years back, had a severe attack of typhoid, combined with pneumonia and signs of delirium at night.

Manilal was restored to health, but I saw that the Girgaum house was not habitable. It was damp and ill-lighted. So in consultation with Shri Ravishankar Jagjivan I decided to hire some well-ventilated bungalow in a suburb of Bombay. I wandered about in Bandra and Santa Cruz. The slaughter-house in Bandra prevented our choice falling there. Ghatkopar and places near it were too far from the sea. At last we hit upon a fine bungalow in Santa Cruz, which we hired as being the best from the point of view of sanitation.

I took a first class season ticket from Santa Cruz to Churchgate, and remember having frequently felt a certain pride in being the only first class passenger in my compartment. Often I walked to Bandra in order to take the fast train from there direct to Churchgate.

I prospered in my profession better than I had

expected. My South African clients often entrusted me with some work, and it was enough to enable me to pay my way.

I had not yet succeeded in securing any work in the High Court, but I attended the 'moot' that used to be held in those days, though I never ventured to take part in it. I recall Jamiatram Nanubhai taking a prominent part. Like other fresh barristers I made a point of attending the hearing of cases in the High Court, more, I am afraid, for enjoying the soporific breeze coming straight from the sea than for adding to my knowledge. I observed that I was not the only one to enjoy this pleasure. It seemed to be the fashion and therefore nothing to be ashamed of.

However I began to make use of the High Court library and make fresh acquaintances and felt that before long I should secure work in the High Court.

Thus whilst on the one hand I began to feel somewhat at ease about my profession, on the other hand Gokhale, whose eyes were always on me, had been busy making his own plans on my behalf. He peeped in at my chambers twice or thrice every week, often in company with friends whom he wanted me to know, and he kept me acquainted with his mode of work.

But it may be said that God has never allowed any of my own plans to stand. He has disposed them in His own way.

Just when I seemed to be settling down as I had intended, I received an unexpected cable from South Africa: 'Chamberlain expected here. Please return immediately.' I remembered my promise and cabled to say that I should be ready to start the moment they put me in funds. They promptly responded. I gave up the chambers and started for South Africa.

*An Autobiography,* (1959), pp. 178-83

# 17

# SOME REMINISCENCES OF THE BAR

Before coming to a narrative of the course my life took in India, it seems necessary to recall a few of the South African experiences which I have deliberately left out.

Some lawyer friends have asked me to give my reminiscences of the bar. The number of these is so large that, if I were to describe them all, they would occupy a volume by themselves and take me out of my scope. But it may not perhaps be improper to recall some of those which bear upon the practice of truth.

So far as I can recollect, I have already said that I never resorted to untruth in my profession, and that a large part of my legal practice was in the interest of public work, for which I charged nothing beyond out-of-pocket expenses, and these too I sometimes met myself. I had thought that in saying this I had said all that was necessary as regards my legal practice. But friends want me to do more. They seem to think that, if I described however slightly, some of the occasions when I refused to swerve from the truth, the legal profession might profit by it.

As a student I had heard that the lawyer's profession was a liar's profession. But this did not influence me, as I had no intention of earning either position or money by lying.

My principle was put to the test many a time in South Africa. Often I knew that my opponents had tutored their witnesses, and if I only encouraged my client or his witnesses to lie, we could win the case. But

I always resisted the temptation. I remember only one occasion when, after having won a case, I suspected that my client had deceived me. In my heart of hearts I always wished that I should win only if my client's case was right. In fixing my fees I do not recall ever having made them conditional on my winning the case. Whether my client won or lost, I expected nothing more nor less than my fees.

I warned every new client at the outset that he should not expect me to take up a false case or to coach the witnesses, with the result that I built up such a reputation that no false cases used to come to me. Indeed some of my clients would keep their clean cases for me, and take the doubtful ones elsewhere.

There was one case which proved a severe trial. It was brought to me by one of my best clients. It was a case of highly complicated accounts and had been a prolonged one. It had been heard in parts before several courts. Ultimately the book-keeping portion of it was entrusted by the court to the arbitration of some qualified accountants. The award was entirely in favour of my client, but the arbitrators had inadvertently committed an error in calculation which, however small, was serious, inasmuch as an entry which ought to have been on the debit side was made on the credit side. The opponents had opposed the award on other grounds. I was junior counsel for my client. When the senior counsel became aware of the error, he was of opinion that our client was not bound to admit it. He was clearly of opinion that no counsel was bound to admit anything that went against his client's interest. I said we ought to admit the error.

But the senior counsel contended: 'In that case there is every likelihood of the court cancelling the whole award, and no sane counsel would imperil his client's case to that extent. At any rate I would be the last man to take any such risk. If the case were to be sent up for a fresh hearing, one could never tell what expenses our client might have to incur, and what the ultimate result might be!'

The client was present when this conversation took place.

I said: 'I feel that both our client and we ought to run the risk. Where is the certainty of the court upholding a wrong award simply because we do not admit the error? And supposing the admission were to bring the client to grief, what harm is there?'

'But why should we make the admission at all?' said the senior counsel.

'Where is the surety of the court not detecting the error or our opponent not discovering it ?' said I.

'Well then, will you argue the case? I am not prepared to argue it on your terms,' replied the senior counsel with decision.

I humbly answered: 'If you will not argue, then I am prepared to do so, if our client so desires. I shall have nothing to do with the case if the error is not admitted.'

With this I looked at my client. He was a little embarrassed. I had been in the case from the very first. The client fully trusted me, and knew me through and through. He said: 'Well, then, you will argue the case and admit the error. Let us lose, if that is to be our lot. God defend the right.'

I was delighted. I had expected nothing less from him. The senior counsel again warned me, pitied me for my obduracy, but congratulated me all the same.

## Sharp Practice?

I had no doubt about the soundness of my advice, but I doubted very much my fitness for doing full justice to the case. I felt it would be a most hazardous undertaking to argue such a difficult case before the Supreme Court, and I appeared before the Bench in fear and trembling.

As soon as I referred to the error in the accounts, one of the judges said:

'Is not this sharp practice, Mr. Gandhi?'

I boiled within to hear this charge. It was intolerable to be accused of sharp practice when there was not the slightest warrant for it.

'With a judge prejudiced from the start like this, there is little chance of success in this difficult case,' I said to myself. But I composed my thoughts and answered:

'I am surprised that your Lordship should suspect sharp practice without hearing me out.'

'No question of a charge,' said the judge. 'It is a mere suggestion.'

'The suggestion here seems to me to amount to a charge. I would ask your Lordship to hear me out and then arraign me if there is any occasion for it.'

'I am sorry to have interrupted you,' replied the judge. 'Pray do go on with your explanation of the discrepancy.'

I had enough material in support of my explanation. Thanks to the judge having raised this question, I was able to rivet the court's attention on my argument from the very start. I felt much encouraged and took the opportunity of entering into a detailed explanation. The Court gave me a patient hearing, and I was able to convince the judges that the discrepancy was due entirely to inadvertence. They therefore did not feel disposed to cancel the whole award, which had involved considerable labour.

The opposing counsel seemed to feel secure in the belief that not much argument would be needed after the error had been admitted. But the judges continued to interrupt him, as they were convinced that the error was a slip which could be easily rectified. The counsel laboured hard to attack the award, but the judge who had originally started with the suspicion had now come round definitely to my side.

'Supposing Mr. Gandhi had not admitted the error, what would you have done?' He asked.

'It was impossible for us to secure the services of a more competent and honest expert accountant than the one appointed by us."

'The Court must presume that you know your case best. If you cannot point out anything beyond the slip which any expert accountant is liable to commit, the Court will be loath to compel the parties to go in for fresh litigation and fresh expenses because of a patent mistake. We may not order a fresh hearing when such an error can be easily corrected,' continued the judge.

And so the counsel's objection was overruled. The Court either confirmed the award, with the error rectified, or ordered the arbitrator to rectify the error, I forget which.

I was delighted. So were my client and senior counsel; and I was confirmed in my conviction that it was not impossible to practise law without compromising truth.

Let the reader, however, remember that even truthfulness in the practice of the profession cannot cure it of the fundamental defect that vitiates it.

*An Autobiography,* (1959), pp. 266-69

## 18

# CLIENTS TURNED CO-WORKERS

The distinction between the legal practice in Natal and that in the Transvaal was that in Natal there was a joint bar; a barrister, whilst he was admitted to the rank of advocate, could also practise as an attorney; whereas in the Transvaal, as in Bombay, the spheres of attorneys and advocates were distinct. A barrister had the right of election whether he would practise as an advocate or as an attorney. So whilst in Natal I was admitted as an advocate, in the Transvaal I sought admission as an attorney. For as an advocate I could not have come in direct contact with the Indians and the white attorneys in South Africa would not have briefed me.

But even in the Transvaal it was open to attorneys to appear before magistrates. On one occasion, whilst I was conducting a case before a magistrate in Johannesburg, I discovered that my client had deceived me. I saw him completely break down in the witness box. So without any argument I asked the magistrate to dismiss the case. The opposing counsel was astonished, and the magistrate was pleased. I rebuked my client for bringing a false case to me. He knew that I never accepted false cases, and when I brought the thing home to him, he admitted his mistake, and I have an impression that he was not angry with me for having asked the magistrate to decide against him. At any rate my conduct in this case did not affect my practice for the worse, indeed it made my work easier. I also say that my devotion to truth enhanced my reputation amongst the members of the profession, and in spite of the handicap of colour I was able in some cases to win even their affection.

During my professional work it was also my habit never to conceal my ignorance from my clients or my colleagues. Wherever I felt myself at sea, I would advise my client to consult some other counsel, or if he preferred to stick to me, I would ask him to let me seek the assistance of senior counsel. This frankness earned me the unbounded affection and trust of my clients. They were always willing to pay the fee whenever consultation with senior counsel was necessary. This affection and trust served me in good stead in my public work.

I have indicated in the foregoing chapters that my object in practising in South Africa was service of the community. Even for this purpose, winning the confidence of the people was an indispensable condition. The large-hearted Indians magnified into service professional work done for money, and when I advised them to suffer the hardships of imprisonment for the sake of their rights, many of them cheerfully accepted the advice, not so much because they had reasoned out the correctness of the course, as because of their confidence in, and affection for, me.

As I write this, many a sweet reminiscences come to my mind. Hundreds of clients became friends and real co-workers in public service, and their association sweetened a life that was otherwise full of difficulties and dangers.

*An Autobiography*, (1959), pp. 269-70

# 19

# HOW A CLIENT WAS SAVED

The reader, by now, will be quite familiar with Parsi Rustomji's name. He was one who became at once my client and co-worker, or perhaps it would be truer to say that he first became co-worker and then client. I won his confidence to such an extent that he sought and followed my advice also in private domestic matters. Even when he was ill, he would seek my aid, and though there was much difference between our ways of living, he did not hesitate to accept my quack treatment.

This friend once got into a very bad scrape. Though he kept me informed of most of his affairs, he had studiously kept back one thing. He was a large importer of goods from Bombay and Calcutta, and not infrequently he resorted to smuggling. But as he was on the best terms with customs officials, no one was inclined to suspect him. In charging duty, they used to take his invoices on trust. Some might even have connived at the smuggling.

But to use the telling simile of the Gujarati poet Akho, theft like quicksilver won't be suppressed, and Parsi Rustomji's proved no exception. The good friend ran post haste to me, the tears rolling down his cheeks as he said: 'Bhai, I have deceived you. My guilt has been discovered today. I have smuggled and I am doomed. I must go to jail and be ruined. You alone may be able to save me from this predicament. I have kept back nothing else from you, but I thought I ought not to bother you with such tricks of the trade and so I never told you about this smuggling. But now, how much I repent it!'

I calmed him and said: 'To save or not to save you is in His hands. As to me you know my way. I can but try to save you by means of confession.'

The good Parsi felt deeply mortified.

'But is not my confession before you enough?' he asked.

'You have wronged not me but Government. How will the confession made before me avail you?' I replied gently.

'Of course I will do just as you advise, but will you not consult with my old counsel Mr—? He is a friend too,' said Parsi Rustomji.

Inquiry revealed that the smuggling had been going on for a long time, but the actual offence detected involved a trifling sum. We went to his counsel. He perused the papers, and said: 'The case will be tried by a jury, and a Natal jury will be the last to acquit an Indian. But I will not give up hope.'

I did not know this counsel intimately. Parsi Rustomji intercepted: 'I thank you, but I should like to be guided by Mr. Gandhi's advice in this case. He knows me intimately. Of course you will advise him whenever necessary.'

Having thus shelved the counsel's question, we went to Parsi Rustomji's shop.

And now explaining my view I said to him: 'I don't think this case should be taken to court at all. It rests with Customs Officer to prosecute you or to let you go, and he in turn will have to be guided by the Attorney-General. I am prepared to meet both. I propose that you should offer to pay the penalty they fix, and the odds are that they will be agreeable. But if they are not, you must be prepared to go to jail. I am of opinion that the shame lies not so much in going to jail as in committing the offence. The deed of shame has already been done. Imprisonment you should regard as a penance. The real penance lies in resolving never to smuggle again.'

I cannot say that Parsi Rustomji took all this quite well. He was a brave man, but his courage failed him for the moment. His name and fame were at stake, and where would he be if the edifice he had reared with such care and labour should go to pieces?

'Well, I have told you,' he said, 'that I am entirely in your hands. You may do just as you like'.

I brought to bear on this case all my powers of persuasion. I met the Customs Officer and fearlessly apprised him of the whole affair. I also promised to place all the books at his disposal and told him how penitent Parsi Rustomji was feeling.

The Customs Officer said: 'I like the old Parsi. I am sorry he has made a fool of himself. You know where my duty lies. I must be guided by the Attorney-General and so I would advice you to use all your persuasion with him.'

'I shall be thankful,' said I, 'if you do not insist on dragging him into court.'

Having got him to promise this, I entered into correspondence with the Attorney-General and also met him. I am glad to say that he appreciated my complete frankness and was convinced that I had kept back nothing.

I now forget whether it was in connection with this or with some other case that my persistence and frankness extorted from him the remark: 'I see you will never take a no for an answer.'

The case against Parsi Rustomji was compromised. He was to pay a penalty equal to twice the amount he had confessed to having smuggled. Rustomji reduced to writing the facts of the whole case, got the paper framed and hung it up in his office to serve as a perpetual reminder to his heirs and fellow merchants.

These friends of Rustomji warned me not to be taken in by this transitory contrition. When I told Rustomji about this warning he said: 'What would be my fate if I deceived you?'

*An Autobiography,* (1959), pp. 270-72

# SECTION III
# THE TRIALS OF GANDHIJI

## 20
## BEFORE THE COURT IN 1907

[Editor's Note: On 22nd November 1905 Messrs. Abdul Gani (Chairman, British Indian Association), Haji Habib (Secretary, Pretoria Committee), E. S. Coovadia, P. Moonsamy Moonlight, Ayub Hajee Beg Mahomed and Gandhiji formed a deputation that waited on Lord Selborne, High Commissioner for Britain in South Africa, and made representations in regard to the repeal of the Peace Preservation Ordinance. The Peace Preservation Ordinance, as its name implied, although framed to keep out of the Colony dangerous characters, was being used mainly to prevent British Indians from entering the Transvaal. The working of the law had always been harsh and oppressive.

The deputation to Lord Selborne, having failed in its efforts to obtain redress, the Indians led by Mahatma Gandhi organized an agitation in England and succeeded in enlisting the sympathy of many Englishmen in the cause of the South African Indians. An influential committee with Lord Ampthill as President, Sir M. M. Bhownaggree as Executive Chairman and Mr. Ritch as Secretary was formed to guard over Indian interests and a deputation from among the leading sympathizers of the cause of British Indians in South Africa was organized to wait on the Earl of Elgin, the Colonial

74

Secretary. The deputation which consisted of Lord Stanley of Alderley, Mr. H. O. Ally, Gandhiji, Sir Lepel Griffin, Mr. J. D. Rees, Sir George Birdwood, Sir Henry Cotton, Mr. Dadabhai Naoroji, Sir M. M. Bhownaggree, Mr. Amir Ali, Mr. Harold Cox and Mr. Thornton, waited on Lord Elgin, on Thursday, November 8, 1906 at the Colonial Office.

Gandhiji's Appeal to Lord Elgin and the efforts of the British Committee in London were successful only to the extent of securing from Lord Elgin a declaration that the Ordinance would be hung up until the matter had received the consideration of the Transvaal Parliament that was shortly to come into being. A constitutional Government was soon formed in the Transvaal and the new measure received the Royal Assent and became Law. The Indian community in Transvaal, seeing that their efforts were all in vain, determined to fight and risk the consequences of disobedience in accordance with the resolution passed at a vast mass meeting of some 3,000 British Indians held at the Empire Theatre, Johannesburg.

On the 26th December 1907, the Royal Assent to the Immigration Act was announced and simultaneously came the news that a number of the leaders of the two Asiatic Communities were warned to appear before the Magistrate to show cause why, having failed to apply for registration, as required by the law, they should not be ordered to leave the Transvaal. They were directed to leave the Colony within a given period, and failing to do so, they were sentenced to simple imprisonment for two months. Gandhiji was one of those arrested and brought to trial.

In Christmas week of 1907, Gandhiji received a telephone message from Mr. H. F. D. Papenfue, Acting Commissioner of Police for the Transvaal, asking him to call at Marlborough House. Upon arriving there, he was informed that the arrests had been ordered of himself and 25 others.

[The following account of the proceedings in Court is taken from the *Indian Opinion*.]

Mr. Gandhi gave his word that all would appear before the respective magistrates at 10 a.m. next day and the Commissioner accepted this guarantee. Next morning when he attended at the British Criminal Court, he was asked by the Superintendent whether he held duly issued registration certificates under Law 2 of 1907 and upon receiving replies in the negative, he was promptly arrested and charged under Section 8 Sub-Section 2 of Act 2 of 1907, in that he was in the Transvaal without a registration certificate issued under the Act. The Court was crowded to excess and it seemed as if at one time the barrier would be overthrown.

Mr. D. G. Shurman prosecuted on behalf of the Grown.

Mr. Gandhi pleaded guilty.

Superintendent Vernon gave evidence as to the arrest.

Mr. Gandhi asked no question but went into the box prepared to make a statement. He said what he was about to state was not evidence but he hoped the Court would grant him indulgence to make a short explanation seeing that he was an officer of that Court. He wished to say why he had not submitted to this.

MR. JORDAN (Magistrate) : I don't think that has anything to do with it. The law is there, and you have disobeyed it. I do not want any political speeches made.

MR. GANDHI : I do not want to make any political speeches.

MR. JORDAN : The question is, have you registered or not? If you have not registered there is an end of the case. If you have any explanation to offer as regards the order I am going to make that is another story. There is the law which has been passed by the Transvaal Legislature and sanctioned by the Imperial Government. All I have to do and all I can do is to administer that law as it stands.

MR. GANDHI : I do not wish to give any evidence in extenuation and I know that legally I cannot give evidence at all.

MR. JORDAN : All I have to deal with is legal evidence. What you want to say, I suppose, is that you do not approve of the law and you conscientiously resist it.

MR. GANDHI : That is perfectly true.

MR. JORDAN : I will take the evidence if you say you conscientiously object.

Mr. Gandhi was proceeding to state when he came to the Transvaal and the fact that he was Secretary to the British Indian Association when Mr. Jordan said he did not see how that affected the case.

MR. GANDHI : I said that before and I simply asked the indulgence of the Court for five minutes.

MR. JORDAN : I don't think this is a case in which the Court should grant any indulgence; you have defied the law.

MR. GANDHI : Very well, Sir, then I have nothing more to say.

The Magistrate then ordered Mr. Gandhi to leave the country in 48 hours.

*Speeches and Writings of Mahatma Gandhi*, 4th Ed., Natesan, Madras, pp. 49-51

## 21

## BEFORE THE COURT IN 1908

[Editor's Note: On the 11th January 1908 Gandhiji appeared before the Court and pleaded guilty to the charge of disobeying the order of the Court to leave the Colony within 48 hours.

The following account of the proceedings in Court is taken from the *Indian Opinion.*]

Mr. Gandhi asked leave to make a short statement and having obtained it, he said he thought there should be distinction made between his case and those who were to follow. He had just received a message from Pretoria stating that his compatriots had been tried there and had been sentenced to three months' imprisonment with hard labour, and they had been fined a heavy amount in lieu of payment of which -they would receive a further period of three months' hard labour. If these men had committed an offence, he had committed a greater offence, and he asked the Magistrate to impose upon him the heaviest penalty.

MR. JORDAN : You asked for the heaviest penalty which the law authorized? MR. GANDHI : Yes, Sir.

MR. JORDAN : I must say I do not feel inclined to accede to your request of passing the heaviest sentence which is six months' hard labour with a fine of £500. That appears to me to be totally out of proportion to the offence which you have committed. The offence practically is Contempt of Court in having disobeyed the order of December 28, 1907. This is more or less a political offence, and if it had not been for the political defiance set to the law, I should have thought it my duty to pass the lowest sentence which I am authorized by the Act. Under the circumstance, I think a fair sentence to meet the case would be two months' imprisonment without hard labour.

Mr. Gandhi was then removed in custody.

*Speeches and Writings of Mahatma Gandhi,* 4th Ed., Natesan, Madras, p. 52

# 22

# BEFORE THE COURT IN 1913

[Editor's Note: While Gandhiji was leading a deputation to England, another deputation led by Mr. Polak came to India to press the question of the repeal of the £3 tax. Then followed an agitation in England and India in 1910-12 which compelled attention of the authorities. Mr. Gokhale subsequently visited South Africa and made special representation to the Union Ministers on this particular question and a definite undertaking was given to him that the tax would be repealed. For a time it appeared that settlement was possible. But General Smuts again evaded and the tension became more when in 1913 a measure was introduced into the Union Parliament exempting women only from its operation. Gandhiji wired to Mr. Gokhale asking whether the promise of repeal was limited to women only. Mr. Gokhale replied that it applied to all who were affected by the tax. Gandhiji reminded the Union Government of the promise and asked for a definite undertaking to repeal it in 1914. The Union Government declined. It was then that Gandhiji organized the great movement advising indentured Indians to suspend work till the tax was repealed. Under his lead the Indian labourers gathered in thousands and they passed mine after mine adding to their numbers. Then commenced the historic march into the Transvaal allowing themselves to be freely arrested. The Government hoping to demoralize the Indians issued a warrant to arrest Gandhiji. The following account of the proceedings in Court is taken from the *Indian Opinion.]*

Mr. Gandhi was on the 11th November 1913 charged on three counts before the Resident Magistrate,

Mr. J. W. Cross, of Dundee, with inducing indentured immigrants to leave the Province. The Court was crowded with Indians and Europeans. Mr. W. Daizell-Turnbell was specially instructed by the Attorney-General to appear for the prosecution and Mr. J. W. Godfrey, Advocate appeared for Mr. Gandhi. Mr. Gandhi pleaded guilty to the charges.

Mr. Turnbell read the section and left the matter in the hands of the Magistrate.

Mr. Godfrey stated that he was under an obligation to the defendant not to plead in mitigation in any way whatsoever. The circumstances which had brought Mr. Gandhi before the Magistrate were well known to all persons, and he was only expressing the desire of the defendant when he stated that the Magistrate had a duty to perform and that he was expected to perform that duty fearlessly and should therefore not hesitate to impose the highest sentence upon the prisoner if he felt that the circumstances in the case justified it.

Mr. Gandhi obtained the permission of the Court and made the following statement :

"As a member of the profession and being an old resident of Natal, he thought that, in justice to himself and the public, he should state that the counts against him were of such a nature that he took the responsibility imposed upon him, for he believed that the demonstration for which these people were taken out of the Colony was one for a worthy object. He felt that he should say that he had nothing against the employers and regretted that in this campaign serious losses were being caused to them. He appealed to the employers also, and he felt that the tax was one which was heavily weighing down his countrymen and should be removed. He also felt that he was in honour bound, in view of the position of things between Mr. Smuts and Professor Gokhale, to produce a striking demonstration. He was aware of the miseries caused to the women and babes in arms. On the whole he felt he had not gone beyond the principles and honour of the profession of which he was a member. He felt that he had only done his duty in advising his countrymen and it was his duty to advise them again, that, until the tax was removed, they should leave work and subsist upon rations obtained by charity. He was certain that without suffering it was not possible for them to get their grievance remedied."

The Magistrate finally in pronouncing sentence said :

"It was a painful duty to pass a sentence upon the conduct of a gentleman like Mr. Gandhi, upon the deliberate contravention of the law, but he had a duty to perform, and Mr. Godfrey, his counsel, had asked him fearlessly to perform that duty. The accused having pleaded guilty, he (the Magistrate) accepted that plea and passed the following sentences : Count 1, £ 20, or three months' imprisonment with hard labour; Count 2, £ 20, or three months' imprisonment with hard labour to take effect upon the expiration of the sentence in respect to Count 1; Count 3, £ 20, or three month's imprisonment with hard labour, this to take effect upon the expiration of the sentence imposed in Count 2."

Mr. Gandhi, in a clear and calm voice, said :

"I elect to go to gaol."

*Speeches and Writings of Mahatma Gandhi,* 4th Ed., Natesan, Madras, pp. 63-64

# 23

# WAS IT CONTEMPT OF COURT ?

## I

### PROCEEDINGS AGAINST MR. GANDHI AND MR. MAHADEV H. DESAI

[Editor's Note: On 22nd April 1919, B. C. Kennedy, the District Judge of Ahmedabad, addressed a letter to the Registrar of the High Court, Bombay, submitting for the determination of the High Court certain questions regarding the conduct of two barristers and three pleaders who had taken Satyagraha pledge, i.e., a pledge "to refuse civilly to obey the Rowlatt Act and such other laws as a committee to be thereafter appointed may think fit". Gandhiji as the editor and Shri Mahadev Desai as the publisher of *Young India,* published the said letter with comments thereon in the issue of *Young India* dated 6-8-1919, while proceedings against those barristers and pleaders under the disciplinary jurisdiction of the High Court were pending. On 11-12-1919, the Registrar of the High Court applied for a rule *Nisi* calling upon the respondents, Mr. Gandhi and Mr. Desai, to show cause why they should not be committed or otherwise dealt with according to law, for Contempt of Court in respect of the publication of the said letter. The rule was granted by Justice Shah and Justice Crump. The rule was heard by the Hon'ble Justices Marten, Hayward and Kajiji on 3-3-1920. Sir Thomas Strangman and Bahadurji appeared for the applicant in support of the rule. The respondents, Mr. Gandhi and Mr. Desai appeared in person. In its judgment delivered on 12-3-1920, the High Court observed that comments on or extracts from any pending proceedings before a Court cannot be published unless the leave of the Court was first obtained. Any act done or writing published calculated to obstruct or interfere with the due course of justice or the lawful process of the Court or to bring a Court or a judge of the Court into contempt or to lower his authority is a Contempt of Court. The Court held that the respondents were guilty of Contempt of Court in publishing the letter pending the hearing of the proceedings and that the comments made on the letter were of a particularly intemperate and reprehensible character and constituted a serious Contempt of Court. The High Court severely reprimanded the respondents and cautioned them both as to their future conduct. The case is reported in 22 Bombay Law Reporter at p. 368 et. seq.]

This rule was heard by the Hon'ble Justices Marten, Hayward and Kajiji on the 3rd inst. (3rd March 1920). The Editor Mr. Gandhi and the Publisher Mr. Desai of *Young India* were to show cause why they should not be committed for contempt having published with comments in the issue of the 6th August 1919 of their paper, a letter addressed by Mr. Kennedy, District Judge of Ahmedabad, to the Registrar of the High Court complaining of the conduct of certain Satyagrahi lawyers of Ahmedabad.

The Hon'ble Sir Thomas Strangman, Advocate-General with Messrs. Bahadurji and Pocock appeared for the applicant, Mr. Gandhi and Mr. Desai appeared in person.

The Advocate-General, in opening the case, said that the proceedings were in contempt against Mr. Gandhi and Mr. Desai, about whose being Editor and Publisher respectively there was no dispute. It appeared that Mr. Kennedy in April last, finding that certain lawyers in Ahmedabad had signed the Satyagraha pledge, asked them to explain why their *Sanads* should not be cancelled for their having signed the pledge, and as he did not consider their explanation satisfactory he addressed a letter to the Registrar of the High Court on the 22nd April 1919. In consequence, two notices were issued by the High Court to the lawyers concerned. A copy of Mr. Kennedy's letter was given by the Registrar to Mr. Divetia, pleader for one of the lawyers, who handed the same to Mr. Kalidas J. Jhaveri, one of the Satyagrahi lawyers, who in turn handed it to Mr. Gandhi. On the 6th of August this letter was published in his paper under the heading. "O'Dwyerism in Ahmedabad" along with an article headed "Shaking Civil Resisters" commenting on the letter. (The Advocate-General at this stage read the letter and the article). It appeared from the article, said he, that by 'O'Dwyer', was meant a disturber of peace. The article said that the District Judge was prejudging the issue. His conduct was described as not only ungentlemanly, but something worse, unpardonable. He was said to be fanning the fire of Bolshevism. Those were shortly the charges made against Mr. Kennedy. Then proceedings took place in the High Court. After the proceedings the Registrar addressed a letter to Mr. Gandhi requesting him to attend the Chief Justice's Chamber to give an explanation as regards the publication of the letter. Mr. Gandhi replied by telegram explaining his inability to attend on the appointed date as he was going to the Punjab, and inquiring if written explanation would be sufficient. The Registrar replied saying that the Chief Justice did not wish to interfere with Mr. Gandhi's appointment and that a written explanation would do. On the 22nd October Mr. Gandhi sent a written explanation in which he stated that the letter was received by him in the ordinary course and that he published it as he believed it was of great public importance and that he thought that he was doing a public service in commenting on it. He, therefore, claimed that in publishing and commenting on the letter, he was within the rights of a journalist. In reply to this the Registrar wrote saying that the Chief Justice was not satisfied with the explanation, but that it would be considered sufficient if an apology in the following terms were published in the next issue of *Young India*.

## Form of Apology

"Whereas on the 6th April 1919 we published in *Young India* a private letter written by Mr. Kennedy, District Judge of Ahmedabad, to the Registrar of the High Court of Justice at Bombay and whereas on the same date we also published certain comments on the said letter and whereas it has been pointed out to us that pending certain proceedings in the said High Court in connection with the said letter we were not justified in publishing the said letter or in commenting thereon, now we do hereby express our regret and apologize to the Hon'ble the Chief Justice and Judges of the said High Court for the publication of the said letter and the comments thereon."

The Advocate-General said that he submitted with some confidence that it was an apology which the opponent should have published. A milder form of apology, he thought, it was difficult to conceive. Mr. Gandhi, however, did not publish the apology and took counsel's opinion and addressed a letter to the Registrar expressing his inability to apologize. Before the receipt of this letter a notice was ordered by the High Court on the 11th of December to be issued for contempt on which the proceedings were based. The text of Mr. Gandhi's letter dated 11th December 1919, is as follows:

"With reference to your letter regarding the publication of the letter of the District Judge of Ahmedabad in the matter of the Satyagrahi lawyers I beg to state that I have now consulted legal friends and given much anxious consideration to the apology suggested by His Lordship the Chief Justice. But I regret to state that I find myself unable to publish the suggested apology. The document in question came into my possession in the ordinary course and being of great public importance I decided to publish and comment upon it. In doing so I performed, in my humble opinion, a useful public duty at a time when there was great tension and when even the Judiciary was affected by the popular prejudice. I need hardly say that I had no desire whatsoever to prejudge the issues that Their Lordships had to decide.

I am anxious to assure His Lordship the Chief Justice that at the time I decided to publish the document in question, I had fully in mind the honour of journalism as also the fact that I was a member of the Bombay Bar and as such expected to be aware of the traditions thereof. But thinking of my action in the light of what has happened I am unable to say that in similar circumstances I would act differently from what I did when I decided to publish and comment upon Mr. Kennedy's letter. Much therefore as I would have liked to act upon His Lordship's suggestion, I feel that I could not conscientiously offer any apology for my action. Should this explanation be not considered sufficient by His Lordship I shall respectfully suffer the penalty that Their Lordships may be pleased to impose upon me.

I beg to apologize for the delay caused in replying to your letter. I have been touring continuously in the Punjab and am not likely to be free before the beginning of the next month."

A few days before the hearing of the rule Mr. Gandhi addressed a letter to the Registrar dated 27th February with which he enclosed copies of statements which he and Mr. Desai desired to submit before the Court. The text of the two statements is given below:

## Mr. Gandhi's Statement

With reference to the Rule *Nisi* issued against me I beg to state as follows:

"Before the issue of the Rule certain correspondence passed between the Registrar of the Honourable Court and myself on the 11th December. I addressed to the Registrar a letter (reproduced above) which sufficiently explains my conduct. I therefore attach a copy of the said letter. I regret that I have not found it possible to accept the advice given by His Lordship the Chief Justice.

Moreover, I have been unable to accept the advice because I do not consider that I have committed either a legal or a moral breach by publishing Mr. Kennedy's letter or by commenting on the contents thereof.

I am sure that this Honourable Court would not want me to tender an apology unless it be sincere and express regret for an action which I have held to be the privilege and duty of a journalist. I shall, therefore, cheerfully and respectfully accept the punishment that this Honourable Court may be pleased to impose upon me for the vindication of the majesty of law.

I wish to say with reference to the notice served on Mr. Mahadev Desai, the Publisher, that he published it simply upon my request and advice."

## Mr. Desai's Statement

"With reference to the Rule *Nisi* served upon me I beg to state that I have read the statement made by the Editor of *Young India* and associate myself with the reasoning adopted by the Editor in justification of his action. I shall therefore cheerfully and respectfully abide by any penalty that this Honourable Court may be pleased to inflict on me."

Continuing the Advocate-General proceeded to cite rulings to show what constitutes Contempt of Court. (1900)2 Q.B. Page 36 showed that there were two kinds of contempt : (1) Any act or writing tending to scandalize the court; (2) any act or writing calculated to obstruct or interfere with the due course of justice or the lawful process of the court. The Advocate General submitted that the publication of the letter and the comments thereon constitutes contempt in two respects : (1) in the language of Lord Hardwicke it scandalized Mr. Kennedy; and (2) it was an attempt to interfere with the course of justice. He further said that the High Court could punish for contempt of an inferior court. The District Court of Ahmedabad was under the superintendence of the High Court and it had no power to commit for contempt except for what was done in the face of the court.

Mr. Justice Marten asked if it was Contempt of Court in a civil action to publish the plaint or the written statement.

The Advocate-General replied it was a contempt. The pleadings did not become public documents until the case was heard. The Advocate-General also referred to (1906) 1. K.B. page 132, and (1903) 2. K.B. He added that publication after trial was different from publication before it. In conclusion the Advocate-General drew the deduction that the gist of Mr. Gandhi's article was that as Mr. Kennedy was fanning the fire of Bolshevism, the High Court, if it acted on his letter, would likewise disturb the peace and fan the fire of Bolshevism.

Mr. Gandhi addressing the Court said that he did not propose to say anything beyond what he had already said in his statement. Esteemed friends had asked him to consider if he was not obstinate in not making the required apology. He had considered the matter over and over again and whatever view the Court held, he asked them to believe him that nothing was farther from his thoughts than obstinacy. He wished to pay all respect to the Honourable Court. On the other hand he did expect that the Honourable Court would not grudge his paying the same respect to his own sense of honour and to the dignity of journalism. He had heard the Advocate-General carefully to see if any thing, he said, could convince him that he had been in the wrong. But he had remained entirely unconvinced. Had he been convinced he would readily have withdrawn his statements and tendered apology. He did not wish to say anything more.

Mr. Justice Marten said that the point of law was against Mr. Gandhi. Mr. Gandhi had said that he was entitled as a journalist to do what he had done. But the Advocate-General had cited authorities against him. Had he any authorities to support his position?

Mr. Gandhi said he differed from the Advocate-General on the point of law, but he did not rest his case such as it was on points of law. He did not wish to argue legal points and go beyond the limits he had set to himself. The Court had before now done justice in many undefended cases and he wished himself to be considered as undefended. He would be entirely content with Their Lordships' finding on points of law.

Mr. Justice Marten reminded Mr. Gandhi that he was himself a member of the Bar and that he could argue out the case from the legal standpoint.

Mr. Gandhi said he was unprepared to do so and

repeated that he would be content to take ruling of the Court with regard to law. But since the Court had coaxed him to argue he would say that what he felt was that he had not prejudiced any party. The Hon. the Advocate-General had said that his comments on the District Judge constituted contempt of a Judge. Mr. Gandhi commented on the District Judge not as a Judge but as an individual.

J. MARTEN: Take the case of a sensational murder trial. Supposing the press commented on the events while the case was going on, what would happen ?

MR. GANDHI: I would respectfully draw distinction as a layman between the two cases. The District Judge writes this letter as a complainant and not as a Judge.

J. MARTEN: He was writing as a Judge exercising jurisdiction over certain lawyers.

MR. GANDHI: I agree. But he was not sitting in court to decide an action. I feel again that I am travelling beyond the limits I set to myself. The whole law of Contempt of Court is that one ought not to do anything which might prejudice proceedings before a Court. But here the Judge does something as an individual. I have not done anything to prejudice in any shape or form the judgment of the Judges.

J. MARTEN: Would it not be dangerous if the press made comments during pendency of proceedings? The Court would cease to be the Tribunal and the press would be the Tribunal instead.

MR. GANDHI: I would again respectfully draw a distinction. If a son wrongly brought a suit against his father then I would be justified in commenting on the son's conduct in bringing such a suit against his father, without in any way thereby prejudicing the decision of the Court. And do our courts prevent public men from inducing litigants to settle their claims outside? I submit I have committed no contempt. I have prejudiced no party and have made no comment on the action of Mr. Kennedy as a Judge. I am anxious to satisfy the Court that there is not an iota of disrespect shown to the Court in commenting on Mr. Kennedy's letter. I may have erred, and in the view of the Court, erred grievously but I have not done so dishonestly or disrespectfully. I need not add that all that I have said applies to the case of Mr. Desai, the publisher.

J. Marten then drew Mr. Gandhi's attention to a decision in England reported in a recent issue of the *London Times* whereby the editor, publisher and printer of a newspaper were fined for contempt.

MR. GANDHI: There also I submit it is possible for me to draw a distinction. While I was in England the famous Mrs. Maybrick's case was going on and the whole newspaper press divided itself into two parties, one condemning Mrs. Maybrick and the other going for the Judge, Mr. Justice Stephen and even suggesting that he was unfit to try the case.

J. MARTEN: But that was all after trial?

MR. GANDHI: No. It was while the case was going on. I followed the proceedings in the case from day to day throughout the many months that it was going on.

J. MARTEN: It did not go on, Mr. Gandhi, for many months. It went on for some days.

MR. GANDHI: Of course here I am speaking subject to correction, but I am quite sure that while the case was going on, the newspaper press was so full with all sorts of innuendoes, insinuations and aspersions, that I am sure I, as a journalist, would not even at this day be able to go to the length they went.

Mr. Desai stated that he entirely associated himself with the sentiment expressed by Mr. Gandhi. He was sure he was infinitely more incapable of arguing the case than Mr. Gandhi and he would not presume to do that. He was prepared to cheerfully and respectfully abide by whatever decision Their Lordships were pleased to give. The judgement was reserved.

*Young India,* 10-3-1920, pp. 6-8

## II
### CONTEMPT CASE JUDGMENT

After stating the facts of the case which are substantially as we have already given, His Lordship Justice Marten observes:

### Cases 'sub judice'

As to the general principles of law to be applied to this case, there can, I think, be no doubt. Speaking generally, it is not permissible to publish comments on or extracts from any pending proceedings in this Court unless the leave of the Court be first obtained. Many good reasons may be advanced for this, but the underlying principle is, I think, that of the due administration of justice for the public benefit, one incident of which demands that as a matter of common fairness, both parties shall be heard at the same time and in presence of each other on proper evidence by an independent and unprejudiced tribunal.

The object would be frustrated if newspapers were free to comment on or to make extracts from proceedings which were still *sub judice.* It matters not whether those comments and extracts favour prosecutors or accused, plaintiff or defendant. The vice is the interference with what is the Court's duty and not a newspaper's, viz. the decision of the pending case.

### Law as to Contempt

After citing numerous English authorities with

respect to Contempt of Court, His Lordship proceeds:

One can easily see the evils which would arise if it were permissible to publish a plaint containing (say) charges of fraud against some respectable man before he could even put in his answer, and long before the charges could be judicially determined.

I may refer to one more case, not because it lays down any new law, but because it brings the English authorities up-to-date and illustrates the restrictions imposed there on the liberty of the press, which, as pointed out by Lord Russell in *Reg. vs. Gray* 1900, 2 Q. B. 36 at p. 40, is on these matters "no greater and no less than the liberty of every subject of the king". The case is *Reg. vs. Empire News Limited* as is reported in the *London Times* of 20th January 1920, and was heard by Lord Chief Justice of England and Mr. Justice Avory and Mr. Justice Sankey. There the newspaper had commented on a pending murder case, but did not attempt to justify its action in so doing, and the proprietors and editor expressed their deepest regret and contrition to the Court. In delivering judgment, the Earl of Reading said:

"The Court could not permit the investigation of murder to be taken out of the hands of the proper authorities and to be carried on by newspapers. The liberty of the individual even when he was suspected of crime and indeed even more so when he was charged with crimes, must be protected, and it was the function of the Court to prevent the publication of articles which were likely to cause prejudice. The only doubt in the case was whether the Court ought to commit the editor to prison. The Court had come to the conclusion that in the circumstances it must mark its sense of the offence committed, which was an offence both by the proprietors and editor, by imposing a fine of £ 1000."

## Application to Present Caw

The principles of law then being clear, how ought they to be applied to the facts of this particular case? In my opinion, those principles prohibited Publication of the District judge's letter pending the hearing of the notices issued by the Bombay High Court. It was contended by the respondent Gandhi that the letter was written by Mr. Kennedy in his private capacity, and not as District Judge. I think that contention is erroneous. The letter is an official letter written by the District Judge in the exercise of his duties as such and submitting the case to the High Court for orders. As my Brother Hayward has pointed out to me, the letter follows the procedure laid down in the *Civil Circulars* of this Court, in cases of alleged misconduct by a pleader (see p. 259). It very properly sets out what the learned Judge considers to be the facts, both for and against the pleaders, and gives his reasons for bringing the matter before the High Court. Indeed, if he had not done so, he would presumably have been asked by the High Court for further particulars before they took any action. The letter is on lines quite familiar to this Court in other cases, where the Sessions Judge, in the exercise of his duties as such, brings some matter before this Court with a view to the exercise of its exceptional powers.

I may instance criminal references where the Sessions Judge for the reasons given in his special letter recommends the revision of some illegal or inadequate sentence which has been passed by a subordinate Court and which the High Court alone can alter in certain contingencies. If, in the present case, the District Judge's letter contained any statements which the respondent pleaders or barristers contended were inaccurate, that would be a matter for decision at the hearing of the notices, when all they had to say would be fully considered. But even if the letter was written by Mr. Kennedy in his private capacity, I do not think it would make any substantial difference as regards mere publication. The letter would still form part and a most important part of the pending proceedings and the record thereon, and I do not think that any substantial difference can be drawn between it and the other classes of documents mentioned in the authorities cited in Oswald and in Halsbury to which I have already referred. In my judgment, therefore, the publication of this letter was a Contempt of Court.

That brings me to the comments made in the newspaper, including the heading "O'Dwyerism in Ahmedabad" under which the letter was published. These comments are not only comments on pending proceedings, but are of a particularly intemperate and reprehensible character. They prejudge the case and tend to undermine any decision which the High Court may come to at the trial. They also amount in my opinion to what Lord Russell describes as "scurrilous abuse of the Judge as such". In this latter connection, the question whether the letter was written by Mr. Kennedy in his private or in his judicial capacity become immaterial, but as I have already stated it was in my judgment written in his judicial capacity.

Accordingly, on the authorities I have already referred to, these comments are clearly Contempt of Court and come within both the classes to which Lord Russell refers and in my judgment they constitute a serious Contempt of Court.

### "No Public Duty"

We have carefully considered the various

statements made by the respondents and invited them at hearing to give any intelligible explanation or excuse for their conduct. None such was forthcoming. In his letter of the 11th December, 1919, the respondent Gandhi contends that in publishing and commenting on the letter he performed a useful public duty at a time when there was a great tension and when even the judiciary was being affected by the popular prejudice. Commonsense would answer that if that tension and popular prejudice existed, it would be increased rather than diminished by abuse of the Local Judge and that this could not be the public duty of any good citizen.

But there would seem to be some strange misconception in the minds of the respondents as to the legitimate liberties of a journalist. Otherwise the respondent Gandhi could hardly have contended before us, as he in fact did, that if a son brought a suit against a father and if a journalist thought that the son's action was wrong, the journalist would be justified in holding the son up to public ridicule in the public press, notwithstanding that the suit was still undecided. I need hardly say that this contention is erroneous. It may however be, that principles which are quite familiar in England are imperfectly known or understood in India, and that the respondents have paid more attention to the liberty of the press than to the duties which accompany that and every other liberty. This has much weighed with me in considering what order the Court ought to pass in this case.

We have large powers and in appropriate cases can commit offenders to prison for such period as we think fit and can impose fines of such amount as we may judge right; but just as our powers are large so ought we, I think, to use them with discretion and with moderation, remembering that the only object we have in view is to enforce the due administration of justice for popular benefit.

In the present case the Court has very seriously considered whether it ought not to impose a substantial fine on one if not both of the respondents, but on the whole, I think it is sufficient for the Court to state the law in terms which I hope will leave no room for doubt in the future, and to confine our order to severely reprimanding the respondents and warning them both as to their future conduct.

## The Order of the Court

That accordingly is the order which I think we should pass in the present case.

The order of the Court will accordingly be: "The Court finds the charges proved. It severely reprimands the respondents and cautions them both as to their future conduct."

## Mr. Hayward's Judgment

Mr. Justice Hayward in a separate but concurrent judgment, after discussing the legal aspect of the case, made the following observations:

"It is difficult to appreciate the position taken up by the respondents. They have expressed their inability to apologize formally but have at the same time represented their readiness to submit to any punishment meted out to them. It is possible that the editor, the respondent Gandhi, did not realize that he was breaking the law and there would be no doubt if that were so, that it was not realized by his publisher, the respondent Desai. The respondents seem to have posed not as law breakers but rather as passive resisters of the law. It would therefore be sufficient in my opinion to enunciate unmistakably for them the law in these matters, to severely reprimand them for their proceedings and to warn them of the penalties imposable by the Right Court."

. Mr. Justice Kajiji concurred.

*Young India,* 24-3-1920, pp. 7-8

# 24

# CONTEMPT OF COURT

The long expected hearing of the case against the editor and the publisher of *Young India* in connection with the publication of a letter* of the District Judge of Ahmedabad regarding Satyagrahi lawyers and my comments thereon has been heard and judgment has been pronounced. Both the editor and the publisher have been severely reprimanded. But the Court did not see its way to pass any sentence upon either of us. If I dwell upon the judgment it is only because I am anxious as a Satyagrahi to draw a moral from it. I wish to assure those friends who out of pure friendliness advised us to tender the required apology, that I refused to accept their advice, not out of obstinacy but because there was a great principle at stake. I had to conserve a journalist's independence and yet respect the law. My own reading of the law was that there was no contempt committed by me. But my defence rested more upon the fact that I could not offer an apology if I was not prepared not to repeat the offence on a similar occasion. Because I hold that an apology

---

* The letter called upon lawyers who took the Satyagraha pledge, to explain why they should not be debarred from practice under the Legal Practitioners' Act for their act in taking the pledges defying law.

tendered to a Court to be true has to be as sincere as a private apology. At the same time I owed a duty to the Court. It was no light thing for me to refuse to accept the advice of the Chief Justice especially when the Chief Justice was so very considerate in the correspondence with me. I was on the horns of a dilemma. I therefore decided not to offer any defence but simply to make a statement frankly and fully defining my position, leaving it to the Court to pass any sentence if thought fit in the event of an adverse decision. In order to show that I meant no disrespect of the Court and that I did not desire to advertise the case, I took extraordinary precautions to prevent publicity and I venture to think that I succeeded eminently in convincing the Court that behind my disobedience, if it was disobedience, there was no defiance but perfect resignation, there was no anger or ill-will but perfect restraint and respect; that if I did not apologize, I did not, because an insincere apology would have been contrary to my conscience. I hold that it was about as perfect an instance of civil disobedience as it ever has been my privilege to offer. And I feel that the Court reciprocated in a most handsome manner and recognized the spirit of civility that lay behind my so-called disobedience. The luminous judgment of Justice Marten lays down the law, and decides against me. But I feel thankful that it does not question the propriety of my action. Justice Hayward's judgment recognizes it as an instance of passive, i.e. civil resistance and practically makes it the reason for not awarding any sentence. Here then we have an almost complete vindication of civil disobedience. Disobedience to be civil must be sincere, respectful, restrained, never defiant, must be based upon some well-understood principle, must not be capricious and above all, must have no ill-

will or hatred behind it. I submit that the disobedience
offered by Mr. Desai and myself contained all these
ingredients.

*Young India,* 24-3-1920, pp. 3-4

## 25

# THE GREAT TRIAL

[Editor's Note: Gandhiji was arrested at the Satyagraha
Ashram, Sabarmati, Ahmedabad on Friday the 10th March,
1922 for certain articles published in his *young India.* On the
11th noon Gandhiji and Shri Shankarlal Banker, the
publisher, were placed before Mr. Brown, Assistant
Magistrate, the Court being held in the Divisional
Commissioner's Office at Shahibagh. The prosecution was
conducted by Rao Bahadur Girdharlal, Public Prosecutor. The
Superintendent of Police, Ahmedabad, the first witness,
produced the Bombay Government's authority to lodge a
complaint for four articles published in *Young India,* dated
the 15th June 1921, entitled "Disaffection a Virtue"; dated
the 29th September, "Tampering with Loyalty"; dated the
15th December, "The Puzzle and Its Solution" and dated the
23rd February 1922, "Shaking the Manes". He stated that the
warrant was issued on the 6th instant by the District
Magistrate, Ahmedabad and the case was transferred to the
file of Mr. Brown. Meanwhile warrants were also issued to
the Superintendents of Police of Surat and Ajmer as Mr.
Gandhi was expected to be at those places. The original
signed articles and issues of the paper in which these
appeared were also produced as evidence. Mr. Gharda,
Registrar, Appellate Side, Bombay High Court. Second
witness, produced correspondence between Mr. Gandhi as the
Editor of *Young India* and, Mr. Kennedy, District Judge,
Ahmedabad. Mr. Chatfield, Magistrate of Ahmedabad was

next witness. He testified to the security deposited by Mr. Gandhi and the declaration of Mr. S. Banker as printer of *Young India.* Two formal police witnesses were then produced. The Accused Mr. Gandhi and Mr. Banker declined to cross-examine the witnesses and thereafter made the following statement.

## Gandhiji's Statement as Recorded in Court

Mr. M. K. Gandhi, 53, Farmer and weaver by Profession, residing at Satyagraha Ashram, Sabarmati, Ahmedabad said:

"I simply wish to state that when the proper time comes, I shall plead guilty so far as disaffection towards the Government is concerned. It is quite true that I am Editor of the *Young India* and that the articles read in my presence were written by me, and the proprietors and publishers had permitted me to control the whole policy of the paper."

Mr. Shankarlal Banker, landed proprietor, Bombay, Second Accused stated that at the proper time he would plead guilty to the charge of having published the articles complained of.

Charges were then framed on three counts under Section 124-A of the Indian Penal Code and the two Accused were committed to the Sessions.

The case having been committed to the Sessions, Gandhiji was taken to the Sabarmati Jail where he was detained till the hearing which was to come off on March 18.

At last the trial came off on Saturday the 18th March, 1922 before Mr. C. N. Broomfield I.C.S., District and Sessions Judge, Ahmedabad. See *Speeches and Writings of Mahatma Gandhi,* 4th Ed., Natesan, Madras, p. 693]

At the Government Circuit House at Shahibagh, Ahmedabad, the trial of Mahatma Gandhi and Mr. Banker commenced at 12 noon on Saturday, the 18th of March, 1922 before C. N. Broomfield Esq., i.c.s.,

District and Sessions Judge, Ahmedabad.

Sir Thomas Strangman, Advocate-General, Bombay assisted by A. C. Wild Esq., Legal Remembrancer to the Government of Bombay, and Rao Bahadur Girdharlal, Public Prosecutor conducted the prosecution. The Accused were undefended. The Judge took his seat at 12 noon, and said there was a slight mistake in the charges framed, which he corrected. The charges under S. 124-A,* Indian Penal Code were then read out by the Registrar, the offence having been committed in three articles[x] published in the *Young India* on September

---

\* Section 124-A of the Indian Penal Code was as under:

Whoever by words, either spoken or written, or by signs, or by visible representation, or otherwise, brings or attempts to bring into hatred or contempt, or excites or attempts to excite disaffection towards His Majesty or the Government established by law in British India, shall be punished with transportation for life or any shorter term, to which fine may be added, or with imprisonment which may extend to three years, to which fine may be added, or with fine.

Explanation I. The expression disaffection includes disloyalty and all feelings of enmity.

Explanation II. Comments expressing disaffection of the measures of the Government with a view to obtain their alteration by lawful means without exciting or attempting to excite hatred, contempt or disaffection do not constitute an offence under this Section.

Explanation III. Comments expressing disapprobation of the administrative or other action of the Government without exciting or attempting to excite hatred, contempt or disaffection do not constitute an offence under this Section.

[x] The complaint in respect of the earlier article "Disaffection — a Virtue", seems to have been dropped subsequently after enquiry, by the Magistrate.

29, 1921, December 15, 1921, and February 23, 1922. The offending articles were then read out: first of them was, "Tempering with Loyalty", the second, "The Puzzle and Its Solution", and the last was "Shaking the Manes". [These three articles have been reproduced in Appendix I.]

The Judge said the Law required that the charges should not only be read out, but explained. In this case, it would not be necessary for him to say much by way of explanation. The charge in each case was that of bringing or attempting to bring into hatred or contempt or exciting or attempting to excite disaffection towards His Majesty's Government, established by law in British India. Both the accused were charged with the three offences under Section 124-A, contained in the articles read out, written by Mr. Gandhi and printed by Mr. Banker. The words 'hatred and contempt' were words the meaning of which was sufficiently obvious. The word disaffection was defined under the section, where they were told that disaffection included disloyalty and feelings of enmity, and the word used in the section had also been interpreted by the High Court of Bombay in a reported case as meaning political alienation or discontent, a spirit of disloyalty to Government or existing authority. The charges having been read out, the Judge called upon the Accused to plead to the charges. He asked Mr. Gandhi, whether he pleaded guilty or claimed to be tried.

MR. GANDHI: I plead guilty to all the charges. I observe that the King's name has been omitted from the charges, and it has been properly omitted.

THE JUDGE : Mr. Banker, do you plead guilty, or do you claim to be tried ?

MR. BANKER: I plead guilty.

## Advocate-General Urges Trial

Sir Thomas Strangman then wanted the Judge to proceed with the trial fully. He said that under Section 271, Criminal Procedure Code, it was open to the Judge to convict the accused on their pleas or to proceed with the trial. The Section says: 'If the accused pleads guilty, the plea shall be recorded and he *may* be convicted thereon.' The words were *'may'*, not 'must'. He asked his honour to proceed with the trial. In the first instance the charges were of a serious character and in the second place it was highly desirable in the public interest that those charges should be fully and thoroughly investigated. From a further and narrower point of view that was in regard to the sentence it was obvious that the Judge could not deal with the accused unless he had the full facts of the case before him. That was the view taken by the Bombay High Court, *(19 Bombay Law Reports,* p. 356). That was an extreme case. (The advocate-general then read out the case to the court and it was in regard to a murder charge in which the accused was sentenced to be hanged.) Those remarks applied to the present case, said Sir Strangman, and he also quoted 23 Madras 151. On these grounds the Advocate-General asked the court to proceed with the trial.

## Court's Reply

The Judge said that he did not agree with what had been said by the Advocate-General. He had full discretion to convict on the plea if he thought it proper to do so, and in this particular case nothing would be gained by going once more into the evidence recorded by the committing Magistrate. As regards the question of the charges they would be fully investigated and as far as he was aware nothing more was needed to establish the offence going to show that Mr. Gandhi was responsible for those particular articles. In the face of the plea it seemed to him that it would be futile to raise the point. As regards the question of sentence, it went without saying that from the time he knew that he was going to try the case, he had thought over the question of sentence and he was prepared to hear anything that the Counsel might have to say, or Mr. Gandhi wished to say, on the sentence. He honestly did not believe that the mere recording of evidence in the trial which the Advocate-General had called for would make a difference to them one way or the other. He, therefore, proposed to accept the pleas.

Mr. Gandhi smiled at this decision.

The Judge said nothing further remained but to pass the sentence and before doing so, he liked to hear Sir Thomas Strangman. He was entitled to base his general remarks on the charges against the accused and on their pleas.

SIR THOMAS STRANGMAN : It will be difficult to do so. I ask the Court that the whole matter may be properly considered. If I stated what has happened before the Committing Magistrate, then I can show that there are many things which are material to the question of the sentence.

The first point, he said, he wanted to make out was that the matter which formed the subject of the present charges formed a part of the campaign to spread disaffection openly and systematically to render Government impossible and to overthrow it. The earliest article that was put in from *Young India* was dated 25th May, 1921, which stated that it was the duty of a non-co-operator to create disaffection towards the Government. The counsel then read out portions of articles written by Mr. Gandhi in the *Young India*.

The Court said, nevertheless, it seemed to it that the Court could accept a plea, on the materials of which the sentence had to be based.

Sir Thomas Strangman said the question of sentence was entirely for the Court to decide. The Court was always entitled to deal in a more general manner in regard to the question of the sentence, than the particular matter resulting in the conviction. He asked leave to refer to articles before the Court, and what result might have been produced, if the trial had proceeded in order to ascertain what the facts were. He was not going into any matter which involved dispute.

The Judge said there was not the least objection to his going into the charges in a general way.

Sir Thomas Strangman said he wanted to show that these articles were not isolated. They formed part of an organized campaign, but so far as *Young India* was concerned, they would show that from the year 1921. The counsel then read out extracts from the paper, dated June 8, on the duty of a non-co-operator, which was to preach disaffection towards the existing government and preparing the country for civil disobedience. Then in the same number, there was an article on disobedience. Then in the same number there was an article on "Disaffection — a Virtue" or something to that effect. Then there was an article on the 28th of July, 1921, in which it was stated that "we have to destroy the system". Again, on September 30, 1921, there was an article headed "Punjab Prosecutions", where it was stated that a non-co-operator worth his name should preach disaffection. That was all so far as *Young India* was concerned. They were earlier in date than the article, "Tampering with Loyalty", and it referred to the Governor of

Bombay. Continuing, he said, the accused was a man of high educational qualifications and evidently from his writings a recognized leader. The harm that was likely to be caused was considerable. They were the writings of an educated man, and not the writings of an obscure man, and the Court must consider to what the results of a campaign of the nature disclosed in the writings must inevitably lead. They had examples before them in the last few months. He referred to the occurrences in Bombay last November and Chauri Chaura, leading to murder and destruction of property, involving many people in misery and misfortune. It was true that in the course of those articles they would find non-violence was insisted upon as an item of the campaign and as an item of the creed. But what was the use of preaching non-violence when he preached disaffection towards Government or openly instigated others to overthrow it ? The answer to that question appeared to him to come from Chauri Chaura, Madras and Bombay. These were circumstances which he asked the Court to take into account in sentencing the accused, and it would be for the Court to consider those circumstances which must involve sentences of severity.

As regards the second accused, his offence was lesser. He did the publication and he did not write. His offence nevertheless was a serious one. His instructions were that he was a man of means and he asked the Court to impose a substantial fine in addition to such term of imprisonment as might be inflicted upon. He quoted Section 10 of the Press Act as bearing on the question of fine. When making a declaration, he said a deposit of Rs. 1,000 to Rs. 10,000 was asked in many cases.

COURT: Mr. Gandhi, do you wish to make a statement on the question of sentence?

MR. GANDHI: I would like to make a statement.

COURT: Could you give it to me in writing to put it on record?

MR. GANDHI: I shall give it as soon as I finish reading it.

## Mr. Gandhi's Oral Statement

Before reading his written statement, Mr. Gandhi spoke a few words as introductory remarks to the whole statement. He said :

"Before I read this statement, I would .like to state that I entirely endorse the learned Advocate-General's remarks in connection with my humble self. I think that he was entirely fair to me in all the statements that he has made, because it is very true and I have no desire whatsoever to conceal from this Court the fact that to preach disaffection towards the existing system of Government has become almost a passion with me, and the learned Advocate-General is also entirely in the right when he says that my preaching of disaffection did not commence with my connection with *Young India,* but that it commenced much earlier; and in the statement that I am about to read, it will be my painful duty to admit before this Court that it commenced much earlier than the period stated by the Advocate-General. It is the most painful duty with me, but I have to discharge that duty knowing the responsibility that rests upon my shoulders, and I wish to endorse all the blame that the learned Advocate-General has thrown on my shoulders in connection with the Bombay occurrences, Madras occurrences and the Chauri Chaura occurrences. Thinking over these deeply and sleeping over them night after night, it is impossible for me to dissociate myself from the diabolical crimes of Chauri Chaura or the mad outrages of Bombay. He is quite right when he says that as a man of responsibility, a man having received a fair share of education, having had a fair share of experience of this world, I should have known the consequences of every one of my acts. I knew that I was playing with fire. I ran the risk, and if I was set free, I would still do the same. I have felt it this morning that I would have failed in my duty, if I did not say what I said here just now.

I wanted to avoid violence, I want to avoid violence. Non-violence is the first article of my faith. It is also the last article of my creed. But I had to make my choice. I had either to submit to a system which I considered had done an irreparable harm to my country, or incur the risk of the mad fury of my people bursting forth when they understood the truth from my lips. I know that my people have sometimes gone mad. I am deeply sorry for it and I am therefore here to submit not to a light penalty but to the highest penalty. I do not ask for mercy. I do not plead any extenuating act. I am here, therefore, to invite and cheerfully submit to the highest penalty that can be inflicted upon me for what in law is a deliberate crime and what appears to me to be the highest duty of a citizen. The only course open to you, the judge, is as I am just going to say in my statement, either to resign your post, or inflict on me the severest penalty, if you believe that the system and law you are assisting to administer are good for the people. I do not expect that kind of conversion, but by the time I have finished with my statement, you will perhaps have a glimpse of what is raging within my breast to run this maddest risk which a sane man can run."

The Statement was then read out.

## Mr. Gandhi's Written Statement

"I owe it perhaps to the Indian public and to the public in England, to placate which this prosecution is mainly taken up, that I should explain why from a staunch loyalist and co-operator I have become an uncompromising disaffectionist and non-co-operator. To the Court too I should say why I plead guilty to the charge of promoting disaffection towards the Government established by law in India.

My public life began in 1893 in South Africa in troubled weather. My first contact with British authority in that country was not of a happy character. I discovered that as a man and an Indian I had no rights. More correctly, I discovered that I had no rights as a man, because I was an Indian.

But I was not baffled. I thought that this treatment of Indians was an excrescence upon a system that was intrinsically and mainly good. I gave the Government my voluntary and hearty co-operation, criticizing it freely where I felt it was faulty but never wishing its destruction.

Consequently when the existence of the Empire was threatened in 1899 by the Boer challenge, I offered my services to it, raised a volunteer ambulance corps and served at several actions that took place for the relief of Ladysmith. Similarly in 1906 at the time of the Zulu 'revolt' I raised a stretcher-bearer party and served till the end of the 'rebellion'. On both these occasions I received medals and was even mentioned in despatches. For my work in South Africa I was given by Lord Hardinge a Kaiser-i-Hind Gold Medal. When the war broke out in 1914 between England and Germany, I raised a volunteer ambulance corps in London consisting of the then resident Indians in

London, chiefly students. Its work was acknowledged by the authorities to be valuable. Lastly, in India, when a special appeal was made at the War Conference in Delhi in 1918 by Lord Chelmsford for recruits, I struggled at the cost of my health to raise a corps in Kheda and the response was being made when the hostilities ceased and orders were received that no more recruits were wanted. In all these efforts at service I was actuated by the belief that it was possible by such services to gain a status of full equality in the Empire for my countrymen.

The first shock came in the shape of the Rowlatt Act, a law designed to rob the people of all real freedom. I felt called upon to lead an intensive agitation against it. Then followed the Punjab horrors beginning with the massacre of Jallianwala Bagh and culminating in crawling orders, public floggings and other indescribable humiliations. I discovered too that the plighted word of the Prime Minister to the Musalmans of India regarding the integrity of Turkey and the holy places of Islam was not likely to be fulfilled. But in spite of the forebodings and the grave warnings of friends, at the Amritsar Congress in 1919, I fought for co-operation and working the Montagu-Chelmsford reforms, hoping that the Prime Minister would redeem his promise to the Indian Musalmans, that the Punjab wound would be healed and that the reforms, inadequate and unsatisfactory though they were, marked a new era of hope in the life of India.

But all that hope was shattered. The Khilafat promise was not to be redeemed. The Punjab crime was white-washed and most culprits went not only unpunished but remained in service and in some cases continued to draw pensions from the Indian revenue, and in some cases were even rewarded. I saw too that not only did the reforms not mark a change of heart, but they were only a method of further draining India of her wealth and of prolonging her servitude.

I came reluctantly to the conclusion that the British connection had made India more helpless than she ever was before, politically and economically. A disarmed India has no power of resistance against any aggressor if she wanted to engage in an armed conflict with him. So much is this the case that some of our best men consider that India must take generations before she can achieve Dominion Status. She has become so poor that she has little power of resisting famines. Before the British advent, India spun and wove in her millions of cottages, just the supplement she needed for adding to her meagre agricultural resources. This cottage industry, so vital for India's existence, has been ruined by incredibly heartless and inhuman processes as described by English witnesses. Little do town-dwellers know how the semi-starved masses of India are slowly sinking to lifelessness. Little do they know that their miserable comfort represents the brokerage they get for the work they do for the foreign exploiter, that the profit and the brokerage are sucked from the masses. Little do they realize that the Government established by law in British India is carried on for this exploitation of the masses. No sophistry, no jugglery in figures can explain away the evidence that the skeletons in many villages present to the naked eye. I have no doubt whatsoever that both England and the town-dwellers of India will have to answer, if there is a God above, for this crime against humanity which is perhaps unequalled in history. The law itself in this country has been used to serve the foreign exploiter. My unbiased examination of the Punjab Martial Law cases has led me to believe that at least ninety-five per cent of convictions were wholly bad. My experience of political cases in India leads me to the conclusion that in nine out of ten the condemned men were totally innocent. Their crime consisted in the love of their country. In ninety-nine cases out of hundred justice has been denied to Indians as against Europeans in the courts in India. This is not an exaggerated picture. It is the experience of almost every Indian who has had anything to do with such cases. In my opinion, the administration of the law is thus prostituted consciously or unconsciously for the benefit of the exploiter.

The greatest misfortune is that Englishmen and their Indian associates in the administration of the country do not know that they are engaged in the crime I have attempted to describe. I am satisfied that many Englishmen and Indian officials honestly believe that they are administering one of the best systems devised in the world and that India is making steady though slow progress. They do not know that a subtle but effective system of terrorism and an organized display of force on the one hand, and the deprivation of all powers of retaliation or self-defence on the other, have emasculated the people and induced in them the habit of simulation. This awful habit has added to the ignorance and the self-deception of the administrators. Section 124A under which I am happily charged is perhaps the prince among the political sections of the Indian Penal Code designed to suppress the liberty of the citizen. Affection cannot be manufactured or regulated by law. If one has no affection for a person or system, one should be free to give the fullest expression to his disaffection, so long as he does not contemplate, promote or incite to violence. But the section under which Mr. Banker and I are charged is one under which mere promotion of disaffection is a crime. I have studied some of the cases tried under it, and I know that some of the most loved of India's patriots have been convicted under it. I consider it a privilege, therefore, to be charged under that section. I have endeavoured to give in their briefest outlines the reasons for my disaffection. I have no personal ill-will against any single administrator, much less can I have any disaffection towards the King's person. But I hold it to be a virtue to be disaffected towards a Government which in its totality has done more harm to India than any previous system. India is less manly under the British rule than she ever was before. Holding such a belief, I consider it to be a sin to have affection for the system. And it has been a precious privilege for me to be able to write what I have in the various articles, tendered in evidence against me.

In fact, I believe that I have rendered a service to India and England by showing in non-co-operation the way out of the unnatural state in which both are living. In my humble opinion non-co-operation with evil is as much a duty as is co-operation with good. But in the past, non-co-operation has been deliberately expressed in violence to the evil doer. I am endeavouring to show to my countrymen that violent non-co-operation only multiplies evil and that as evil can only be sustained by violence, withdrawal of support of evil requires complete abstention from violence. Non-violence implies voluntary submission to the penalty for non-co-operation with evil. I am here, therefore, to invite and submit cheerfully to the highest penalty that can be inflicted upon me for what in law is a deliberate crime and what appears to me to be the highest duty of a citizen. The only course open to you, the Judge, is either to resign your post and thus dissociate yourself from evil, if you feel that the law you are called upon to administer is an evil and that in reality I am innocent; or to inflict on me the severest penalty if you believe that the system and the law you are assisting to administer are good for the people of this country and that my activity is therefore injurious to the public weal."

MR. BANKER : I only want to say that I had the privilege of printing these articles and I plead guilty to the charge. I have got nothing to say as regards the sentence.

## The Judgment

The following is the full text of the judgment:

"Mr. Gandhi, you have made my task easy in one way by pleading guilty to the charge. Nevertheless, what remains, namely the determination of the just sentence, is perhaps as difficult a proposition as a judge in this country could have to face. The law is no respecter of persons. Nevertheless, it will be impossible to ignore the fact that you are in a different category from any person I have ever tried or am likely to have to try. It would be impossible to ignore the fact that, in the eyes of millions of your countrymen, you are a great patriot and a great leader. Even those who differ from you in politics look upon you as a man of high ideals and of noble and of even saintly life. I have to deal with you in one character only. It is not my duty and I do not presume to judge or criticize you in any other character. It is my duty to judge you as a man subject to the law, who by his own admission has broken the law and committed what to an ordinary man must appear to be grave offence against the State. I do not forget that you have consistently preached against violence and that you have on many occasions, as I am willing to believe, done much to prevent violence. But having regard to the nature of your political teaching and the nature of many of those to whom it was addressed, how you could have continued to believe that violence would not be the inevitable consequence, it passes my capacity to understand.

There are probably few people in India, who do not sincerely regret that you should have made it impossible for any government to leave you at liberty. But it is so. I am trying to balance what is due to you against what appears to me to be necessary in the interest of the public, and I propose in passing sentence to follow the precedent of a case in many respects similar to this case that was decided some twelve years ago, I mean the case against Bal Gangadhar Tilak under the same section. The sentence that was passed upon him as it finally stood was a sentence of simple imprisonment for six years. You will not consider it unreasonable, I think, that you should be classed with Mr. Tilak, i.e., a sentence of two years' simple imprisonment on each count of the charge; six years in all, which I feel it my duty to pass upon you, and I should like to say in doing so that, if the course of events in India should make it possible for the Government to reduce the period and release you, no one will be better pleased than I."

THE JUDGE TO MR. BANKER: "I assume you have been to a large extent under the influence of your chief. The sentence that I propose to pass upon you is simple imprisonment for six months on each of the first two counts, that is to say, simple imprisonment for one year and a fine of a thousand rupees on the third count, with six months' simple imprisonment in default."

## Mr. Gandhi on the Judgment

MR. GANDHI: "I would say one word. Since you have done me the honour of recalling the trial of the late Lokamanya Bal Gangadhar Tilak, I just want to say that I consider it to be the proudest privilege and honour to be associated with his name. So far as the sentence itself is concerned, I certainly consider it is as light as any judge would inflict on me, and so far as the whole proceedings are concerned, I must say that I could not have expected greater courtesy."

When the Judge left the court the friends of Mr. Gandhi crowded round him and fell at his feet. There was much sobbing on the part of both men and women. But all the while, Mr. Gandhi was smiling and cool and giving encouragement to everybody who came to him. Mr. Banker also was smiling and taking this in a light-hearted way. After all his friends had taken leave of him, Mr. Gandhi was taken out of the court to the Sabarmati Jail.

And thus the great trial finished.

*Young India,* 23-3-1922, pp. 165 *et. seq.*

# SECTION IV
# LAWYERS AND SATYAGRAHA

## 26
## COURTS AND SCHOOLS

The Non-co-operation Committee has included in the first stage, boycott of law-courts by lawyers and of Government schools and colleges by parents or scholars as the case may be. I know that it is only my reputation as a worker and fighter which has saved me from an open charge of lunacy for having given the advice about boycott of courts and schools.

I venture however to claim some method about my madness. It dees not require much reflection to see that it is through courts that a government establishes its authority and it is through schools that it manufactures clerks and other employees. They are both healthy institutions when the government in charge of them is on the whole just. They are deathtraps when the government is unjust.

### First as to Lawyers

No newspaper has combated my views on non-co-operation with so much pertinacity and ability as the Allahabad *Leader*. It has ridiculed my views on lawyers expressed in my booklet *Indian Home Rule,* written by me in 1908. I adhere to the views then expressed. And if I find time I hope to elaborate them in these

118

columns. But I refrain from so doing for the time being, as my special views have nothing to do with my advice on the necessity of lawyers suspending practice. I submit that national non-co-operation requires suspension of their practice by lawyers. Perhaps no one co-operates with a government more than lawyers through its law-courts. Lawyers interpret laws to the people and thus support authority. It is for that reason that they are styled officers of the court. They may be called honorary office-holders. It is said that it is the lawyers who have put up the most stubborn fight against the Government. This is no doubt partly true. But that does not undo the mischief that is inherent in the profession. So when the nation wishes to paralyze the Government, that profession, if it wishes to help the nation to bend the Government to its will, must suspend practice. But, say the critics, the Government will be too pleased, if the pleaders and barristers fell into the trap laid by me. I do not believe it. What is true in ordinary times is not true in extraordinary times. In normal times the Government may resent fierce criticism of their manners and methods by lawyers, but in the face of fierce action they would be loath to part with a single lawyer's support through his practice in the courts.

Moreover, in my scheme, suspension does not mean stagnation. The lawyers are not to suspend practice and enjoy rest. They will be expected to induce their clients to boycott courts. They will improvise Arbitration Boards in order to settle disputes. A nation, that is bent on forcing justice from an unwilling government, has little time for engaging in mutual quarrels. This truth the lawyers will be expected to bring home to their clients. The readers may not know that many of the most noted lawyers of England suspended their work during the late war. The lawyers, then, upon temporarily leaving their profession, became whole-time workers instead of being workers only during their recreation hours. Real politics are not a game. The late Mr. Gokhale used to deplore that we had not gone beyond treating politics as a pastime. We have no notion as to how much the country has lost by reason of amateurs having managed its battles with a serious-minded, trained and wholetime-working bureaucracy.

The critics then argue that the lawyers will starve, if they leave their profession. This cannot be said of the Sinhas of the profession. They do at times suspend work for visiting Europe or otherwise. Of those who live from hand to mouth, if they are honest men, each local Khilafat Committee can pay them an honorarium against full-time service.

Lastly, for Mohammedan lawyers, it has been suggested that if they stop their practice, Hindus will take it up. I am hoping Hindus will at least show the negative courage of not touching their Muslim brethren's clients, even if they do not suspend their own practice. But I am sure no religious minded Musalman will be found to say that they can carry on the fight only if the Hindus stand side by side with them in sacrifice. If the Hindus do as they must, it will be to their honour and for the common good of both. But the Musalmans must go forward whether the Hindus join them or not. If it is a matter of life and death with them, they must not count the cost. No cost is too heavy for the preservation of one's honour, especially religious honour. Only they will sacrifice who cannot abstain. Forced sacrifice is no sacrifice. It will not last. A movement lacks sincerity when it is supported by unwilling workers under pressure. The Khilafat movement will become an irresistible force

when every Musalman treats the peace terms as an
individual wrong. No man waits for other's help or
sacrifice in matters of private personal wrong. He seeks
help no doubt, but his battle against the wrong goes on
whether he gains help or not. If he has justice on his
side, the divine law is that he does get help. God is the
help of the helpless. When the Pandava brothers were
unable to help Draupadi, God came to the rescue and
saved her honour. The Prophet was helped by God
when he seemed to be forsaken by men.

*Young India,*  11-8-1920, pp. 4-5

## 27

## LAWYERS AND NON-CO-OPERATION

[Extract from a speech on Non-co-operation delivered by
Gandhiji at Madras on 12-8-1920]

I have suggested another difficult matter, viz. that
the lawyers should suspend their practice. How should
I do otherwise knowing so well how the Government
had always been able to retain this power through the
instrumentality of lawyers. It is perfectly true that it
is the lawyers of today who are leading us, who are
fighting the country's battles, but when it comes to a
matter of action against the Government, when it
comes to a matter of paralyzing the activity of the
Government, I know that the Government always looks
to the lawyers, however fine fighters they may have
been, to preserve their dignity and their self-respect. I
therefore suggest to my lawyer friends that it is their
duty to suspend their practice and to show to the
Government that they will no longer retain their
offices, because lawyers are considered to be honorary
officers of the courts and therefore subject to their

disciplinary jurisdiction. They must no longer retain
these honorary offices if they want to withdraw co-
operation from Government. But what will happen to
law and order? We shall evolve law and order through
the instrumentality of these very lawyers. We shall
promote arbitration courts and dispense justice, pure,
simple, home-made justice, Swadeshi justice to our
countrymen. That is what suspension of practice
means.

*Speeches and Writings of Mahatma Gandhi,* 4th
Ed., Natesan, Madras, pp. 528-29

## 28

# THE HALLUCINATION OF LAW COURTS

If we were not under the spell of lawyers and law
courts and if there were no touts to tempt us into the
quagmire of the courts and to appeal to our basest
passions, we would be leading a much happier life than
we do today. Let those who frequent the law courts—
the best of them—bear witness to the fact that the
atmosphere about them is foetid. Perjured witnesses
are ranged on either side, ready to sell their very souls
for money or for friendship's sake. But that is not the
worst of these courts. The worst is that they support
the authority of a government. They are supposed to
dispense justice and are therefore called the palladile
of a nation's liberty. But when they support the
authority of an unrighteous Government they are no
longer palladile of liberty, they are crushing houses to
crush a nation's spirit. Such were the martial law
tribunals and the summary courts in the Punjab. We
had them in their nakedness. Such they are even in
normal times when it is a matter of dispensing justice

between a superior race and its helots. This is so all the world over. Look at a trial of an English officer and the farcical punishment he received for having deliberately tortured inoffensive Negroes at Nairobi. Has a single Englishman suffered the extreme penalty of the law or anything like it for brutal murders in India ? Let no one suppose that these things would be changed when Indian judges and Indian prosecutors take the place of Englishmen. Englishmen are not by nature corrupt. Indians are not necessarily angels. Both succumb to their environment. There were Indian judges and Indian prosecutors during the martial law regime, who were generally guilty of just as bad practices as the Englishmen. Those who tortured the innocent women in Amritsar were Indians, if it was a Bosworth Smith in Manianwala who insulted its women. What I am attacking is the system. I have no quarrel with the Englishmen as such. I honour individuals among them today as I did before my discovery of the unimprovableness of the existing system. If anything, Mr. Andrews and other Englishmen I could name, are nearer to me today than before. But I could not tender my homage even to him who is more than a brother to me, if he became the Viceroy of India. I would distrust his ability to remain pure if he accepted the office. He would have to administer a system that is inherently corrupt and based on the assumption of our inferiority. Satan mostly employs comparatively moral instruments and the language of ethics, to give his aims an air of respectability.

I have digressed a little for the purpose of showing that this Government, if it was wholly manned by Indians but worked as it now is, would be as intolerable to us as it is now. Hence it is that the knowledge of

Lord Sinha's appointment to a high office fails to fill me with a glow of satisfaction. We must have absolute equality in theory and in practice, and ability to do away with the British connection if we so wish.

But to revert to the lawyers and the law courts, we cannot gain this desirable status, so long as we regard with superstitious awe and wonder the so-called palaces of justice. Let not individuals who get satisfaction of their greed or revenge for their just claims, be blind to the ultimate aim of Government which they represent. Without its law courts the Government must perish in a day. I admit that under my plan this power of subjugating the people through the courts will still remain even when every Indian lawyer has withdrawn and there are no civil suits in the law courts. But then they will cease to deceive us. They will have lost their moral prestige and therefore the air of respectability. It is strange but it is true that so long as we believed in the gradual transference of the power of the English to the people, appointments to high posts in the law courts were hailed as a blessing. Now that we believe that the system is incapable of being gradually mended, every such appointment by reason of its deceptiveness must be regarded as an evil. Therefore every lawyer suspending his practice to that extent undermines the prestige of the law courts and to that extent every suspension is a gain for the individual as for the nation.

The economic drain that the law courts cause has at no time been considered. And yet it is not a trifle. Every institution founded under the present system is run on a most extravagant scale. Law courts are probably the most extravagantly run. I have some knowledge of the scale in England, a fair knowledge of the Indian and an intimate knowledge of the South

African. I have no hesitation in saying that the Indian is comparatively the most extravagant and bears no relation to the general economic condition of the people. The best South African lawyers — and they are lawyers of great ability — dare not charge the fees the lawyers in India do. Fifteen guineas is almost a top fee for legal opinion. Several thousand rupees have been known to have been charged in India. There is something sinful in a system under which it is possible for a lawyer to earn from fifty thousand to one lakh rupees per month. Legal practice is not — ought not to be — a speculative business. The best legal talent must be available to the poorest at reasonable rates. But we have copied and improved upon the practice of the English lawyers. Englishmen find the climate of India trying. The habits imbued under a cold and severe climate are retained in India, ample margin is kept for frequent migrations to the hills and to their island home and an equally ample margin is kept for the education of an exclusive and aristocratic type for their children. The scale of their fees is naturally therefore pitched very high. But India cannot bear the heavy drain. We fancy that, in order to feel the equals of these English lawyers, we must charge the same killing fees that the English do. It would be a sad day for India if it has to inherit the English scale and the English tastes so utterly unsuitable to the Indian environment. Any lawyer looking at the law courts and the profession of law from the view-points I have ventured to suggest cannot keep coming to the conclusion that if he wants to serve the nation to the best of his ability, the first condition of service is suspension of his practice. He can come to a different conclusion only if he successfully changes the statement of facts I have made.

*Young India,* 6-10-1920, pp. 2-3

# 29

## COBBLERS V. LAWYERS
[From "Notes"]

Babu Motilal Ghosh,* whose mind is fresh like that of a youth, though he is too frail even to move, summoned Maulana Mohomed Ali and me chiefly to urge us to invite the lawyers to the Congress fold and in effect to restore them to their original status of unquestioned leadership of public opinion. Both the Maulana and I told him that we did want the lawyers to work for the Congress, but that those who would not suspend practice could not and should not become leaders. Motibabu said that my mention of cobblers in the same breath as lawyers had offended some of them. I felt sorry to hear this. I remember the note in these pages, and it was certainly not written to offend. I have said many hard things about lawyers, but I have never considered them to be guilty of caste prejudices. I am sure that the lawyers have appreciated the spirit of my remark. I hope I am never guilty of putting a sting in any of my writings. But I certainly meant no offence in the paragraph referred to by Motibabu. Having been myself a lawyer, I could not so far forget myself as wantonly to offend members of the same profession. Nor can I forget the brilliant and unique services rendered to the country by lawyers such as Pherozeshah Mehta, Ranade, Taiyabjee, Telang, Manamohan Ghose, Krishna-swami Iyer, not to speak

---

* Well-known, old Indian Nationalist; ex-Editor of the *Amrita Bazar Patrika* of Calcutta.

of the living ones.

When no one else had the courage to speak, they were the voice of the people and guardians of their country's liberty. And, if today the majority of them are no longer accepted as leaders of the people, it is because different qualities are required for leadership from what they have exhibited hitherto. Courage, endurance, fearlessness and above all self-sacrifice are the qualities required of our leaders. A person belonging to the suppressed classes exhibiting these qualities in their fullness would certainly be able to lead the nation; whereas the most finished orator, if he have not these qualities, must fail.

And it has been a matter of keen satisfaction to me to find the lawyers all over India, who have not been able to suspend practice, readily assenting to the proposition and being content to work as humble camp-followers. A general will find his occupation gone, if there were no camp-followers in his army.

"But," said Motibabu, "there is a great deal of intolerance that has crept into our movement. Non-co-operators insult those lawyers who have not suspended practice." I fear that the charge is true to a certain extent. Intolerance is itself a form of violence and an obstacle to the growth of a true democratic spirit. Arrogant assumption of superiority on the part of a non-co-operator who has undergone a little bit of sacrifice or put on Khadi is the greatest danger to the movement. A non-co-operator is nothing if he is not humble. When self-satisfaction creeps over a man, he has ceased to grow and therefore has become unfit for freedom. He who offers a little sacrifice from a lowly and religious spirit quickly realizes the miserable littleness of it. Once on the path of sacrifice, we find out the measure of our selfishness, and must continually wish to give more and not be satisfied till there is a complete self-surrender.

And this knowledge of so little attempted and still less done must keep us humble and tolerant. It is our exclusiveness and the easy self-satisfaction that have certainly kept many a waverer away from us. Our motto must ever be conversion by gentle persuasion and a constant appeal to the head and the heart. We must therefore be ever courteous and patient with those who do not see eye to eye with us. We must resolutely refuse to consider our opponents as enemies of the country.

Lawyers and others who believe in non-co-operation but have not, from any cause, been able to non-co-operate in matters applicable to them, can certainly do silent work as lieutenants in the matter of Swadeshi. It requires the largest number of earnest workers. There is no reason why a practising lawyer should not make Khadi fashionable by wearing it even in courts. There is no reason why he and his family should not spin during leisure hours. I have mentioned one out of a variety of things that can be done by practising lawyers for the attainment of Swaraj. I hope, therefore, that no practising lawyer and for that matter no co-operating student will keep himself from serving the movement in every way open to him. All cannot become leaders, but all can be bearers. And non-co-operators, I hope, will always make it easy for such countrymen to offer and render service.

*Young India,* 29-9-1921, p. 305 at p. 306

# 30

# HOW MANY LAWYERS AND STUDENTS HELP
[From "Notes"]

Everywhere I have been asked whether lawyers and students who do not carry out the Congress resolution affecting them can help the movement in any other way. The question is rather strange for it assumes that if a lawyer or a student cannot non-co-operate as such, he cannot help at all. There are undoubtedly hundreds of students and scores of lawyers who are not suspending their normal studies or their practice, as the case may be, only out of weakness. A lawyer who cannot suspend practice can certainly help with money, he can give his spare hours to public service, he can introduce honesty and fair dealings in his profession, he can cease to consider clients as fit prey for his pecuniary ambition, he can cease to have anything to do with touts, he can promote settlement of cases by private arbitration, he can at least do spinning himself for one or two hours per day, he can simplify the life of his family, he can induce the members of the family to do spinning religiously for a certain time daily, he can adopt for himself and his family the use of Khaddar. These are only some of the things that can be done by every lawyer. Because a man cannot or will not carry out a particular part of the non-co-operation programme, he need not be shy about the other items. One thing a practising lawyer may not do; he may no longer figure as a leader on public platforms. He must be content to be a silent worker. What I have said about practising lawyers

applies to students also who cannot or will no
withdraw from schools. Most of our volunteers are
drawn from the student world. Volunteering is a
privilege and a student who has not been able to
withdraw from Government schools cannot receive
privileges from the nation. They too must be content to
be unambitious servants of the nation. Even if we
cannot completely boycott schools and colleges, we must
destroy their prestige. That prestige has almost gone
and is daily decreasing. And we must do nothing that
would restore their prestige till they are nationalized
and answer the requirements of the nation.

*Young India,* 23-2-1921, p. 57

## 31

## PRACTISING LAWYERS

The *Patrika* devotes a leading article to an
examination of the position taken up by me regarding
lawyers and strongly dissents from it. The *Patrika*
thinks that, practising lawyers may continue to lead
public opinion on Congress platform. I respectfully
suggest that any such deviation from the non-co
operation resolution will be a serious mistake. I am
aware that the *Patrika* thinks that the Congress has
not called upon all lawyers to suspend practice.
venture to differ from the interpretation. The resolution
calls upon all lawyers to make greater effort to suspend
practice. And, in my opinion, those lawyers who have
not yet succeeded in suspending their practice, cannot
expect to hold office in any Congress organization or
lead opinion on Congress platforms. Will titled men be
elected as office-bearers, although they may not have
given up their titles? If we do not face the issues boldly

we stand in danger of corrupting the movement. We must exact correspondence between precept and practice. I hold that a lawyer president of Provincial Committee cannot lead his province to victory, if he does not suspend his practice. He simply will not carry weight. I have noticed this again and again during my tours. Lawyers, who have hitherto led public opinion, have either renounced practice or public life.

The *Patrika* errs in comparing practising lawyers to merchants. Not many merchants have yet led public opinion, but where they have come forward, they have certainly renounced dealing in foreign cloth. The public will not, I am glad to be able to say, tolerate divorce between profession and practice. But not to seek, or give up public position is one thing, and to help the movement as a weak but humble follower is another. Thousands are unable to carry out the full advice of the Congress and are yet eagerly helping as silent camp followers. That is the position that practising lawyers should take up. It will be honourable, dignified and consistent. We may not, in our progress towards Swaraj, consider the lead of any class or individual as essential to success.

The *Patrika* goes beyond the scope of the paragraph of *Young India* when it presents as an alternative to suspension, derision and insult. He would be an unworthy non-co-operator who would deride or insult a lawyer, or any one else who is too weak or otherwise unable to respond to the Congress call. Because we may not elect such persons as office-bearers, we may not be intolerant and insulting to them. On the contrary, those who are honestly unable to follow the Congress resolution are in every way, worthy of sympathy.

Nor is the *Patrika* right in thinking that, before

practising lawyers cease to be leaders, there should be a complete boycott of law courts; and as that is impossible without a rebel government, and as we do not contemplate rebellion, practising lawyers may safely lead opinion as hitherto. There is an obvious fallacy underlying this suggestion. Carried to its logical extent, it would mean that no leader need practise what he preaches. The fact is that, although law courts may not be completely boycotted by the sacrifice of Messrs. Nehru and Das, and by our refusal to give any public status to practising lawyers and others who have not carried out the Congress resolution, we have successfully demolished the prestige of these institutions, and, therefore to that extent, of the Government. If we restore titled men, lawyers and others to their status even though they have not responded, we commit national suicide. Lastly, the *Patrika* is wrong in arguing that the Congress has called for suspension in order to secure the lawyers' services. The motive as the preamble of the original resolution clearly states, is to undermine the Government's prestige by the non-co-operation of parties to the institutions on which the prestige is built. *Young India,* 30-3-1921, pp. 98-99

## 32

## A PROTEST

"The Editor, *Young India*, Ahmedabad

Sir,

The other day when you left Jubbulpore for Cuttack, you had an interview with Gunada Babu at Calcutta. I have seen that interview in the Independent of the 2nd instant, which appears to have borrowed it from the *Servant*. I refer you to a statement in that article attributed to you.

It runs thus:

'At Jubbulpore, from where he (Mahatma Gandhi) was coming, two young men (sons of rich merchants) were leading the movement very successfully against a whole host of lawyers. Being businessmen, they were carrying on the work of organization most effectively.'

This statement is incorrect.

The facts are:

These young men are not merchants. They are foundation-stones of the British Government in India. They are Malguzars. Their trade is to realize Rs. 100 from the poor tenants, give the Government Rs. 55 and keep Rs. 45 with themselves as commission and guarantee to recover the money even in the worst times. What a non-co-operation with the Government ! If these Malguzars are not co-operators, no one else is a co-operator. The Malguzari system was an invention of Todarmal by which means people could be systematically dominated by the rulers through their mercenaries. These mercenaries are the Malguzars, who, you have said, are leading the movement.

If a lawyer who has not suspended his practice is not a proper person to be an office-bearer, certainly a Malguzar too should not be an office-bearer. A Malguzar is more attached to the Government than a lawyer.

In Jubbulpore these young men, Malguzars, are not leading the movement.

The movement in Jubbulpore is being led by the lawyers and the whole host of them are supporting it.

You did not give sufficient time to Jubbulpore, else the members of the Bar would have gladly seen you and discussed the matter with you. I fully believe that it will never be wealth which will lead the movement. It will always be the intellect and I hope you will correct the wrong impression created by the interview.

I suspended my practice in November last.

I am, etc.,
G. C. VARMA
Bar-at-Law."

Jubbulpore, 10-4-21

I am glad of Mr. Varma's energetic protest. And I hope that the lawyers of Jubbulpore are leading the N.C.O. Movement. I must however adhere to my statement that the lawyers were conspicuous by their absence on the day I visited Jubbulpore, and that the two young men referred to by me, were in charge of the whole management. That they are sons of land-holders is true enough. Theirs today is cooperation of necessity. The Congress has not yet called upon land-holders to surrender their lands to the Government nor is it ever likely to. These youngmen, like some land-holders' sons elsewhere are taking an honourable part in the national uplift and they deserve every encouragement from lawyers. There are no two opinions about the fact that intellect rather than riches will lead. It might equally be admitted by the correspondent that the heart rather than the intellect will eventually lead. Character, not brains, will count at the crucial moment. And I fancied that these young men showed character. I should be sorry to find otherwise.

*Young India,* 20-4-1921, pp. 127-28

# 33

## PRACTISING LAWYERS
[From "Notes"]

Letters continue to pour in regarding practising lawyers holding offices in Congress Committees. Ever since my arrival in Bengal, the question has been still more pressingly put to me. An ex-student from Dhubri writes to ask whether I expect the movement to succeed under the leadership of practising lawyers. I cannot conceive the possibility of the movement, which is one of self-sacrifice, succeeding if it is led by lawyers who do not believe in self-sacrifice. I have not hesitated to advise that electors rather than be ably led by such lawyers should be content to be more humbly guided. I can certainly imagine a brave and believing weaver or cobbler more effectively leading than a timid and sceptical lawyer. Success depends upon bravery, sacrifice, truth, love and faith; not on legal acumen, calculation, diplomacy, hate and unbelief.

*Young India*, 25-8-1921, p. 265 at p. 266

# 34

## ABOUT LAWYERS
[From "Notes"]

The Jamnalal Bajaj Fund of one lakh of rupees that was given last year for the support of lawyers who had suspended practice as a result of the Nagpur resolution is nearly, as it was intended to be, exhausted. The lawyers cannot go back to practice with

135

any show of decency, and I am sure that many will not countenance even the idea of a return when the country is showing such wonderful example of self-sacrifice.

But it would not be proper to leave the lawyers to their own resources. I would therefore certainly suggest to the Provincial Committees that they should take up the burden subject to assistance from the Central Fund, if it was at all found necessary. The rearrangement should be quickly made so as to avoid suspense and delay in the even tenor of national work.

This, however, is the least among the difficulties that surround the lawyer class at the present moment. They are eager to take part in a national awakening. The spirit is willing, the flesh is weak. I still feel that practising lawyers cannot lead. They cannot but weaken a movement which demands complete, almost reckless, sacrifice. The whole cause can be lost if top men weaken at a supreme crisis. But the Congress has purposely opened an honourable door for them. The original draft was perhaps uncertain as to any but full non-co-operators being entitled to sign the volunteer pledge. The conditions for them are easy of fulfilment, being mostly matters of belief. The use of Khadi may cause some little inconvenience at first, but I feel sure that they will not mind it, if otherwise they believe in the requirements of the pledge. And, as among non-co-operators' imprisonment covers a multitude of defects, practising lawyers who go through the fire of imprisonment will by that one fact come to occupy the position of honour which once was theirs. There is also the general resolution appealing to and inviting all including full co-operators to take up such activities as do not admit of any sacrifice or any difference of opinion. I hope therefore that lawyers will, to the best of their ability and opportunity, respond to the country's call in many of the various ways open to them. Where all are expected to help none should be found wanting or indifferent. Non-co-operators on their part instead of priding themselves upon their achievements, should be humble enough to receive all the aid that might be rendered to the country's cause. The spirit of toleration should take the place of intoleration and exclusiveness. It can do no credit to the movement or good to the cause if a man, who has nothing or little to sacrifice, claims, by reason of his putting on Khadi, the right of slighting practising lawyers or others who may be honestly and according to their lights serving the country in various ways. Whatever is offered upon the altar of service to the motherland with a willing heart must be thankfully received.

*Young India,* 12-1-1922, p. 9 at p. 15

## 35

# THE SATYAGRAHI LAWYERS

[Editor's Note: As a protest against the passing of the Anarchical and Revolutionary Crimes Act (XI of 1919), known popularly as the Rowlatt Act, certain barristers and pleaders practising in the Courts of the Ahmedabad District joined a movement called the Satyagraha Sabha and signed a pledge whereby they undertook "to refuse civilly to obey these laws (viz., the Rowlatt Act) and such other laws as a committee to be hereafter appointed may think fit". B. C. Kennedy, the District Judge of Ahmedabad, called upon these barristers and pleaders to explain their conduct in signing the pledge. The respondents offered an explanation of their conduct which the District Judge considered unsatisfactory. On a reference from the District Judge, the High Court of Bombay issued notice against the respondent barristers and pleaders to show cause why they should not be dealt with under the disciplinary jurisdiction of the High Court for taking the pledge. The notice came up for hearing before the Hon'ble Chief Justice Sir Norman Macleod and Mr. Justice Heaton and Mr. Justice Kajiji. On hearing Bahadurji, acting Advocate-General who appeared in support of the notice and the Counsel for the respondent barristers and pleaders who appeared to show cause the High Court delivered judgment on 15-10-1919. It was held by the High Court that the barristers and pleaders had, by signing the pledge, rendered themselves amenable to the disciplinary jurisdiction of the High Court. The High Court further held that under the circumstances it was not necessary to take any disciplinary action against the respondents but a mere warning to them was enough. The judgment of the High Court is reported in 22 *Bombay Law Reporter* at page 13.]

The judgment of the (Bombay) High Court in the case of the Satyagrahi lawyers is, to say the least, highly unsatisfactory. It has shirked the issue. The logical outcome of the judgment should have been punishment and not a postponement of it. The lawyers in question had shown no repentance. So far as the public know, they will be ready to offer civil disobedience should the occasion arise. The issue having been raised, the lawyers did not ask for mercy but a clear decision. As it is, they do not know where they are.

The learned Judges have laid down principles of legal conduct which, in our humble opinion, are open to question. For instance, what is the meaning of "those who live by the law must keep the law" ? If it means that no lawyer may ever commit a civil breach without incurring the displeasure of the court, it means utter stagnation. Lawyers are the persons most able to

appreciate the dangers of bad legislation and it must
be with them a sacred duty by committing civil breach
to prevent a criminal breach. Lawyers should be
guardians of law and liberty and as such are interested
in keeping the statute book of the country 'pure and
undefiled'. But the Judges of the Bombay High Court
have presented to them a mercenary view of their
profession and have even confounded the functions of
judges and lawyers. The only escape from the
intolerable situation created by the judgment is for the
respondents to have the case restored to the board, re-
argued and to ask for a final decision. Fortunately the
Judges have left the course open to the Satyagrahi
lawyers.

*Young India,* 22-10-1919, p. 1


## 36

## MYSORE LAWYERS

Several Mysore lawyers who had taken part in the
Mysore Satyagraha struggle have been disbarred by the
Mysore Chief Court. The last victim is Shri H. C.
Dasappa, a most respected Mysorean and a practitioner
of twenty years' standing. Serious as the disbarring of
a member belonging to a liberal profession must be, such
cases have happened before now on insufficient or purely
political grounds. Such injustices have to be borne with
resignation and fortitude. But the order of the Chief
Judge in Shri Dasappa's case as reported in *The Hindu*
has made for me most painful reading. Shri Dasappa
had the hardihood to defy a magistrate's order not to
address meetings in a part of Mysore, and had the equal
hardihood under my instructions to advise Satyagrahi
prisoners, to boycott the departmental inquiry by Justice

Nageswara Iyer. For these grave offences Shri Dasappa
has been disbarred for ever. He will be reduced to
penury, if the Judges could help it and if their verdict
has any potency beyond the paper on which it is written.
Shri Dasappa becomes a man without a character to be
despised and shunned by society. I happen to know Shri
Dasappa personally. I hold him to be a man of spotless
character and unimpeachable honesty. He has been
manfully striving to practise non-violence to the best of
his ability. He has done what many patriot lawyers or
no lawyers have done in British India. And nowadays
the judges take no notice of their conduct, and the public
have made of them heroes. Advocate Bhulabhai has been
Advocate-General of the Bombay High Court. He has
defied laws. So has Advocate Munshi, and so has
Chakravarti Rajagopalachari. They have not been
disbarred. Two of them have been Ministers in their
Provinces. Public inquiries have been boycotted before
now with impunity. Neither the honour nor the
character of those who have brought about such boycotts
have been impugned. In my opinion the Judges of the
Mysore Court have forgotten themselves in delivering
their judgment. Shri Dasappa has not suffered. He will
rise in the estimation of the people of Mysore. But I
make bold to say the Mysore Judges have suffered by
allowing themselves to be carried away by prejudice.

Such travesty of justice has happened before now.
A Durban Magistrate who was carried away by some
stupid prejudice had condemned an innocent man. His
judgment was reversed, and the Supreme Court
condemned it in such scathing terms that the
Magistrate had to be removed. The Judges of the
martial law days in the Punjab were not removed, but
many were thoroughly disgraced because they had
pronounced judgments which could not be supported by

evidence before them. This Mysore judgment is worse than the Punjab judgments. Then there was panic. Murders had been committed by the mob, and eminent men were tried not by ordinary courts but by martial law tribunals. In Mysore nothing of the kind has happened. The Chief Judge's order is a cool and calculated attack on the honour of a man who could not defend himself against reckless statements from the Bench. Judges sometimes forget, as these Mysore gentlemen have done, that there is the bar of public opinion which is no respecter of persons.

My condolence and pity go out to the Judges who have delivered a judgment which, let me hope, in their cooler moments they will regret. For Shri Dasappa and his colleagues who have been disbarred I have nothing but congratulations. I would ask them to turn the punishment into a blessing. It is well that they cannot appear before judges who can be so grossly prejudiced as the Mysore Judges have proved themselves to be. Let these lawyers be proud of their poverty which will be probably their lot now. Let them remember Thoreau's saying that possession of riches is a crime and poverty a virtue under an unjust administration. This is an eternal maxim for Satyagrahis. The disbarred lawyers have a rare opportunity of so remodelling their lives that they can always be above want. Let them remember that practice of law ought not to mean more taking daily than, say, a village carpenter's wage. Let them make redoubled efforts to produce such a state of affairs in Mysore that the travesty of the nature I have described may become impossible. It is no pleasure to me to have to write as strongly as I have done. But I could do no less if I was to serve Truth.

*Harijan,* 13-7-1940, p. 205

# 37

# SHRI DASAPPA'S CASE

(Originally appeared under the title "A Note" by M. D.)

Perhaps a brief note of facts is necessary to explain Gandhiji's remarks on the extraordinary order of the Mysore Chief Judge directing Shri H. C. Dasappa to be struck off the rolls of the High Court. The first charge against Shri Dasappa was that he had disobeyed the Kolar District Magistrate's order prohibiting him from addressing meetings in a certain area. The other and, in the Judge's opinion more serious, charge was that Shri Dasappa as President of the Mysore Congress advised the Congressmen not to participate in an inquiry appointed by Government. The inquiry was to be made into serious allegations of torture made by the Congress against police officials. It was entrusted to a Judge of the Mysore Court. The Mysore Congress, acting on Gandhiji's advice, decided not to participate in the inquiry, as it was not of an impartial and independent character. This action on the part of Shri Dasappa as President of the Congress could by no stretch of imagination be described as having anything to do with his conduct as a lawyer, but it was regarded by the Chief Justice as "a defect of character unfitting him to be an advocate of the High Court".

He was asked by the High Court to explain his conduct. He naturally questioned the procedure as irrelevant, but described in a statement the circumstances leading to the decision for non-participation in the inquiry. This is what Shri Dasappa said in the course of his statement :

> "The Government appointed Justice A. R.
> Nageswara Iyer to carry on what was admittedly a
> departmental inquiry, not open to the press or the
> public. Attempts made to have the inquiry postponed
> with a view to arrive at an amicable settlement in the
> matter, were of no avail. It was then that the Mysore
> Congress was advised by Mahatma Gandhi to negotiate
> for a change in the personnel of the inquiry. . . . The
> opponent submits that the inquiry was only a
> departmental one and there was no court constituted for
> the purpose. There was no legal obligation whatever on
> the part of Congressmen to tender evidence at the
> inquiry. The moral obligation would only arise in case
> the tribunal was satisfactory."

It is these words that provoked the ire of the Chief
Justice, and in criticizing them he has made certain
statements of astounding audacity: "To make a foul
allegation against one's neighbour and to refuse either
to withdraw it or substantiate it, was a conduct to
which no decent-minded man who had not lost all sense
of fairness would descend or advise others to descend."
Again: "I understand from the respondent's statement
that the aim of his political  association is to get
responsible government established in this State. This
is a form of government which many of us would
admire, and all of us, who are not judges, are at liberty
to advocate. This is not an occasion on which it would
be proper to discuss the advantages or disadvantages
of that form of government. But I think we shall agree
that that form of government can have no chance of
success in any country in which there is not a general
spirit of fairness    throughout   the   country.   The
respondent, in this matter of deterring his followers

from withdrawing or substantiating their charges against their fellow-subjects, has shown himself devoid of that spirit of fairness. He has stated in one part of his statement that he did so at the dictates of a person outside the State. No man fit to be an advocate of this Court can submit his conscience to any one else in that way. It is no excuse for such conduct." Again, the Chief Justice, proceeding, observed, says *The Hindu* report, that, "it was surprising that the respondent, the professed votary of truth, should have behaved in such a way. Perhaps it is because truth is so often degraded in this country into nothing more than a political catchword that the respondent has lost all appreciation of its meaning and value. It was a sad thing indeed for anyone to have so degraded himself and to have lowered his moral standards. It would not be fair to require other members of this honourable profession to associate in the work of the courts with a man who had allowed his morals to be so debased, nor would it be safe to allow litigants to allow their cases in his hands. In my opinion it is quite clear that the respondent has become by defect of character unfit to remain an advocate of this court."

*Harijan,* 13-7-1940, pp. 205-206

## 38

## BABU KALINATH ROY

By the courtesy of the *Young India* Syndicate, composed as it is largely of Satyagrahis, since the deportation of Mr. Horniman I have been permitted to supervise the editing of this journal. I asked for such supervision because I was anxious that nothing should appear in it that was in any way inconsistent with the general principles of Satyagraha, i.e., of truth and non-violence to person or property. In pursuance of the plan I have hitherto also written some leading articles in the usual editorial style. But for this issue I wish to take the sole responsibility, if there be any, of writings on the case of Babu Kalinath Roy, the editor of the now defunct *Tribune*. Personally, I consider that even from the point of view of the authorities, there is nothing wrong or out of the way in what I am about to say. But lest they may think otherwise, it is due to the public and to the *Young India* Syndicate that the authorship of this writing should be known.

With reference to the Punjab disturbances, by my complete silence over them I have allowed myself to be misunderstood by many friends and, as is now well known, I have been deprived of the co-operation, though never the friendship, of so respected and renowned a leader and co-worker as Sannyasi Swami Shri Shraddhanandaji. But I still believe that I have done well in persisting in my silence, for I had no conclusive data to go upon. No public declaration of mine could have in any way affected for the better the action of the authorities. But Babu Kalinath Roy's case materially alters the situation. In my humble opinion the case represents a manifest and cruel wrong. I have not the honour of knowing him personally. When I took up the judgment in the case, I approached it with a feeling that there would be at least a *prima facie* case made out against the accused on some isolated passages in his writings. But as I proceeded with it, the impression grew on me that it was a kind of special pleading in order to justify a conviction and heavy sentence. In order to check myself I took up the numbers of the *Tribune* referred to in the judgment and on which the serious charge against Babu Kalinath Roy under Sec.

124 A of the Indian Penal Code was based, and a careful reading of everyone of the writings in the *Tribune* more than confirmed the impression produced by a perusal of the judgment and led me to think that the martial law court had allowed its judgment to be warped and clouded by the atmosphere of suspicion and distrust surrounding it. The best proof of my statement must be the judgment and the writings on which it is based. They are therefore reproduced in this issue in full. I have prefaced the judgment and the offending articles in the *Tribune* with extracts from the other numbers, showing the whole tendency and tone of the writings, from the beginning of April just after the Delhi affairs. They are not extracts torn from their context, but they are representative of the issues of the *Tribune* published after the 30th March last. The dominant note pervading all the issues is that the agitation against the Rowlatt Legislation should be conducted with sobriety, truth and non-violence. I could nowhere trace in them ill-will, either against Englishmen in general, or against the English Government in particular. Indeed, it would be difficult to surpass the *Tribune* in calmness and self-restraint in the face of circumstances brought about by the Delhi affairs.

This is the test that the Special Tribunal put before itself for its guidance:

"You will have to consider whether this publication was or was not a calm and temperate discussion of the events that had occurred. The people have a right to discuss any grievances that they may have to complain of, but they must not do it in a way to excite tumult. . . . You may point out to the Government their errors. . . . The question is always as to the manner. A question is made whether they (writings) show an intention to instruct by appealing to the judgment or to irritate and excite to sedition. In other words, whether they appeal to the sense of the passions."

Judged by the standard set before the court the articles complained against do not warrant a conviction. They cannot excite tumult, when daily during a period of exceeding stress, the writer asks his readers to refrain from all violence telling them in unmistakable terms that disturbance can only damage their cause. The editor has continuously appealed to the judgment of the readers by asking them not to prejudge, but to await the results of an inquiry which he persistently asked for. The court's discussion of the passages and articles fails to convince one of the propriety of its decision. The court has resented the use of the term "Delhi Martyrs" in the issues of the 6th and the 8th April. When you read the contents under the headings, the one has reference to prayers at the Jumma Masjid and the other to a relief and Memorial Fund. The crime in the language of the court was that "the accused chose to emphasize the memorial for martyrs and not the relief," and the court proceeds, "the inference from this is plain." The plain inference from this is that whoever put the heading felt that those who were shot down at Delhi were so dealt with, without sufficient cause. Why this should be considered seditious passes comprehension. And if such inference shows, as it undoubtedly does, that the action of the Magistrate who gave the order for firing was wrong, is the drawing of such a deduction to be punished? We are told by the court that one may point out to Government their errors. I submit that Mr. Roy justly points out the error of one of the local authorities. (Incidentally I may mention that there is not such editorial headings as "Memorial to Delhi Martyrs" referred to in the judgment.)

The next indictment consists in the editor having used the word "dupe" in connection with the action of some Honorary Magistrates and Municipal Commissioners who tried to dissuade shopkeepers from closing their shops. This is what the article describing the demonstration of the 6th April says:

> "The masses of India are no fools... That they cannot be successfully duped ought to be clear from the very ignominious failure in this very case of certain Municipal Commissioners and Honorary Magistrates and several others who went round the city trying to persuade shopkeepers to keep their shops open."

This is a bare statement of fact as the accused knew it. Then follows an examination of the other articles as to which the gravamen of the charge is the assertion of the editor that the action of the Punjab Government was both "unjust and unwarranted", and that it had "exposed itself to the severest criticisms at the bar of public opinion". Here, too, the editor has, after having reasoned to the reader, led him to the conclusion to which he himself has arrived, — a procedure held to be entirely justifiable under the test accepted by the court itself. The wrong would undoubtedly be if the editor had misstated facts. But in every case, as would appear from the articles reproduced herewith, the writer has fortified himself with what he believed to be facts, and which, so far as the judgment allows us to see, have not been controverted.

The other two articles referred to by the court are "Delhi Tragedy" in the issue of the 9th, and "Blazing Indiscretion" in the issue of the 10th April. The "Delhi Tragedy" is a dispassionate review of the tragedy of the 30th March, and ends with an exhortation to the Government of India to appoint a public inquiry.

"Blazing Indiscretion" is undoubtedly an indictment against Sir Michael O'Dwyer about his speech before the Punjab Legislative Council. The speech, analysed in the article in question, certainly contains more than one "blazing indiscretion". The truth of the matter is that the wrong man was in the wrong box; the right man to have been in the box of the accused should certainly have been Sir Michael O'Dwyer. Had he not made inflammatory and irritative speeches, had he not belittled leaders, had he not in a most cruel manner flouted public opinion and had he not arrested Drs. Kitchlew and Satyapal, the history of the last two months would have been differently written. My purpose, now is not to prove Sir Michael O'Dwyer's guilt, but it is to prove Babu Kalinath Roy's complete innocence, and to show that he has suffered a grievous wrong in the name of British justice, and I do not hesitate to ask Englishman as I ask my countrymen to join me in the prayer for Babu Kalinath Roy's immediate release. As Mr. Norton had shown, and quite recently Sir P. S. Shivaswamy Aiyer, a Martial Law Tribunal was never contemplated to be one for the trial of cases involving delicate interpretations of difficult sections of ordinary enactments. Such tribunals are properly designed only for summary justice being meted out to men who are caught red-handed in acts of rebellion or crimes which mean, if left unchecked, complete disruption of society.

One thing more remains to be considered. Why should this case be singled out for special treatment when it is highly likely that an independent and impartial committee is likely to be appointed to overhaul the Martial Law administration in the Punjab and so revise the sentences passed by the Martial Law Court? My answer is that Mr. Roy's case does not admit of any doubt about it. It is capable of being immediately considered by the Government and if the articles on which the charge against Mr. Roy was based do not amount to sedition — as I hold they do not — he should be immediately set free. Moreover time is an important consideration in this case, for Mr, Roy, as Mr. Andrews has pointed out, has a very delicate constitution.

*Young India,* 11-6-191.9

## 39

## LALA RADHA KRISHNA'S CASE

When Babu Kalinath Roy's case was taken up in these columns, I was asked by several Punjabi friends why I had not taken up Lala Radha Krishna's case which was equally strong, if not stronger than Babu Kalinath Roy's. I respectfully told the friends that I did not know Lala Radha Krishna's case and that I would be glad to study it if the papers were sent to me. I have now received the papers, namely, the charge, the defence statement, the judgment, Lala Radha Krishna's petitions and the translations of portions of the *Pratap* from which the statements in the charge-sheet were taken. These are all published in this issue.\* The reader, therefore, has complete data for coming to a definite conclusion.

In my humble opinion the judgment is a travesty of justice. The case is in some respects worse even than Babu Kalinath Roy's. There are no startling headlines as in the *Tribune* case. The accused has been sentenced not on a section of the Indian Penal Code but on a rule

---

\* These articles are not included in this book.

temporarily framed as a war measure. My meaning will be clear when the reader has the rule itself before him. Let me remind him that it is not a rule passed by the Legislative Council. It is a rule promulgated by the Government under the powers granted to it by the Defence of India Act. Here is the whole of it:

"(1) Whoever by words, either spoken or written or by signs, or by visible representations, or otherwise publishes or circulates any statement, rumour or report—

(a) which is false and which he has no reasonable ground to believe to be true, with intent to cause, or which is likely to cause, fear or alarm to the public or to any section of the public; or

(b) with intent to jeopardize, or which is likely to jeopardize, the success of His Majesty's forces by land or sea, or the success of the forces of any power in alliance with His Majesty; or

(c) with intent to prejudice, or which is likely to prejudice, His Majesty's relations with Foreign Powers; or

(d) with intent to promote, or which is likely to promote, feelings of enmity and hatred between different classes of His Majesty's subjects:

shall be punishable with imprisonment of either description for a term which may extend to three years, and shall also be liable to fine, or if it is proved that he did so with intent to assist the King's enemies, with death, transportation for life or imprisonment for a term which may extend to ten years.

(2) No court shall take cognisance of any offence against this rule save upon complaint made by order of,

or under authority from, the Governor-General in Council, the Local Government or some officer empowered by the Governor-General in Council in this behalf."

It will be noticed that the rule is so drastic that an offence against it could not be taken cognisance of except under special orders of the Government or some officers appointed in this behalf.

Let us turn to the indictment. Now a charge-sheet should contain no avoidable inaccuracies and no innuendoes. But we find that this indictment contains material inaccuracies. One of the three statements claimed by the Prosecution to be false is that the accused said in his paper that "they (the crowd) were fired at in Delhi without any cause". Now this is a dangerous inaccuracy. The passage in question reads, "they were, *at least from their point of view,* fired at without any cause." The words italicized have been omitted from the charge thus giving a different meaning to the writing from the one intended by the writer. From the third item too the relevant portion which alters the accused's meaning in his favour has been omitted. The third count concludes, "the people threw stones and brickbats at the time when the authorities had already taken the initiative." The relevant and qualifying sentences in the article from which the above is extracted are-

"But it is possible that somebody among this huge crowd might have thrown stones on the police officers (before they resorted to firing). Even admitting this to be true, we say that the wisdom and prudence of the authorities demanded that some other method than firing guns should have been adopted with a view to suppress this disturbance."

This sentence with the portion italicized again alters the whole meaning. If such an omission was made by a defendant, it would amount to *suppressio veri* and he would rightly put himself out of court. Done by the prosecution, the omission has passed muster, but in reality it is far more dangerous than *suppressio veri* on the part of a defendant. The Crown by a material omission, intended or otherwise, may succeed in bringing about an unjust conviction, as it appears to have done in this case.

The last paragraph of the charge contains an unpardonable innuendo. "The accused has published a number of seditious and inflammatory articles, but the Crown prefers to proceed under Rule 25." The suggestion that the accused has written "seditious and inflammatory articles" could only be calculated to prejudice the defence. I have never seen an indictment so loosely drawn up and so argumentative as this. In a properly constituted court of law, I venture to think, that it would have been ruled out of order, and the accused set free without having to enter upon any defence.

The judgment, too, I am sorry to say, leaves the same impression on one's mind that the charge does an impression of prejudice and haste. It says, "The prosecution have also established that each of these statements is false." Now I have, I hope, already demonstrated that two of the statements in the indictment would not be proved to be false for they are statements *torn from their context* and *incomplete.* No amount of evidence to prove the falsity of such incomplete statements could possibly be permitted to injure the accused. There remain only two statements to be examined. The first statement is: "By the evening of the 31st March forty Hindus and Musalmans had been killed." Now it would be quite clear to anybody pursuing the judgment that even now it is not known how many persons were killed. I suggest that the deciding factor in examining the falseness or otherwise of the above statement is not the number killed, but whether any people were killed at all. If anything could then alarm the people, it was the fact of firing, not necessarily the number killed. And the fact of firing is not denied. As to the number, the newspapers including the Anglo-Indian press had different versions. The learned Judge dismisses the plea that other respectable papers contained about the same statements that the *Pratap* did. I submit that it was a relevant plea in order to establish the defendant's *bona fides* with a view to show that he had reasonable grounds for believing the statements he published. The second statement made by the accused is: "It cannot be denied that most who were killed or wounded were innocent." Lala Radha Krishna in his petition pertinently observed that 'the Delhi authorities themselves took this view and in order to provide for the innocent sufferers in the riots opened a public fund'. Let me add to this that no attempt was made by the Crown to show that even one man killed or wounded among the crowd was guilty of any act of violence himself. The court seems merely to have relied upon the fact that those who were killed were 'members of a violent and dangerous mob'. That fact docs not necessarily prove that those actually killed were guilty of violence nor has the accused in his articles complained that the innocent suffered with the guilty. His complaint naturally was that the firing was at all resorted to.

It is now necessary to examine the rule under which the accused was charged. Lala Radha Krishna was charged under sub-clause (a) of sub-section 1 of rule 25. In order to establish the guilt of the accused it is necessary to prove

      (a) That the statement is false;

      (b) That the accused 'has no reasonable ground to believe it to be true';

      (c) That it is published 'with intent to cause' or it 'is likely to cause tear or alarm to the public'.

It has been made abundantly clear in the foregoing that the statements have not been proved to be false, and that even if they were, it has not been proved thai the accused 'had no reasonable ground for believing them to be true'. On the contrary the defence statement gives clearly the grounds of his belief and lastly the Prosecution never proved that there was any 'intent to cause fear or alarm', or that 'there was likely to be any fear or alarm caused'. The judgment however says, "Without going into the question whether he intended to cause fear or alarm to the public, we are satisfied that the publishing and circulating of these false statements did actually cause fear and alarm to the public." L. Radha Krishna observes on this point, "The prosecution witnesses were unable to cite any specific instances of such alarm having been caused by the articles in question."

The judgment takes no note of the antecedents of Lala Radha Krishna, of the fact that although there was not the slightest reason for expressing regret for anything he had written, he expressed it in his statement to the court for any unconscious exaggerations and of the very material fact that the error, if error it was, regarding the number of the dead was corrected by him as soon as the official *Communique* was published and that he published too the *Civil and Military Gazette* version. This seems to be a question of manifest injustice. We understand that Lala Radha Krishna's petition for release is still engaging the attention of His Honour the Lieutenant Governor of the Punjab. We hope that the public and the Press throughout India will support the prayer for justice and that it will not go in vain.

*Young India,*  12-7-1919

40

# THE LAHORE JUDGMENT

"Whoever wages war against the Queen, or attempts to wage war, or abets the waging of such war, shall be punished with death or transportation for life, and shall forfeit all his property." Section 121, Indian Penal Code.

Lala Harkishan Lal, Bar-at-Law, Chaudhary Rambhaj Dutt, Vakil, and Mr. Duni Chand Bar-at-Law and Messrs. Allah Din and Motasingh have been convicted by one of the Special Tribunals, under sections 121 and 121 A of the Indian Penal Code and have been sentenced to transportation for life and forfeiture. The reader may dismiss from his mind section 121 A for the time being. Having convicted the accused under Section 121, the Tribunal had no option but to pronounce the sentence of transportation for life and forfeiture. That, it will be seen, is the lowest penalty the court could inflict, the highest being the penalty of death by hanging. The Judges felt the severity to be so great in the last two cases that they were constrained to remark, "Allah Din and Motasingh are minor offenders, and had it been in our power, we should in their cases, have awarded much lighter sentences." The learned Judges had in their powers not to convict any of the accused at all or to convict them on other charges. But they have said, "We do not consider it necessary to record findings on other charges."

Though the judgment covers twenty-seven sides of the foolscap size, it is being presented to the readers of *Young India,* and I would urge every reader to go through it word by word. For the judges have made it the *cause celebre* of all the cases and shown to the world what the Punjab, and incidentally the whole of India, is in their estimation.

This judgment, read together with the Amritsar one, forms the saddest commentary on British justice, when the judges are ruled by passion and prejudice and not by a sense of justice. To me the judgments are a proof of the contention I have ventured to urge that we need not be enamoured of British justice and that it, in its essence, is no better than any other justice. We deceive ourselves into a false belief when we think that British courts are the palladia of liberty. Justice in British courts is an expensive luxury. It is often 'the longest purse that wins'. It is the crucial moments which provide the surest test. The judges' business is to rise superior to their surroundings. The Punjab Tribunal, in my opinion, has signally failed to do so. Mr. Winston Churchill at the time of the education crusade permitted himself to admit that even the judges were not free from political bias. It is possible, though highly improbable, in this case, that the Privy Council will or can set the matter right, but if it does, what then? At what cost will it have been done? How many of tens of thousands feeling, and having cause to feel, aggrieved by decisions of lower courts can afford to go to appellate courts and finally to the Privy Council? It is much to be wished that people would avoid litigation. 'Agree with thine adversary quickly' is the soundest legal maxim ever uttered. The author knew what he was saying. But it will be asked, what when we are dragged, as we often are, to the courts? I would say, 'Do not defend.' If you are in the wrong, you will deserve the sentence whatever it may be. If you are wrongly brought to the court and yet penalized, let your innocence soothe you in your unmerited suffering. Undefended, you will in every case suffer the least and what is more, you will have the satisfaction of sharing the fate of the majority of your fellow-beings who *cannot* get themselves defended.

But I have digressed. I do not wish to inflict on the reader my special views on law courts, though I hold them to be thoroughly sound. This Lahore judgment shows clearly what our duty is as to the Rowlatt Act and as to the sentences. The judgment is designed to condemn the Rowlatt Legislation agitation.

The opening paragraphs of the judgment set forth in some detail the "public agitation against the Rowlatt Bills" which "began with a protest meeting held at the Bradlaugh Hall on the 4th February, 1919". They refer to my letter of the 1st March including the Satyagraha Vow and bring up the events to the 15th April, including the firing at Delhi, the disturbances at Amritsar, and the meetings at the Badshahi Mosque and say, "Such are the main facts and the Prosecution sets out to combine and connect these facts with *the* accused in such a way as to show that there was a conspiracy to secure the repeal of the Rowlatt Act by criminal means." The court indicates the criminal means in the very next sentence. "The defence has asked us to believe that there was no sort of organization of the *hartal* and that every individual shopkeeper in Lahore, Muzang, and Bhagwanpura decided of his own accord that he must close his shop as a protest." It then describes what it calls two violent posters in order to show that the *hartal* was organized. I can see no violence in any of them, but I can detect in them the agony of an embittered soul. The criminality consists in the *hartal* having been organized and continued, *langarkhanas* having been opened during its continuance and meetings having been held during the time. I venture to think that *hartal* is the inherent right of the people when they are deeply grieved by any action of the authorities. From time immemorial it has been held to be meritorious to organize *hartal* without using force as a means of protest against acts of the governing authority. And when merit becomes a crime, it is a sacred duty to commit that crime, and imprisonment for it, instead of being a disgrace, becomes an honour that every good citizen should cherish. And the least that he can do is to continue the agitation against the Rowlatt Legislation so intense and formidable that Government must withdraw the liberty of the agitators. And were I not afraid of an outbreak of violence in the present state of tension, I would certainly advise *hartals* again.

The tension was no doubt brought about, not by the advent of Satyagraha, but by the folly of the Government in precipitating and almost inviting violence by arresting me whilst I was proceeding to Delhi, and if necessary to Lahore and Amritsar, with the deliberate intention of calming the atmosphere and bringing about peace. The Government invited violence by the mad act of arresting Drs. Kitchlew and Satyapal, who were leaders of the people but who, whilst they were no doubt carrying on a stubborn agitation against the Rowlatt Legislation, were able to curb the temper of the people and were entirely on the side of law and order. The tension must some day go. And if the Government persist in the folly of retaining the Rowlatt Legislation they must prepare for a repetition of *hartals,* well organized but without any force being used and without a drop of blood being shed by the people. When the masses have imbibed the message of Satyagraha, we shall repeat from a thousand platforms Chaudhary Rambhaj Dutt's formula which has been interpreted into threat by the Tribunal in order to prove the existence of criminal conspiracy. The formula is "Remove our sufferings or we close our shops, suspend our business and we ourselves shall starve." There is no doubt that a great and effective demonstration was degraded by the cries such as *"Hai Hai Rowlatt Bill",* *"Hai Hai George mar gaya",* or by an inspector of the C. I. D. having been beaten and driven out, or by disgraceful sheets like the *Danda Akhbar,* or by the destruction of pictures of their Majesties. The accused could not be held responsible for them any more than Mr. Shafi and others who were endeavouring to bring about the peace. What right had the Government to launch out a prosecution for criminal conspiracy or, what is worse, for waging war against the King in respect of men who are not proved to have brought about any of these excesses, whose whole character and status make them almost proof against any such incitements? Whatever may be the technical view of the expression "waging war", to dub a powerful agitation against an odious law an act of war is a descent to the ludicrous. One might as well incriminate a Government for the unauthorized crimes of its servants. If the acts of Lala Dunichand, Lala Harkishanlal and his co-accused were acts of war, no organized agitation is possible in the country. And as organized agitation must be the breath of public life when there is stagnation in the body politic, whether of a social, economic, or political character, it must be counted as a 'merit' to wage war after the style of the Lahore accused.

The whole of the judgment is tinged with a political bias. This is how the Judges dismiss from their consideration the previous record of the accused:

"Before proceeding to consider the case of each accused it is necessary to remark that each of them according to their station in life have been able to produce testimonials from more or less eminent members of society to their moderation and loyalty, These could doubtless have been multiplied as often as they wished. Some of them again have been able to show that in recent times they have not merely prayed for the success of the British arms but have advocated War Loans, helped in recruiting and have even given relatives to the Indian Defence Force or clerks for Mesopotamia. Perhaps all of these efforts were not very valuable, and it has to be remembered that some of the accused are men who are always in the lime-light; but we have no doubt that everyone of them, however much he may dislike the existing Government, at least preferred it to the prospect of German rule. None of these things, however, really affect the matter before us."

When one's judgment is so warped, as is evident was the Judges', from the passages above quoted, it is impossible to expect an impartial decision.

The issue raised by the case is abundantly clear, though not stated. Can we or can we not, legally cany on a sustained powerful agitation involving processions, *hartals,* fasting etc. but eschewing, always and invariably, violence in any shape or form? The implication in the judgment is that we may not do so. If the sentences are allowed by the Government to stand, it is quite clear that they are of the same opinion as the Judges. I, for one, would not welcome the release of the accused on any side-issue or as an act of clemency. There is nothing in the judgment to show that any of the accused either directly or indirectly encouraged violence. And where there is absence of intention to do violence, it is absurd to call a peaceful combination a criminal conspiracy, even though uncontrollable spirits may find their way into that combination and do mischief. The happening of untoward incidents may be used as a warning to leaders. They may be used for justifying the declaration of Martial Law, but they ought not to be used for the purpose of making out peaceful, law-abiding citizens as criminals and liars. The duty of the Indian public is clear: By a quiet, persistent and powerful agitation, but without violence and irritation, to secure repeal of the Rowlatt Legislation and the reversal of the sentences.

*Young India,* 23-7-1919

# 41

## JAGANNATH'S CASE

It is not without extreme sorrow that I have to invite public attention to a third miscarriage of justice in the Punjab. This time it is not a case of a celebrity like Babu Kalinath Roy or a lesser light like Lala Radha Krishna, the Editor of the *Pratap.* The case of which the papers have been furnished me relates to one Mr. Jagannath, unknown to fame and unconnected with any public activity. He has been sentenced by one of the Martial Law Tribunals to transportation for life, with forfeiture of property, under section 121 of the Indian Penal Code, i.e., for waging war against His Majesty. The facts of the case are lucidly set forth in his petition to be found elsewhere*. It is addressed to

---

*This petition is not included in this book.

the Hon. Sir Edward Maclagan, the Lieut. Governor of
the Punjab. The reader will find also the judgment in
the Gujaran-walla case in respect of fifteen accused of
whom Mr. Jagannath was one. The following is the text
in the judgment dealing with the case:

> "Jagannath, accused 10, had the notices convening
> the meeting of the 5th, printed in Lahore and was
> present at the meeting. He denies his presence at the
> meetings of the 12th and the 13th. But we have no
> hesitation in holding that he was present at both and
> that his defence is worthless. There is ample evidence
> to show that on the 14th April, he took a very active
> part in having the shops closed. We are satisfied of his
> guilt and convict him under sec. 121, I. P. C."

I submit that it was no crime on the accused's part
to have the notice convening the meeting of the 5th
printed, nor to have been present at the meeting,
unless the notices or the meetings were of an
incriminating character. This is what the court has to
say about the meeting of the 5th April:

> "It is alleged that the people of Gujaranwalla knew
> little and cared less about the Rowlatt Act and that on
> the 4th April certain of the accused decided to start an
> agitation against this Act on the same lines as had been
> adopted in other parts of the country at the instance of
> Gandhi. A mass meeting was accordingly convened and
> held on the evening of the 5th April when the Rowlatt
> Act was condemned."

Under no Statute known could these facts be held
to involve any crime. The Judges themselves have
stated as much:

> "We are not however satisfied in this case, that
> prior to the 12th April any indictable conspiracy had

come into existence. We therefore feel constrained to
acquit those of the accused who are shown only to have
taken part in the proceedings prior to that date."

It is difficult therefore to understand the reference
of the court to the accused's presence at the meeting
of the 5th or his having been an agent for getting the
notices printed. The court proceeds, "On the evening of
the 12th and during the day of the 13th certain of the
accused in consultation with Bhagat agreed that they
should follow the example set at Amritsar of burning
bridges and cutting telegraph wires." Now these facts,
it is plain, undoubtedly prove a criminal conspiracy but
the court is silent as to which accused agreed upon the
crimes recited in the paragraph. It should be
remembered that there was a meeting on the 12th, of
the District Congress Committee held prior to the
evening meeting of the 12th referred to in the sentence
quoted above. I submit that it was necessary for the
court definitely to find that the accused was present at
the agreement alleged to have been arrived at, for
burning bridges and cutting telegraph wires. But there
is nothing in the finding of the court beyond a vague
general statement about the accused's presence at the
meetings of the 12th and 13th. I would suggest that
even if the accused was in Gujaranwalla on the 14th
April and took a very active part in having the shops
closed, it would be no offence, unless he could be proved
to have been party to the criminal agreement referred
to.

Whilst, therefore, the judgment seems to afford no
evidence of the accused's crime, statements, most
damaging to the court and conclusive in favour of the
accused, have yet to follow. The accused's defence
rested upon an *alibi*. He stated that he left
Gujaranwalla on the 12th April by the 5 p.m. train *en*

*route* for Kathiawad where he had a case. Now I admit that it is as easy to set up an *alibi* as it is difficult to prove it. But anyone reading the petition can only come to one conclusion, viz., that the defence of *alibi* was completely established. Mr. Jagannath produced local respectable witnesses to show that he had left Gujaranwalla on the 12th. He applied for subpoena to summon witnesses from Kathiawad to show that he was in Dhoraji on the 16th April. The court rejected the application, but granted interrogatories, put the accused, a poor man, to the expense of Rs. 250 for the expenses of the Commission, and yet strange as it may appear, pronounced judgment against the accused without waiting for the return of the Commission. He made an application for the stay of argument, till after the receipt of replies to interrogatories. The application was rejected. In a second application he urged that the court should ascertain by telegram the result of the interrogatories. Even that application was proved unavailing. The accused has rightly contended in the petition that on this ground alone the conviction was illegal and ought to be set aside. The petition refers to the register of the *Foujdar* of Dhoraji saying that he reached Dhoraji on the 16th April. The accused shows also by the examination of 10 independent witnesses that he was in Dhoraji on that date. He shows further by extracts from Railway Time Tables, that it takes 44 hours to reach Dhoraji from Delhi by the fastest train, and shows conclusively that it was physically impossible for him to be in Gujaranwalla after 6 p.m. on the 13th; though as a matter of fact he shows by other conclusive evidence that he left Gujaranwalla on the 12th. He produces proceedings of Jetpur Court where he had his case in Kathiawad. There is, therefore, no ground whatsoever for keeping the accused in jail for a single moment.

The accused on his own showing is "a petty shopkeeper at Gujaranwalla, paying no income tax, being ignorant of Urdu as well as English and not possessed of any influence in a big town like Gujaranwalla with a population of 30,000 persons. He, being a man of humble position and status in life, with no education, has never taken part in politics, nor was he a member of the local District Congress Committee or any other political body or association." The humbleness of his position makes the injustice all the more galling and makes it doubly incumbent on the public to see that the meanest of the subjects of the King suffers no wrong. The decision of His Honour the Lieut. Governor in the case of Lala Radha Krishna raises the hope that speedy justice will be done in this case. Bad as Babu Kalinath Roy's and Lala Radha Krishna's cases were, this, if possible, is worse in that Martial Law Judges in their impatience, shall I say, to convict, declined to wait for a return of the Commission they themselves had granted—a Commission on whose return hung the liberty, and might have been, even the life of the accused.

*Young India,* 30-7-1919

## 42

## ANOTHER SCANDAL

It is my unpleasant duty to present another batch of cases to the reader from the Punjab which reveal a state of things that is utterly unbearable. It is to be wished that H. E. the Viceroy will end the growing anxiety by appointing the promised Committee of Inquiry without delay. Mr. Montagu has said from his

place in the House of Commons that at least two out
of the three Judges of the Punjab Special Tribunals
were Judges of the High Court of three years standing.
The public have been recently informed that where the
members were not High Court Judges, they were
eligible for that high post. The poignancy of the sorrow
that the atrocious injustices such as I have had the
painful duty of exposing have caused, is increased by
the knowledge that perpetrators of these injustices are
judges in whose judgments the people have been
accustomed to put the utmost faith. This unevenness of
temperament can only be accounted for by the
supposition that the trained judicial intellect of the
Judges must have suffered temporary aberration by the
events of the Punjab. The desire to secure for
Englishmen almost absolute immunity from physical
harm from the 'natives', by inflicting exemplary
punishments on some one or other, appears to have
been the master passion overruling discretion, wisdom
and justice. It is not possible for me to understand the
judgments that have come under my notice on any
other hypothesis. These reflections are caused by a
perusal of the judgment and the evidence in the Hafizabad case. The full text of the judgment and the
evidence material to the case to be examined, will be
found printed elsewhere in this issue.* During the
whole course of my practice of law, by no means
inconsiderable, extending over an unbroken period of
nearly twenty years, I have never come across cases in
which capital punishment has been so lightly
pronounced, on the flimsiest evidence taken down in a
most perfunctory manner, as appears to me to have

---

*The judgment and notes of evidence are not included
in this book.

been done in the Hafizabad case.

The case has been sent to me in regard to only one of the nineteen accused tried viz. Karamchand, the nineteenth accused—a student of the Dayanand Anglo-Vedic College. But I have no hesitation in saying that there was no evidence before the court to warrant a conviction against any of the accused for waging war. The Judges had a choice of offences for conviction. The accused were charged under Sections 121, 147, 307, 486(?), and 149 of the Indian Penal Code. Section 147 relates to rioting, carrying with it a maximum penalty of two years' imprisonment. Section 149 renders members of an unlawful assembly liable to the same penalty as any other member thereof. Section 307 relates to attempts to murder carrying the maximum penalty of ten years. Section 486 appears to be an erroneous copy, it has no relevance to the evidence led before the court. It was thus easy enough to convict on any of the milder sections if the Judges had so chosen. They however 'scented' war in every act of the crowd during those three or four days of April.

Whilst therefore it is clear to me, as I hope it will be clear to every impartial student of the case, that the charge of 'waging war against the King' is unsustainable, in the absence of the specific evidence against the other accused, it is difficult to form a conclusive opinion as to their cases on the minor charges. I cannot however conceal from myself or the reader the very strong suspicion that the full text of the evidence will not disclose any ground for the statement of the Judges to the effect that "the orators had incited the crowd to take immediate and vigorous steps to overthrow the Government by raising as much opposition to it as possible.".Nowhere have I seen any attempt during those days of April to 'overthrow the Government'.

But I must confine myself to the case of Karam-chand. These are the full remarks in the judgment about him:

> "Karamchand, No. 19, was peculiarly guilty. He brought down the news of the Lahore riots. He gave a most garbled account of it. And by representing that the Lahore crowd had succeeded in beating the military, he gave the Hafizabad crowd reason to believe that their insurrection would be successful."

"We think," the Judges proceed, "that these four men deserve the extreme penalty." The three men who are bracketed together with him for capital punishment are supposed to have been among the active assailants of Lieutenant Tatam. Not so Karamchand, as is clear from the passage from the judgment just quoted.

Let us look at the evidence against the accused. Two of the prosecution witnesses who were on the train that carried Lieutenant Tatam have given only identifying evidence. They are unable to say that Karamchand himself did anything at all. Prosecution witness No. 5 first identified Karamchand 18 or 20 days after the 14th April. Witness No. 6 identified him 10 or 12 days after the said date. Both the witnesses, it is admitted, were utter strangers to Karamchand. The gravamen of the charge against Karamchand is, not that he did anything on the 14th, but that he brought some news from Lahore on the 11th. This is the exclusive evidence about Karamchand given by the Head Master of the D. B. School:

> "Karamchand is a student of the D. A. V. College, Lahore. I saw him on the 11th evening. He was talking about the riots of Lahore that the people are being fired upon with a machine-gun at Lahori Gate are not retreating." (I have taken the sentence exactly as it

occurs in the original copy before me—M. K. Gandhi.).
"He was going to say more but I stopped him. I advised
him that it is not good to say such things at Hafisabad.
He was my old pupil. 6 or 7 people were present. This
was outside the town on a footpath. He was excited. I
left on the 12th."

CROSS EXAMINATION: Accused does not belong to
Hafizabad. He went away when I warned him. I had not
asked him what had happened at Lahore."

Prosecution witness 27 gave evidence corroborating
that of the Head Master. This is all the evidence
against Karamchand. It stands out clear as daylight
that Karamchand's alleged talk about the Lahore riots
took place on the 11th, that he spoke outside the town
on a footpath in the presence of 6 or 7 people and that
he stopped as soon as his old school master advised
him to do so and went away; and that he does not
belong to Hafisabad. I hold that the Judges' paraphrase
of the above evidence is totally unwarranted. There is
nothing in all the evidence about Karamchand to show
that the crowd near the Railway station on the 14th
was the same as the 6 or 7 people before whom he
talked outside the town on the 11th about the Lahore
riots. One fails to see what peculiarity the Judges found
in Karamchand's case.

Let me note here that the Head Master and the
corroborating witness give us no information regarding
Karamchand's doings or whereabouts on the 14th April.
Even if, therefore, Karamchand was present on the
14th April at the station, so far as the evidence enables
one to see, he was a silent spectator of the cowardly
conduct of the mob. But Karamchand says he was not
there. He says he went to his village on the 12th. He
produced four witnesses to prove that he was in his
village Udhoki on the 14th April. I venture to suggest

that there is just as much probability of Karamchand and his witnesses having told the truth as there is of the two witnesses for the prosecution being mistaken about the identity of Karamchand, regard being had to the fact that they had never seen him before, that they were taken to the jail to identify him 10 or 18 days after the event and specially when they never saw Karamchand doing anything active. Add to this the fact that the prosecution witnesses were only for a few minutes in the midst of the crowd and whilst, according to the evidence of the Grown, stones were being thrown at the first class compartment. It is not justice to sentence a man to be hanged on the very inconclusive testimony as to identify. Karamchand's father gives me further details to prove that the former was at his village on the 14th April. Naturally I am unable to make use of this - extraneous, though important— evidence to prove his innocence. The father says in his letter that Karamchand's sentence has been commuted to 10 years' rigorous imprisonment. He is naturally not satisfied with it. I hope that His Honour the Lieutenant Governor of the Punjab will study the case personally, and if he does, I doubt not that Karamchand will be discharged. I hope too, that his co-accused who were sentenced to be hanged are at least alive so that their cases may be reviewed by the forthcoming Committee of Enquiry.

We, who are living in the Presidency, cannot but contrast the Punjab proceedings with those at present going on in Ahmedabad. Nothing that was done in Hafizabad could surpass the wicked and wanton cruelty of the mad mob at Viramgam. And yet this Tribunal, I am thankful to be able to note, has carried on the enquiry with judicial calmness, giving every opportunity to the counsel for the defence to bring every fact to light and have not found it in their hearts to impose the capital punishment on a single person in that case. So far as I know, its judgments have not provoked much hostile criticism, whereas almost every judgment of the Punjab Tribunals that has come to light has been subjected to the severest comment. Only the promised Committee of Inquiry can solve the discrepancy. Meanwhile I hope the public will demand full and unconditional discharge in cases of palpable injustice like that of poor Karamchand.

*Young India,* 20-8-1919

## 43

## VICTIMS, NOT GUILTY

The readers will recall our Lahore correspondent's remarks about the Ramnagar cases. I have a file of papers in these cases but I was unprepared to discuss them until I got at least the text of the judgment. This is now before the readers. The able petition on behalf of Lala Karamchand — not the same as the lad Karamchand who was sentenced to be hanged— presented by his old mother Gangadevi shows the graphic language of his son Devidas's letter that the accused in the case are, 'victims, not guilty'. If the simple narrative of Lala Karamchand's son be true, and I think there is no reason to doubt its accuracy, the whole proceedings were a farce. They constituted not a legal trial but a mockery of it. The accused, twenty-eight in number, were all tried together, the trial was finished in one day during which altogether 150 defence witnesses were examined, the accused were not informed of the charge against them except through the mouths of the prosecution witnesses. How the Judge could examine so many witnesses in a day passes comprehension. In spite of repeated applications, copy of notes of evidence or the statements of the accused is not furnished. The only inference is that no notes were kept.

Why were these cases rushed so? The accused were arrested eight days after the alleged offence. Order was completely restored throughout the Punjab by that time. The trial took place on the 22nd May, five weeks after the alleged offence. There was no occasion then for indecently rushing through the trial.

On the 17th April a police officer notes in his diary that all was quiet, save that there was a partial *hartal*. It is rightly suggested in the papers that mention would surely have been made in the diary of any serious offence. The offence alleged is not such as could be committed in secret. It is stated to have been openly committed. Here at least there is enough to throw doubt on the prosecution story. But the judge had no doubt about it!

The story of the prosecution is varied from time to time. Five maunds of fuel said to have been required for burning His Majesty's effigy became reduced to a few straws!

At best all but one of the accused appear to have been mere spectators.

These facts are common to all the accused. I have been supplied also with the papers regarding Lala Daulatram. The facts therein set forth tally with those furnished in Lala Karamchand's case. I am convinced that twenty-eight innocent men have been ignorantly condemned. They should be set free.

Lala Karamchand is an old retired servant. He has never taken part in politics. For years past, he has been passing his time between Ramnagar and

Hardwar, devoting it to religious pursuits. Lala Daulatram is the son of one who has rendered meritorious service to the Government for a long period. In fact the whole family seems to belong to the official class. It is cruel to think that such men should have been so shamelessly punished.

The judgment is self-condemned. It breathes vindictiveness and anger. The rejection of the defence evidence, the explaining away of the weak points in the prosecution, the punishment of solitary confinement, the heavy fines point unmistakably to loss of balance and unfitness to judge. The cases are now before His Excellency the Viceroy. Let him do unto these humble men even as he would wish to be done unto himself, if he were in their place.

*Young India,* 3-9-1919

## 44

## DR. SATYAPAL'S CASE

Dr. Satyapal's statement, which is published in another column*, shows what a gross injustice has been done in his case as in that of Dr. Kitchlew. They had to be absolved from any participation in the violence that occurred after their arrest. What violence there ever was in Amritsar took place after they were arrested. They were, therefore, accused of all sorts of things which they had never done, of speeches they had never made. Dr. Satyapal's clear, emphatic and courageous statement is a categorical denial of the whole string of charges against him. He shows clearly that the speeches he made were incorrectly reported by

---

* This statement is not included in this book.

the C.I.D. officials, and that every time he spoke he preached the gospel of truth and non-violence, and unceasingly warned the people against losing their temper and going in for any excesses.

I have purposely refrained from printing a spirited letter addressed to me by Dr. Satyapal's father in which he gives his own impressions of the case. I cannot, however, resist the temptation of quoting some of the facts stated in it. For instance, he says:

> "At first time it was not the intention of the Government to prosecute Drs. Kitchlew and Satyapal who had been deported on the 10th April and therefore his (the approver's) confessional statement before the Magistrate of Amritsar did not incriminate them. But as soon as there was a change in the intention of the Government, an additional statement by way of an 'improvement' was obtained which implicated both of these gentlemen."

If this allegation is true, it is a severe reflection on the methods of prosecution and it vitiates the whole of the proceedings. Again this letter says:

> "Dr. Satyapal was restricted from public speaking etc. on the 29th March. The Commissioners have sentenced him to transportation for life on the ground that he was a member of a conspiracy formed for disseminating sedition. But it is curious to the highest degree that he did not even attend the meeting of the 30th March—not to say of his having addressed the meeting —as held by the judges, and it is the meeting in which sedition has been said to have been disseminated in pursuance of the conspiracy."

It is true that Dr. Satyapal signed the handbill convening the meeting that was held on 30th March.

That was on the 28th March. But if there was any conspiracy, it became one not on the 28th but on the 30th. A platform ticket agitation carried on by Dr. Satyapal in January and February last was shamelessly brought into the trial to prejudice him, an agitation that was entirely harmless and successful, and about which Dr. Satyapal even received thanks from the station authorities.

The letter concludes:

"For your information I may mention that Dr. Satyapal offered himself for military service in 1915 and was granted a temporary commission as a lieutenant I.M.S. He was posted at Aden where under very trying circumstances he worked for one year to the satisfaction of his superior officers who gave him eulogizing testimonials at the time of his departure. In 1918 he again volunteered for service but the arrangement fell through. During the influenza and malaria epidemics he did his level best in his humble way to mitigate the suffering of his fellow townsmen, and was awarded non-official *sanads*. It is indeed a befitting sequel to be convicted under section 124A after such a record of services to the Government and public both."

As I have already observed, the Lahore and Amritsar cases are not cases in which a commutation can carry any merit or give satisfaction. It is not mercy that the distinguished accused ask for. It is justice that they seek and on which public must insist. Reduction in the sentences is a blind, however unintended it may be. It must not be allowed to lull the public to sleep. There can be no contentment unless there is a complete and honourable discharge, for the leaders of Lahore and Amritsar.

*Young India,* 3-9-1919

# 45

# LALA LABHU RAM

Bad as are the cases from the Punjab which it has been my misfortune to examine from time to time, that of Lala Labhu Ram is no better. Isolated cases of injustice will happen in the best regulated society and under a model Government. But when injustice becomes the order of the day, it is time for honest men not merely to protest against it but to withdraw their support from a system of Government under which such organized injustice is possible, unless that system is changing and systematic injustice becomes an impossibility. I have no desire to exaggerate the picture. Nothing can be further from my intention than to exacerbate the relations between the two races. And if I could prevent exacerbation by remaining silent, I should do so with the greatest gladness. But I should fail in my duty if I did not draw the attention of the Government to injustices as they come under my notice. They are like poison corrupting the whole system. The poison must be expelled or the body perishes.

What is this case of Lala Labhu Ram then? The evidence for the defence does not appear to be complete and yet it seems to be the whole of the evidence received by Lala Labhu Ram's solicitors. It is quite possible that that evidence was not recorded; for does not the judgment of the court commence with the pregnant sentence: "The evidence for the defence is worthless" ? In one place the notes of evidence contain the remark, "Cross-examination for accused No. 9. Nothing relevant"! The Judges might have considered the defence evidence too as irrelevant. Fortunately one has the exhaustive petition of Mrs. Labhu Ram to fall back upon. It must be accepted as a correct statement of the evidence in the absence of contradiction.

Mr. Labhu Ram is not a poor student lad like Karamchand or a petty trader like Jagannath. He is a Civil Engineer, he belongs, says Malandevi, "to a very respectable and loyal family of Lahore. Several relations of his occupy responsible position in the service of Government." He finished his studies in Glasgow. He returned from England in 1912. He was for some time State Engineer in the Poonch State, "where he not only discharged his professional duties to the entire satisfaction of his superiors but materially helped the authorities in recruiting work. He was not a member of any political society or of any Samaj or Sabha nor did he even take part in any propaganda of any kind whatsoever. He was not in the habit of attending any lectures even. He took no part whatever in the recent *hartal*." I have dealt with Mr. Labhu Ram's position in society somewhat fully, because the case at the worst turns upon the credibility of witnesses. Several of the accused, of whom Lala Labhu Ram was one, pleaded an *alibi* and, as I have had to remark in connection with one case, courts always look upon the defence of *alibi* with considerable distrust. It is therefore necessary to dispose of the case at its worst and give the court credit for fairness in weighing evidence. I submit then that unless the court has overwhelming and unimpeachable testimony against that of Lala Labhu Ram, who said he was not present at the Badshahi Mosque meeting and who was respectably supported, the court was bound to accept his evidence and grant him an honourable discharge. In such cases the status of the accused is a material consideration in coming to a decision and I claim that Lala Labhu Ram enjoyed a status in society which should have stood him in good stead.

But the reader may dismiss the plea of respectability from his mind. It would not be perhaps an unfair reasoning on the part of the opponents—the up-holders of the Punjab proceedings—to say that when the very best of men in the Punjab were under severe suspicion and were drawn into the turmoil of April last, the question of respectability should be ruled out of account. But the Punjab Commissions have gone infinitely further and in many cases, as the readers of these pages have by this time seen, ruled out practically the whole of the defence. Mr. Labhu Ram was arrested on the 20th April, i.e. eight days after the day of the alleged offence. He is supposed to have been one of the hundred men who were charged with a simultaneous assault on one of the police officers. He was not known to this officer before, nor was there a single prosecution witness who had known the accused at all intimately before. Identification is difficult at best of times. It is most difficult, if not almost impossible, when it is a matter of picking out men from an excited crowd of several thousands. Mr. Labhu Ram's name does not occur in the police diary in which the names of the assaulters were noted down. Out of 11 prosecution witnesses 6 had nothing to say about the accused Mr. Labhu Ram. "Witnesses," says Mrs. Labhu Ram, "who identified the petitioner's husband are police employees or interested in them. Most of them have appeared as prosecution witnesses in other Martial Law cases also." This is a most damaging statement, if it is true. It means that they were professional witnesses. One would think that as the accused was arrested eight days after the event, there would be some explanation given by the prosecution of the delay. This is what the petitioner says about it : "The name of the petitioner's husband not having been entered in the diary of the complainant, it is not stated how and when the police came to know of his complicity." This is a sample of the case for the prosecution. The case for the defence is overwhelming. "Dr. Bodhraj, a well-known physician of Lahore, Dr. Bholaram and his compounder gave evidence that Labhu Ram was busy with them in connection with the treatment of his ailing son at the time of the alleged assault."

The reader will be shocked to know that Mr. Labhu Ram's sentence of transportation, with forfeiture of property has been commuted to fourteen years. Though I can appreciate and fully share a wife's sorrow and agony over an unmerited separation from her husband and therefore while I understand Mr. Labhu Ram's position in asking for a commutation, if a complete discharge might not be possible, I am unable to derive the slightest satisfaction from the fact of the commutation. Mr. Labhu Ram is not a child. He is a man of the world, of culture and fully aware of his responsibility. If he took part in a cowardly assault on an inoffensive man who was but doing his duty he deserves stern justice and no mercy. For to the crime of an assault he had added that of deliberate perjury. If therefore his case is not true, it is not one for mercy, and if it is true, justice would be hardly satisfied when he is discharged.

I do not deal with the monstrous method of the court in taking judicial notice of a "state of rebellion". It is really an abuse of legal terms to consider the state of Lahore on the 12th of April as one of rebellion and a martial proclamation of the Government to be a document for judicial notice in the manner it has been.

The evidence before the court does not sustain a charge of waging war against the King. Only recently the people of Liverpool went much further than the Badshahi Mosque meeting. But the long expected Commission has now been appointed, and if the reference includes the power to revise the sentences, the members of the Commission will have an opportunity of pronouncing upon cases like Mr. Labhu Ram's. But I submit to the Punjab Government as also to the Government of India that in cases where the recorded evidence itself shows a patent miscarriage of justice, they are bound in honour to discharge the accused without hiding themselves behind the Commission.

*Young India,* 10-9-1919

## 46

## GUJARATIMAL'S CASE

Gujaratimal is a lad eighteen years old, having received no more than middle school education. At the age of sixteen he got himself appointed as a dresser in the Military Department. After working for about a year in Multan Cantonment, he went to Egypt and spent one year there, also on service. He subsequently returned to the Punjab taking one month's leave. He reached Madhranwala, his native village, five miles from Hafizabad, on the 8th April. He remained at his village getting his shop repaired. But "to our astonishment some policemen came there on the 16th with warrants issued against him, and prosecuted him accordingly, leaving us in utter amazement, for we could not understand what the matter was." Thus writes the seventy years old father of Gujaratimal.

This is not one of those cases in which a stranger can arrive at a firm decision merely on reading the evidence, which was reproduced in the last issue of *Young India*. It will be remembered that the case of Gujaratimal is one out of nineteen tried together. I had occasion to analyse the judgment in the case in connection with that of Karamchand, and all I have said about that judgment naturally applies in this case, as in that of the lad Karamchand. But upon reading the evidence it is not possible to come to a positive conclusion that the defence of *alibi* was completely established. The whole of the evidence, as the reader must have observed, has been taken in such a scrappy manner that one is unable to know what has been omitted. It is also clear from the evidence that the prosecution witnesses are mostly policemen or connected with the police, and that the accused were not arrested red-handed, but most of them were arrested some time after the affair. Certainly Gujaratimal, who is said to have been the principal speaker and one of the assailants, was not arrested red-handed, but two days after the date of the alleged assault. Gujaratimal was sentenced to be hanged. His sentence was subsequently commuted to transportation, and still more subsequently, according to what his father has heard, to seven years' rigorous imprisonment. It is a serious matter to sentence a lad of eighteen years, who denies his guilt, who denies having been present at the scene itself and who has only lately rendered service to the Crown, to be hanged on the strength of the very questionable evidence of identification by witnesses of no standing.

To these observations I would add a summary of the facts supplied by the father of Gujaratimal, and respectfully submit that if the facts supplied by the father be true he is entitled to complete discharge without further investigation. And even without those the whole case requires a thorough investigation. The father says, "On the 23rd May, i.e. five weeks after the event, the Deputy Commissioner of the District ordered all the residents to assemble in one place to be identified by the prosecution witnesses, and Lieutenant Tatam." Gujaratimal was also among the crowd. Now comes the most material part of the father's statement. "At this occasion none of the prosecution witnesses Nos. 3, 4, 7, 8, 9, 15, 16, 18, 19, who afterwards gave evidence against him could identify him, nor even Lieutenant Tatam." If this is true, Gujaratimal has certainly been wrongly convicted. And what shall we say of the value of the identification evidence when we read such a shocking deposition as this of prosecution witness No. 13: "Mr. Tatam identified Karam Sing, Jiwan Kishen, Mulchand. Mr. Tatam even pointed me out as one of the assailants, and when the Deputy Commissioner said that I was Tehsildar, Mr. Tatam said that the man he remembered was fatter than I." If this is true —and the prosecution surely cannot question its truth—this is a circumstance which must raise gravest doubts about the value of the identification evidence led by the prosecution. The father adds that the prosecution witness No. 3 says that Gujaratimal delivered an oration at the station, whereas P.W. No. 16 says that it was Gian Singh who delivered it. This discrepancy can be proved from the recorded evidence. Again the father says, prosecution witness No. 15 who could not identify Gujaratimal on the 3rd May says at the trial that Gujaratimal carried a flag, etc. The father has submitted already several petitions to the authorities. He is a man of poor circumstances. The accused is an insignificant lad. In my opinion, therefore, the case becomes all the stronger for a searching inquiry. His Excellency the Viceroy was pleased to say in his speech "for those cases which have come before the Government of India, I have no hesitation in claiming that they received the most careful consideration, and that orders were passed with the greatest possible despatch." The letter before me says that the father has petitioned His Excellency also. It is not impertinent to inquire what was the result of the "most careful consideration" given to the most damaging statements made in the father's petition. If his statements were considered to be worthless, he was and still is entitled to know on what ground the decision was based.

*Young India,* 13-9-1919

## 47

## LABH SINGH, M.A., LL.B., (CANTAB),
### Bar-at-Law

"No mere reduction of sentence, it is most humbly submitted, can be a consolation to Your Excellency's memorialist or in an adequate measure will right the wrong that has been done him or meet the ends of justice."

This is an extract from the latest petition of Mr. Labh Singh, Bar-at-Law. I am sure this petition will not fail to evoke from the reader both sympathy and admiration; sympathy because of the wrong that has been done him and admiration because the jail has not broken the spirit of the young Barrister. He asks for no mercy, he pleads for justice, if he can secure it. But in spite of H.E. The Viceroy's remarks to the contrary, the spirit of justice is moving so slow and there seems

to be such a disinclination even in the high quarters
to do real justice that one almost despairs of getting it.
Look at Sir Edward Maclagan's speech in reply to the
Hon. Pandit Malaviyaji's resolution for the appointment
of a Commission. He recalls the warning of the Viceroy
against the temptation "to minimize the events of last
April". "I do not think," His Honour proceeds, "that
even while the disorders were in progress, people
outside the Punjab fully realized the extreme gravity of
the situation." He adds, "Had it not been for the
rapidity with which the disturbances were made, had
they been allowed to proceed but a little further than
they did, the lives and property of all classes of people
would have been in the most imminent danger." This
is merely begging the question and anticipating the
verdict of the Committee of Enquiry. Regarding the
sentences, His Honour again begs the question by
saying that the findings of the Special Courts should
be accepted, because "they represent the unanimous
conclusions, in each case, of three experienced officers".
But the unanimity and experience are beside the point
when behind them lies a temporary aberration of the
intellect. His Honour, however, attempts to silence his
critics by saying, "Although I have examined many
cases, I have not found one in which I felt justified in
impugning the substantial correctness of the findings of
the court." In the face of this emphatic opinion I
despair of securing or expecting justice either for Mr.
Labh Singh or for any of the great Punjab leaders, who
are at present adorning the Punjab jails. I do however
feel tempted to say with due deference to the Lieut.
Governor of the Punjab that if he has not found a
single case for challenging the correctness of the
findings of the Special Courts, of all the many cases
that have come before the public, it has not been my

good fortune to find many judgments to inspire confidence in their correctness. Let me illustrate my point by taking this very case of Mr. Labh Singh. He is not a man of straw. This is the full text of the Judges' remarks in his case :

> "Labh Singh, accused 4, took an active part in the inception of the agitation against the Rowlatt Act and was present at meeting of the 12th and 13th. On the latter date, he is said to have at first opposed the commission of acts of violence, but finally agreed. He was seen in several places with the mob on the 14th but appear to have rendered assistance to the authorities on that date. We find him guilty under Section 121, I. P. C."

The whole of this judgment, the reader will find reproduced in the issue of *Young India* of July 30th. I ask where is, in the above remarks, anything but good, said even by the Judges about Mr. Labh Singh, except the expression "but finally agreed"? On the Judges' own showing there was nothing indictable in the acts prior to the 12th April. The whole of the conviction is based upon the uncorroborated testimony of an approver, notwithstanding the fact that there was incontestible evidence to show that he "endeavoured to render assistance to the authorities" (I am quoting the Judges' words) after the supposed approval by him of acts of violence. But in order to accept the approvers' testimony the court says at the end of the judgment, "Labh Singh evidently repented of his action." Let the reader remember that this is the same judgment in which poor Jagannath was sentenced in the face of a clearly established *alibi,* and even before replies to the interrogatories issued by the Commissioner had been received. No wonder Mr. Labh Singh says, "the order of the Lieut. Governor, it is humbly submitted, goes only to confirm and perpetuate what is a great and serious miscarriage of justice." It is admitted that beyond signing the notice for the 5th April. Mr. Labh Singh neither convened nor addressed a public meeting "at Gujaranwalla or elsewhere at any time within 12 to 15 months preceding the occurrence of the 14th April." Mr. Labh Singh further says, "The court proceeded to the judgment with inordinate haste and without waiting for the answers to the interrogatories issued to some of the witnesses for the defence."

I do not wish to burden these notes with more quotations from the very able an convincing statements of Mr. Labh Singh and his two petitions, but I would ask every lover of India and every public man to carefully study these documents together with the judgment in the case. I think that we owe a very plain duty to Mr. Labh Singh and his co-prisoners. According to Sir Edward Maclagan they are all clearly guilty. According to the evidence before the public, they are all clearly innocent. We may not allow young men of brilliant ability and moral worth to have their careers blasted for life by our indifference. Posterity will judge us by our ability to secure justice in the cases such as I have had the painful duty of placing before the public. For me, justice for the individual, be he the humblest, is everything. All else comes after. And I hope that the public will take the same view. If the convictions stand, it will not be because we are unable to secure justice but because we are unwilling and incompetent, for I feel that even the Government of India and the Punjab Government will find it hard to withstand a unanimously expressed public opinion based on facts and couched in the language of moderation.

*Young India,* 18-9-1919

# 48

## MORE PUNJAB TRAGEDIES

It is my misfortune to have to present two more cases from the land of sorrow to the readers of *Young India*. I call Punjab the land of sorrow, because I find on the one hand a series of cases in which, if the records of cases are to be believed, a manifest injustice has been done, and on the other, an apparent determination on the part of the Punjab Government not to undo the wrong. For as I have already said in these columns, a mere reduction of sentences without admission of at least an error of judgment is no comfort to the men who protest their innocence or to the people at large who believe in their innocence and wish to see justice done. I must confess that I am uninterested in reduction of sentences if the prisoners are guilty and it is a crime to keep them in duress if they are innocent. The reader will see the petitions* on behalf of Mr. Gurudayal Singh and Dr. Mahomed Bashir. Both are high-spirited men — one a Sikh of culture, and other a Mohamedan doctor having before him a life full of promise. If they have waged war, if they have incited to murder, there can be no question of remission of the sentences passed against them. Therefore, the fact that Dr. Bashir's sentence of death has been commuted, whilst it must be a matter of some feeble consolation to Mrs. Bashir, can be none to Dr. Bashir or to the public.

Let us glance at Mr. Gurudayal Singh's case. His

---

*These petitions are not included in this book.

brother has sent me a long letter asking me even to publish it. As the main facts are contained in the petition, I refrain from publishing the letter for fear of tiring the reader, but I will make use of such statements from it as may be necessary to demonstrate the enormity of the injustice done in the case. "He only attended," says the brother, "the constitutional and the orderly meeting of the 6th April. He was on the 14th and 15th confined to bed. The local sub-assistant surgeon (Government employee) attended on him, gave his prescription, which I am sending to you in original along with the papers." I have seen this prescription. "Seriously sick with appendicitis, my brother could not join the so-called unruly mob in breaking the glass panes of the Tahsil windows." As regards prosecution witnesses against my brother I have only to add that my brother was not informed of the names of such persons. He knew them by seeing them in the court. . . . My brother was, as a matter of fact, not informed of the charge against him except through the mouth of the prosecution witnesses."

I hold that if this statement is correct, it is enough to ensure Mr. Gurudayal Singh's discharge. No accused could thus be taken by surprise and expected where and when to plead. Surely he was entitled to see the charge, and not gather it through the prosecution witnesses. The letter in my possession then analyses the antecedents of the witnesses for the prosecution and shows the animus they had against the accused. Naturally the public cannot be expected to judge the credibility of witnesses upon *ex parte* statements made by or on behalf of the accused, but these statements show, if they are true, that an immense amount of perjury must have taken place on the part of the prosecution witnesses. ' I admit that this case is not as clearly established on behalf of the prisoners as many others I have examined, for I have not the whole of the papers for presentation to the public. Bat assuming the truth of the statements made authentically on behalf of the prisoner, it is clear that the case required looking into.

Dr. Mahomed Bashir's is another such case. The pathetic petition by his wife and Dr. Bashir's statement itself before the court, which sentenced him to death, if true, show that the court's judgment had been completely warped. Dr. Bashir may or may not have lied, but the court had most decidedly nothing before it to warrant the remark that the defence evidence was worthless; for, Dr. Bashir, as will be seen from the statement published in another column,* categorically denied many of the statements and facts imputed to him. I do not intend to burden this criticism with any extracts from the very brief and business-like statement presented to the court by Dr. Bashir, but I would commend it to the careful attention of the reader. He cannot help the conclusion that the statement deserved a better fate than a contemptuous dismissal from the court.

*Young India,* 24-9-1919

# 49

# HOW NOT TO DO IT?

At the very earnest request of Mayadevi, 16 years old wife of Kesar Mal, I reproduce elsewhere her picturesque petition** praying for the release of her

---

* This statement is not included in this book.
** This petition is not included in this book.

young husband, 21 years old. The case presented seems to me to be unanswerable but a good cause has been spoiled by a bad advocate. Though the petition is that of Mayadevi, it is quite clear that it is the handiwork of a draftsman who has written in a fit of rage against what he has, undoubtedly and with good cause, believed to be a monstrous injustice. But anger is short madness and noblest causes have been damaged by advocates affected with temporary lunacy. The petition is overlaid with useless adjectives and declamations. Whilst it has been a pleasure to me to dissect the many businesslike petitions that have come from that land of sorrow, in the present instance I have been obliged to labour through violent language to what I consider to be a right conclusion. I do not happen to know the draftsman of the petition. Mayadevi, who has sent a covering letter equally violently worded, gives me no information about the draftsman. But I do wish as a practised draftsman to warn writers of petition, whether they be pleaders or otherwise, to think of the cause they may be espousing for the time being. I assure them that a bare statement of facts embellished with adjectives is far more eloquent and effective than a narrative glowing with exuberant language.

Petition writers must understand that they address busy men, not necessarily sympathetic, sometimes prejudiced, and almost invariably prone to sustain the decisions of their subordinates. In the case of the Punjab they approach a Viceroy and a Lieutenant-Governor who have preconceived ideas. Petitions have to be read and analysed by public workers and journalists who have none too much time at their disposal. I know to my cost how difficult it is for me to do full justice to the value of the papers that pour in upon me week to week from the Punjab. I make a present of my valuable experience to young patriots who wish to try the art of advocating public cause by writing petitions or otherwise. I had the privilege of serving under the late Mr. Gokhale and for a time under the G. O. M.* of India. Both told me that if I wanted to be heard I must be brief, I must write to the point and adhere to facts, and never travel beyond the cause under notice, and I must be most sparing in my adjectives. And if some success has attended my effort it is due to my acceptance of the golden advice given to me by the two illustrious deceased. With this preface and warning I proceed to the analysis of the case of young Kesar Mal.

I am anxious that the excellent case of young Kesar Mal might not be overlooked by reason of bad draftsmanship of the petition. The wonder to me is that so many petitions have been written with marked ability and amazing self-restraint. But when a badly drawn document comes their way it is the business of public workers to sift the grain from the chaff and present the former to the public.

Let it be remembered that this is one of the Hafizabad cases arising out of the tumult that took place at Hafizabad station during which Lieut. Tatam is alleged to have been the object of the mischievous attention of the crowd that had gathered at that station. Kesar Mal was sentenced to be hanged, the sentence being subsequently commuted to ten years' imprisonment. The wife's petition says, "It is justice which Your Excellency's petitioner most humbly seeks and on justice Your Excellency's petitioner insists." And on that account she asks for the release of her young husband. The grounds as can be collected from the petition are:

---

* Grand Old Man, i.e. Dadabhai Naoroji.

(1) The prosecution evidence is inconsistent with itself.

(2) The charge against Kesar Mal is that he was trying to snatch Lieut. Tatam's child from him, but according to the petition, the police produced Kesar Mal a dozen times before the Lieutenant, but Mr. Tatam would as many times nod his head meaning positive and complete nay and added each time, "none tried to snatch the child from me!"

(3) Lieut. Tatam did not identify Kesar Mal even as one of the men concerned in assaulting him.

(4) Identification parade was held some time after the occurrence.

(5) Lieut. Tatam is reported to have said, "Your Deputy Commissioner Lieut. Col. O'Brien is a very strong man and he has unnecessarily compelled me to make too much of the case."

(6) The petition charges the police with having given colour to the proceedings which they did not deserve.

(7) The prosecution witnesses were nearly all Government servants, i.e., *chaprasis*, *moharrirs*, railway staff, police staff, and also pedlars, confectioners etc. who are alleged to have been made to give evidence.

(8) Prosecution witnesses against Kesar Mal were either prejudiced or themselves feared "implications" or expected favours.

(9) Lieut. Tatam himself had nothing against Kesar Mal. Bashir Haiyat stated, "Only Kesar Mal was wounded by the glass of the window." Haveli Ram identified Kesar Mal, but the Commission remarked about him, "demeanour bad — not to be trusted". Similar was the case with Wadhawa Mal. Kishan Dayal was another prosecution witness who is stated to have

perjured himself and given evidence flatly in contradiction of Lieut. Tatam's. Kishan Dayal appears to have been a boon companion of Kesar Mal and yet is said to have stated to the court that he did not know Kesar Mal before. Chapter and verse are given in the petition to prove Kishan Dayal's intimacy with Kesar Mal. Kisan Dayal is stated to have yielded to police influence and, it is said, he is now sorry "for his wrong and cruel statement".

(10) The defence evidence was entirely ignored although the defence witnesses were impartial men of position.

(11) Young Kesar Mal belongs to a family which rendered services to the Government.

If these allegations are true, it is clear that Kesar Mal has been wrongly convicted and is entitled to be discharged. Cases like this prove the great need there is for an impartial Commission to investigate them. Sir William Vincent has sprung a surprise upon the community by stating that two judges would be appointed to investigate such cases and report upon them to the Government. One would have thought that Lord Hunter's Committee would be able to do this work. But I take it that the public would be satisfied with this separate committee, provided that the judges to be appointed are strong, independent and able men. Sir William Vincent might have been more communicative than he was. He evidently does not realize the pain and the torture under which the relatives of men who, in their opinion, are wrongly convicted, are passing their days.

## An Unworthy Defence

One almost despairs of getting justice when one reads the debates that have taken place in the

Viceregal Council and the defence put forth for every vile and vindictive act done in the Punjab in the name of prestige, law and order. Even the 'hands and knees' order has been sought to be justified by Lieut. General Sir Havelock Hudson. The action of the crowd against an innocent lady doctor cannot be condemned too strongly or too vehemently. I do not know whether all the facts stated by the gallant General are true, but for the purpose of my argument, I shall assume them to be true. I venture to submit, however, that no act on the part of an infuriated mob can possibly be held to justify the issuing of a barbarous order in cold blood requiring that "those who wished to pass the scene of the assault on Miss Sherwood should be made to crawl on their hands and knees." The scene of assault was not an out-of-the-way corner which nobody need visit or which people could avoid if they chose. There was, therefore, no question of people's wishing to pass the scene of the assault. It was one of *being obliged* to pass the scene. Why should people who had no hand in the act of violence have 'to crawl on their hands and knees' in passing the scene of the assault? The General proceeds thus to justify the order:

> "I think that the Council will agree that it is not surprising that the officer in command at Amritsar took the view that some unusual measures were necessary to bring home to the mob that such acts of violence directed against defenceless women could not be tolerated. Something was required to strike the imagination and impress on all the determination of the military authorities to protect European women."

The whole of the speech is worth reading as an example of bad taste. It is speeches such as .Sir Havelock Hudson's which create bad blood and give unbridled licence to the soldiery. I was totally unprepared for this defence from high quarters of acts of vengeance, unworthy of true soldiers. Surely there are nobler methods of ensuring protection for European women. Have their lives been in such danger in India as to require any special protection? Why should the life of a European woman be held more sacred than that of an Indian woman ? Has she not the same sense of honour, the same feelings? What is the British flag worth if a British soldier wearing the King's uniform rises from his seat in the Viceregal Council and insults the people of India by language such as Lieut. General Sir Havelock Hudson has used ? I still do not approve of the cry against the Indemnity Bill. I think, with due deference to the great experienced leaders of opinion in India, that to put it at its worst it was bad tactics to have opposed the Indemnity Bill but the speech of General Hudson, if it reflects, as I fear it does, the sentiments of the English members of the Council, must cause the gravest misgivings as to the ultimate result of Lord Hunter's Committee and its off shoot.

*Young India,* 27-9-1919

# 50

## FINING THE LABOURERS

Ahmedabad, the Government has decided, has to pay a fine of nearly nine lakhs of rupees in connection with the April disturbances. This is under the same section of the British Police Act as Nadiad has been dealt with. A law that allows a Government thus arbitrarily to impose a penalty is a bad law. All laws that place a Government above law and enable them to impose their will upon people without consultation

with them or without the authority of a properly
constituted judicial tribunal are bad, and should not be
tolerated where there is an enlightened and liberal
Government or where the people are jealous of their
freedom. But it is not my purpose to discuss the
badness of the law. My object at the present moment
is to bring to public notice an unwise and untimely and
an almost despotic application of that bad law. The
principle that the wanton damage done to life and
property by crowds of people should be made good by
them is beyond dispute. But acceptance of that
principle cannot and does not involve acceptance of
arbitrary powers. In the case of the Ahmedabad
millhands a fine of 176 thousand rupees has been fixed.
Recovery is to be made from all millhands employed
during September 1919, within the municipal limits.
Now the disturbances took place in April last. It is a
notorious fact that millhands have changed somewhat
and newcomers constantly come in. Why should those
who joined after the disturbances and have no
connection with them be made to pay anything
whatsoever? Why should women and children of whom
there is a considerable number in the mills have to
pay? There are probably sixty thousand labourers in
the mills. Is it right to fine them nearly two lakhs of
rupees?

The manner of collection and the time chosen are
still more unfortunate. The order is dated 26th
September, 1919 and on the same day the following
was served upon the millowners:

"The Collector of Ahmedabad hereby calls upon the
Agents of the ... mill to pay to the Huzur Deputy
Collector, Ahmedabad, on Monday, September 29th
before 3-00 p.m. an amount equal to one week's wages

of the manual labourers employed during September, 1919 in the mill out of the amount held by him as caution money on their account."

The law contemplates the possibility of an appeal to the Government against such orders by the parties aggrieved. The order has not been served upon the millhands. They have not been given the chance of appeal nor have they been given the option of paying the fine themselves. The caution money, that is, the money retained by the millowners out of the wages due to the millhands, has been summarily attached without notice to or consent of the labourers concerned. Such treatment of labourers debases them, needlessly irritates them and keeps them in a helpless condition. This manner of dealing with the labourers shows that they are not considered responsible human beings.

It is almost like collecting fine from owners of cattle for trespass without reference to the latter, the difference being that the labourers are not dumb like cattle and unlike cattle the burden ultimately falls on their shoulders. It is surprising that the millowners have, as I understand they have, become willing parties to such a monstrous procedure.

Information in my possession goes to show that the millowners are to recoup themselves for the above payment out of the wages immediately to fall due. This means that the enormous sum of one hundred and seventy-six thousand rupees (Rs. 1,76,000) is to be collected during a festival season common to both the Hindus and Mohamedans. The impropriety of such a step can hardly be questioned. The coincidence is no doubt unintended but the unsophisticated labourers will conclude that the festival season has been intentionally chosen to wound their feelings.

The Collector of Ahmedabad is a gentleman. He has given every satisfaction to the inhabitants of the district. At a time of intense excitement, he acted with remarkable coolness. He is a man full of broad humanity. It is a matter, therefore, of special regret to me to have to criticize his actions and I cannot help saying that if he was not a slave to a system which makes arbitrary procedure possible at almost every step of national life, he could not have helped seeing the absurdity and the injustice of the action taken by him. The matter is now before His Excellency the Governor and I venture to express the hope that the wrong done to the labourers of Ahmedabad will be redressed. The sum apportioned for the labourers is too much for them. It should be reduced. Women and boys should be exempted and the payment received by easy stages. I admit the difficulty of collection by instalment from a large number of labourers but that difficulty is nothing compared to the infliction of a serious injustice upon a large number of human beings. Terrorizing punishment is hardly the best method of weaning offenders from wrong-doing, and in the present instance the punishment will fall upon many innocent shoulders.

The authorities have recognized the delicacy of the situation in that they have drafted special police to Ahmedabad and taken extraordinary precautions in order to avoid unruliness on the part of the labourers and to cow them down into submission.

*Young India,*  4-10-1919

# 51

# THE AMRITSAR APPEALS

[Editor's Note: On July 24, 1919, the Privy Council had granted leave of appeal to 21 citizens of Amritsar convicted by the Court Martial at Lahore in connection with the Amritsar riots of April 1919. They appealed on the ground that the Viceroy had no power to issue the Martial Law ordinances and that the procedure followed by the Summary Courts was irregular.]

So these appeals have been dismissed in spite of the advocacy of the best counsel that was obtainable. The Privy Council has confirmed lawless procedure. I must confess that the judgment does not come upon me quite as surprise, though the remarks of the judges, as Sir Simon was developing his argument on behalf of the appellants, led one to expect a favourable verdict. My opinion, based upon a study of political cases, is that the judgments even of the highest tribunals are not unaffected by subtle political considerations. The most elaborate precautions taken to procure a purely judicial mind must break down at critical moments. The Privy Council cannot be free from the limitations of all human institutions which are good enough, only for normal conditions. The consequences of a decision favourable to the people would have exposed the Indian Government to indescribable discredit from which it would have been difficult [for it] to free itself for a generation.

Its political significance can be gauged from the fact that as soon as the news was received in Lahore all the preparations that were made to accord a fitting welcome to Lala Lajpat Rai were immediately cancelled and the capital of the Punjab was reported to be in deep mourning. Deeper discredit, therefore, now attaches to the Government by reason of the judgment, because rightly or wrongly the popular opinion will be that there is no justice under the British Constitution when large political or racial considerations are involved.

There is only one way to avoid the catastrophe. The human and especially the Indian mind quickly responds to generosity. I hope that without the necessity of an agitation or petitions the Punjab Government or the Central Government will immediately cancel the death sentences and, if at all possible, simultaneously set the appellants free.

This is required by two considerations, each equally important. The first is that of restoring, public confidence which I have already mentioned. The second is fulfilment of the Royal Proclamation (of December 1919) to the letter. That great political document orders the release of all the political offenders who may not by their release prove a danger to society. No one can possibly suggest that the twenty-one appellants will, if they are set free, in any shape or form constitute a danger to society. They never had committed any crimes before. Most of them were regarded as respectable and orderly citizens. They were not known to belong to any revolutionary society. If they committed any crimes at all, they were committed only under the impulse of the moment and under what to them was grave provocation. Moreover, the public believe that the majority of the convictions by the Martial Law Tribunals were unsupported by any good evidence. I, therefore, hope that the Government, which have so far been doing well in discharging political offenders even when they were caught in the act, will not hesitate to release these appellants and thus earn the goodwill of the whole of India. It is an act of generosity done in the hour of triumph which is the most effective. And in the popular opinion this dismissal of the appeal has been regarded as a triumph for the Government.

I would respectfully plead with the Punjab friends not to lose heart. We must calmly prepare ourselves for the worst. If the convictions are good, if men convicted have been guilty of murders or incitements to murder, why should they escape punishment? If they have not committed these crimes as we believe most at least have not, why should we escape the usual fate of all who are trying to rise a step higher? Why should we fear the sacrifice if we would rise ? No nations have ever risen without sacrifice and sacrifice can only be spoken of in connection with innocence and not with crime.

*Young India*, 3-3-1920

# 52

# THE PUNJAB SENTENCES

The Commissioners appointed by the Congress Punjab Sub-committee have in their report accused His Excellency the Viceroy of criminal want of imagination. His Excellency's refusal to commute two death sentences out of five is a fine illustration of the accusation. The rejection of the appeal (See "The Amritsar Appeals", *Young India*, 3-3-1920) no more proves the guilt of the condemned than their innocence could have been proved by quashing the proceedings before the Martial Law Tribunal. Moreover, these cases

clearly come under the Royal Proclamation (of
December 1919) in accordance with its interpretation
by the Punjab Government. The murders in Amritsar
were not due to any private quarrel between the
murderers and their victims. The offence, grave though
it was, was purely political and committed under
excitement. More than full reparation has been taken
for the murders and arson. In the circumstances
common sense dictates reduction of the death
sentences. The popular belief favours the view that the
condemned men are innocent and have not had a fair
trial. The execution has been so long delayed that
hanging at this stage would give a rude shock to Indian
society. Any Viceroy with imagination would have at
once announced commutation of the death sentences —
not so Lord Chelmsford. In his estimation, evidently,
the demands of justice will not be satisfied if at least
some of the condemned men are not hanged. Public
feeling with him counts for nothing. We shall still hope
that either the Viceroy or Mr. Montagu will commute
the death sentences.

But if the Government will grievously err, if they
carry out the sentences, the people will equally err if
they give way to anger or grief over the hanging if it
has unfortunately to take place. Before we become a
nation possessing an effective voice in the councils of
nations, we must be prepared to contemplate with
equanimity, not a thousand murders of innocent men
and women but many thousands before we attain a
status in the world that shall not be surpassed by any
nation. We hope therefore that all concerned will take
rather than lose heart and treat hanging as an ordinary
affair of life.

(Since the above was in type, we have received the
cruel news. At last H. E. the Viceroy has mercilessly

given the rude shock to Indian society. It is now for the latter to take heart in spite of the unkindest cut. —Editor, *Young India*.)

*Young India*, 7-4-1920

# 53

# A HARD CASE

I have received the following telegram from the families of Messrs Bugga and Ratanchand:

> Bugga and Ratto under orders transfer Andamans. Bugga, suffering hernia and piles since ten years. Was operated upon. Ratto aged over forty and therefore should not be sent Andamans under Jail Manual Rule 721.

The readers will remember that these were the accused on whose behalf appeals were made to the Privy Council in common with others and whose appeals were rejected on technical grounds. (See "The Amritsar Appeals", Young India, 3-3-1920)

The Hon'ble Pandit Motilal Nehru has analysed the cases and shown that they are no more guilty than the others who have been discharged. But several who were originally sentenced to death had their sentences commuted to imprisonment and are now set free. What is it that distinguishes these two cases from the others? Is it the fact of the appeal itself? If they had not appealed, or rather, if a philanthropic lawyer out of pity had not taken up their case, fought for them against tremendous odds, they would not have escaped the hangman's noose. H. H. the Lieutenant-Governor of the Punjab has been showing a generous discretion in releasing many who suffered between April and June last year. Although he had the opportunity, after the dismissal of the appeal, to hang Messrs Bugga and

Ratanchand, H. E. the Viceroy, it is equally true, has commuted the sentence of death to one of transportation. But I venture to submit that if the Royal Proclamation is to be given effect to in the fullest measure, Messrs Bugga and Ratanchand are entitled to their liberty. They are no more a danger to the State than Lala Harkishen Lal, Pandit Rambhuj Dutt Chowdhari and others of that distinguished company. But for the time being, strong as the case is for their discharge, I am pleading not for a complete release but for keeping them in the Punjab and if they have been sent away already, for bringing them back, if for nothing else, out of consideration for the wives of these poor men. Let not the public think that the acts of the Government of the day are dictated only by fear and expedience, not by logic and high principles of justice,

*Young India,* 26-5-1920

## 54

## LAWYERS' DUTY

I have never minced words in criticizing lawyers. Mahadev, during his short reign, castigated them to his heart's content. But the lawyers did not misunderstand him. They saw that the shafts he aimed at them were shafts of love. Though the lawyers deserve criticism, their contribution to the fight for freedom is no mean one. Pherozeshah Mehta, the uncrowned king of Bombay, was an eminent lawyer. The Lokamanya was a lawyer. Manmohan Ghosh, Lalmohan Ghosh and Lalaji, the Lion of the Punjab, all of them were lawyers. Deshbandhu, who sacrificed lakhs in the service of the country, was also a lawyer. Motilalji, Malaviyaji, Vithalbhai Patel, Sardar, Jairamdas,

Rajagopalachari, Prakasam, Venkatapayya, Santhanam, Munshi, Kamdar, Purushottamdas Trikumdas and Broker, all these are lawyers, and the President of the Congress himself is a lawyer. This list is not exhaustive. I have mentioned only the names which occur to me at the moment, but many others can be mentioned.

The lawyers have, therefore, no reason to feel ashamed of their contribution, but there is none to feel elated either. If despite the sacrifices of all these lawyers people speak ill of lawyers—even I have done so—there is reason for that.

People expect every lawyer to be a patriot, as they expect every Brahmin to possess spiritual knowledge. A lawyer, by his very profession, is an advocate of people's rights, an expert in law and politics and one who saves the victims of oppression by the State. When, therefore, a class of people who should regard service of the country as their profession give themselves up to the pursuit of self-interest, lead a life of self-indulgence or have no other aim than making money by encouraging litigation, people naturally speak ill of them. Though, taken absolutely, the number of patriotic lawyers named above will not appear insignificant, if we have regard to the total number of lawyers and the magnitude of their task, it will appear small indeed.

Lawyers have not remained untouched by the present awakening. The sacrifices of Shri Munshi and other lawyers stem from the present struggle. I see that lawyers who dare not or cannot give up practice, still wish to do some service. I hear that many lawyers in Bombay have stopped wearing hats and foreign clothes. Some lawyers in Gujarat have come forward to investigate the cases of those against whom atrocities are being committed. All this is welcome indeed. But, leaving aside the question of their giving up practice, the important thing is that they should come forward in large numbers to offer civil disobedience and remain undeterred if the courts cancel their *sanads*. They cannot betray the country for the sake of their *sanads*. If in consequence of their doing national work they lose their *sanads,* they should welcome this as if they had been cleansed of dirt. If lawyers thus become fearless, they can help the people of their districts in many ways. If they shed fear, lawyers can

1. keep accounts of public funds;
2. explain legal intricacies to the people;
3. enquire into civil disobedience cases which have been arbitrarily dealt with and bring them to light;
4. be present at places where there is fear of violence;
5. explain to the people all cases of arbitrary use of authority;
6. enquire into injustices being perpetrated at present and point out to the public the Government's misdeeds;
7. help in manufacturing khadi;
8. help the women in bringing about boycott of foreign cloth;
9. since in every province almost all the prominent leaders have been arrested, lawyers can lead the people and encourage the present spirit of fearlessness.

I have suggested these items only by way of illustration. Those who are keen on doing service will think up many fields in which they may do it.

[From Gujarati] *Navajivan,* 4-5-1930 *The Collected Works of Mahatma Gandhi*, Vol. XLIII pp. 383-384

# SECTION V
# MISCELLANEOUS

## 55

## HOW TO SPIRITUALIZE THE PROFESSION
[From "In Ceylon" by M. D.]

While in Colombo we had a pretty little encounter with the law students. They had promised to go to Gandhiji's residence to present their purse to him. Later it seems they got jealous of the smaller institutions that Gandhiji was visiting, changed their mind, and gave a sort of notice to the Reception Committee that they should either bring Gandhiji to their college or sacrifice a 'substantial purse'! The threat however was lost on the Committee, and the students thought it discreet to keep their previous promise. So they came, but lodged their complaint against the Reception Committee for taking Gandhiji to private houses and to minor educational institutions and ignoring the Law College! But they had counted without their host. Gandhiji twitted them first with inaccuracy about facts, in that they had stated that Gandhiji had visited private houses, whereas he had called only on Mrs. DeSilva and that as a hawker, and with their inability to understand that Gandhiji should naturally give preference to those who were yet children and fathers of tomorrow over those who in all probability were fathers of today. The joke was enough to put them in proper humour, and they made amends by recognizing the difficulty of the Reception Committee, and proceeded to turn the little time they had with Gandhiji to good account. 'How to spiritualize the legal profession' was the point on which they sought advice which Gandhiji readily gave them:

"I am glad you have put this question. For I may say that if I cannot speak on this subject with authority, no one else can. For throughout my career at the bar, I never once departed from the strictest truth and honesty. Well, then the first thing which you must always bear in mind, if you would spiritualize the practice of law, is not to make your profession subservient to the interests of your purse, as is unfortunately but too often the case at present, but to use your profession for the service of your country. There are instances of eminent lawyers in all countries who led a life of self-sacrifice, who devoted their brilliant legal talents entirely to the service of their country, although it spelt almost pauperism to them. In India you have the instance of the late Man Mohan Ghose. He took up the fight against the indigo planters and served his poor clients at the cost of his health, even at the risk of his life, without charging them a single pie for his labours. He was a most brilliant lawyer, yet he was a great philanthropist. That is an example that you should have before you. Or better still you can follow Ruskin's precept given in his book *Unto This Last*. 'Why should a lawyer charge fifteen pounds for his work' he asks, 'whilst a carpenter, for instance, hardly gets as many shillings for his work?' The fees charged by lawyers are unconscionable everywhere. I confess, I myself have charged what I would now call high fees. But even whilst I was engaged in my practice, let me tell you, I never let my profession stand in the way of my public service.

"And there is another thing which I would like to warn you against. In England, in South Africa, almost everywhere I have found that in the practice of their profession lawyers are consciously or unconsciously led into untruth for the sake of their clients. An eminent English lawyer has gone so far as to say that it may even be the duty of a lawyer to defend a client whom he knows to be guilty. There I disagree. The duty of a lawyer is always to place before the judges, and to help them to arrive at, the truth, never to prove the guilty as innocent. It is up to *you* to maintain the dignity of your profession. If you fail in your duty what shall become of the other professions? You, young men, claiming as you have just done to be the fathers of tomorrow, should be the salt of the nation. If the salt lose its savour wherewith shall it be salted?"

*Young India,* 22-12-1927, pp. 427-28

## 56

## BIRDS OF A FEATHER (?)

[From: "In the Frontier Province—VI" by Pyarelal]

The Bar Association of Peshawar utilized Gandhiji's presence in the City by presenting him with an address at the Premier's residence in which they proudly claimed him as one of their confraternity and incidentally also managed to do a little trumpet blowing for themselves by adverting to the splendid services in the political field rendered by leading lights of the profession. Gandhiji, in a witty little speech, while thanking them for the honour that they had done him, observed that he was hardly entitled to that privilege, in the first place because, as they all knew, he had been disbarred by his own Inn, and secondly because he had long forgotten his law. Of late he had more often been engaged in breaking laws than in expounding or interpreting them in the courts of the land. Still another and perhaps,˙ his most vital reason was his peculiar views about lawyers and doctors which he had recorded in his booklet, *The Indian Home Rule*. A true lawyer, he told them, was one who placed truth and service in the first place and the emoluments of the profession in the next place only. He did not know whether they had all adopted that ideal but if they pledged themselves to render service through their legal acumen in an altruistic spirit he would be the first to pay them his homage.

*Harijan,* 26-11-1938, p. 351

## 57

## A JUDGE'S INDICTMENT

I condense the following from a newspaper report:

"It is extremely common for advocates for the defence in criminal cases to argue that the prosecution story is an entire concoction by the police, and in the vast majority of cases no evidence whatever, whether elucidated in cross-examination or offered in examination-in-chief, is ever produced in support of this argument. Now either the contention is raised on direct instructions of the client, or it is deliberately raised by counsel without any instructions from the client. In the former case the accused has aggravated the heinousness of the offence with which he is charged. In a clear case of this kind the tribunal trying the case should take this into account as a circumstance warranting an increase in the sentence. In the latter case where the legal practitioner has acted without reasonable cause he is guilty of the grossest professional misconduct. Cross-examination on these lines is often grossly abused, and it is the duty of the trying judge, if he has any suspicion when an advocate begins an attack upon the prosecutor or a witness, to demand from the advocate an assurance that he has good grounds for making the suggestion. If such is not forthcoming, cross-examination on these lines should be promptly stopped. If an assurance is given, but if it appears on the termination of the trial that no such grounds has existed, the tribunal should bring the conduct of the advocate to the notice of the High Court. I make these observations in order that a check may be placed on a growing and serious evil."

These are the remarks of the Chief Justice of the Patna High Court.

I have said enough in these columns to show that justice is practically unobtainable in the so-called courts of justice in India. But I was unprepared for a Chief Justice (assuming that he is correctly reported) becoming the framer of a gratuitous indictment against lawyers and their clients. These remarks of the Chief Justice of the Patna High Court, in my opinion, amount to a threat to the accused persons and their counsel. If the fear of an increase in sentence or being disbarred hangs like Damocles' Sword on the accused person or his counsel as the case may be, it would be impossible for either to impugn the conduct of the police. Whatever the learned Chief Justice's experience may be, the experience of the man in the street is, that in a vast number of cases the police story *is* manufactured, and the growing evil is *not* in the accused or his counsel, but it *is* in the police who therefore need to be checked in their excessive zeal to fasten a particular crime upon some one. The ordinary policeman is in mortal fear of degradation or dismissal, if he cannot secure convictions.

It becomes therefore his interest to manufacture a case in the absence of reliable evidence. The judge, therefore, whose duty is to presume the innocence of every accused person coming before him, would think twenty times before he puts a single obstacle in his way. Where is the lawyer who has not often felt the truth of the statement which he makes but which he is unable to prove? And even a Charles Russell will be hard to put to it to demonstrate the truth that he feels within himself if, for fear of being disbarred in case he fails to prove his charge, he is hampered in the course of his cross-examination or examination-in-chief. The Piggot forgeries would never have been proved but for his fiery cross-examination. A lawyer who believes in the innocence of his client, whether he is prompted by him or no, is bound, in order to discover the truth, to impugn by way of cross-examination or otherwise the prosecution story. This however is commonsense and common law, but both are at a discount in India's courts of justice. When it is a question of the prestige of the Government which, in its turn, depends upon the prestige of the police, the judges consider it their duty to protect that prestige by turning prosecutors themselves. It is sad, but it is true. The Chief Justice of the Patna High Court is to be congratulated upon his boldness in emphasizing the fact.

*Young India,* 19-9-1929, p. 308

## 58

## AN UNJUDICIAL DICTUM

A correspondent sends me a press cutting containing a report of an Allahabad judgment of two English Judges sitting as appellate court. In delivering their judgment allowing the appeal Their Lordships are reported to have said:

"The case is unsatisfactory because we have no less than five persons who were in effect, if their evidence can be relied upon, eye-witnesses, and yet, having regard to the slight value placed upon truth in this country, we have seriously to apply our minds as to whether they can be believed."

This is an extraordinary pronouncement from a bench of Judges. What legal basis had these two Judges for the sweeping statement made by them as to the character of a whole nation? The inference is that in other countries a higher value is placed upon truth. Now if this was a universally accepted proposition, perhaps the Judges would have been justified in taking legal notice of it. There is, however, not only no such acceptance but experienced observers have testified that on the whole, greater value is put upon truth in India than elsewhere. But no judge should be influenced one way or the other by such observations as have no judicial value. I would go further and say that such observations ought not to be made by any responsible person, even on political platforms. They can never be proved. But when they are made by Judges they vitiate their Judgments and may lead to miscarriage of justice. Be it noted that the Allahabad Judges have made use of their bias in coming to their decision and have thus proved their incapacity to hold responsible posts. The case in which the observation was made affected poor people. But the fact that only poor persons were involved makes it all the more necessary to take public notice of the judges' strictures. Who knows in how many cases this bias of theirs has resulted in defeating justice?

*Harijan,* 2-4-1940, p. 116

## 59

# UNTRUTH IN LAW COURTS
[From "The Question Box"]

Q. I have followed with interest the controversy that has grown round your article in *Harijan* "Fourfold Ruin". Whatever one may say about the arguments used on either side in this controversy, one thing I am in a position to assert without fear of contradiction, from my experience as a judicial officer of the present system of our law. Courts and the institution of lawyers are mainly responsible for the moral and spiritual degradation of our village peasantry in particular and the public in general. Even 'respectable' people, whom one has learnt to regard as the soul of honour in their ordinary every-day life, will tell barefaced lies for a trifle in a law court and think nothing of it. The canker is eating into the vitals of our village life. Would you suggest as to what a person in my position (viz. a judge), who has to record evidence and give judicial decisions, can do to check this evil?

A. What you say is too true. The atmosphere round law courts is debasing as any visitor passing through them can see. I hold radical views about the administration of justice. But mine, I know, is a voice in the wilderness. Vested interests will not allow radical reform, unless India comes into her own through truthful and non-violent means. If that glorious event happens, the administration of law and medicine will be as cheap and healthy as it is today dear and unhealthy. The heroic advice will be for you to descend from the bench, embrace poverty and serve the poor.

The prosaic will be for you to do the best you can in the very difficult circumstances in which you find yourself, reduce life to its simplest terms and devote your savings for the service the poor.

*Harijan,* 17-2-1940, pp. 7-8

## 60

## HINDU LAW AND MYSORE

Sjt. Bhashyam Aiyengar of Bangalore writes:

"The principles of Hindu Law as at present administered are antiquated and opposed to our sense of equity and justice. I shall give a few instances:

1. Near and dear relations like the sister's daughter, the daughter-in-law, the brother's widow and the stepmother are altogether denied the right of inheritance. If a man were to leave a widowed daughter-in-law as his only surviving relation, his properties escheat to the Government, and the poor girl who staked all her life and fortune on the family of her husband gets out into the street

2. Even such near relations as are included in the list of heirs do not get a chance because of the priorities of distant agnates. The sister is an heir; but if only the deceased has left a fifth descendant of a great-great-grand-father of his, the latter takes the property and the sister gets nothing. So too the son's daughter, the sister's son and the brother's daughter.

3. Women are not allowed to exercise full rights of ownership in properties inherited by or gifted to them. A widow should carefully handle her husband's property and if only she spends more or incurs a debt on the security of the property, may be for her own livelihood, a distant *dayada* can drag her to the court and coerce

her into giving up her rights. *Mitakshara* which is the prevailing authority here clearly and definitely says that all properties which a woman may get in any manner whatsoever are her *stridhana* and she can dispose of them at her will. The Privy Council refused to follow it stating that Indians always treated women as incapable and the author of *Mitakshara* is a fire-eater,

4. The deaf and the dumb are excluded from inheritance. In this we are beating the lame man with bis own crutches.

5. The legality of widow-remarriage is not recognized in Mysore, as in British India.

6. It is doubtful whether post-puberty marriage is legal. The age of consent should be raised to 14 in the case of girls.

7. Divorce may be provided for if people agree. We. had it in India formerly. We find Parashara mentioning the circumstances under which a wife may marry a second husband during the lifetime of the first.

8. Inter-caste marriages are not allowed under the present law. They must be legalized. It was an institution freely recognized by our ancients. Many of our sages such as Vasishtha; Vyasa, Narada and Parashara were the offspring of inter-caste marriages. If I may marry a Christian wife lawfully why may not I be permitted to marry a Hindu wife though of another caste?

9. An orphan is declared ineligible for adoption. If ever a boy be fit for adoption it is the orphan, and yet we have the prohibition.

10. Widows are not allowed to adopt unless they have been authorized by the husband or the consent of *sapindas* is taken. Authority should be presumed and the widow allowed to adopt unless directed by the husband not to do so. This is the law in Bombay.

There are many more such instances. I have chosen only a few.

Thinking people feel the oppressiveness and desire reform. The only way of changing the law is by legislation. The legislature is unable to pass any law without consulting public opinion. And public opinion can only be consulted by a committee appointed for the purpose. Hence I moved a resolution in the last Budget session of our Assembly asking for the appointment of a committee to go into the question, take evidence and report thereon formulating suggestions for legislative action. It was unanimously passed by the House.

The committee has not yet been appointed though people all over the State desire it. The fear seems to be that British India not having moved in the matter yet, it may be that any attempt by Mysore might be laughed at. This is absurd as you said. Mysore is peculiarly fitted to undertake the work, whereas there are real difficulties with British India. Mysore has peculiar advantages which it would be unwise on our part to ignore. We have now a most enlightened ruler and an equally earnest and progressive Dewan. If we cannot effect the desired reforms now we never can hope to do it.

Can you not take up this matter in *Young India?*"

The prominence I have given to the foregoing need not imply that I endorse every one of the reforms suggested by the writer. That some of them require immediate attention I have no doubt. Nor have I any doubt that all of them demand serious consideration from those who would rid Hindu society of its anachronisms.

In pre-British days there was no such thing as rigid Hindu Law governing the lives of millions. The body of regulations known as Smritis were indicative

rather than inflexible codes of conduct. They never had
the validity of law such as is known to modern lawyers.
The observance of the restraints of the Smiritis was
enforced more by social than legal sanctions. The
Smritis were, as is evident from the self-contradictory
verses to be found in them, continually passing, like
ourselves, through evolutionary changes, and were
adapted to the new discoveries that were being made
in social science. Wise kings were free to procure new
interpretations to suit new conditions. Hindu religion or
Hindu Shastras never had the changeless and
unchanging character that is now being sought to be
given to them. No doubt in those days there were kings
and their councillors who had the wisdom and the
authority required to command the respect and
allegiance of society. But now the custom has grown up
of thinking that Smritis and everything that goes by
the name of Shastras is absolutely unchangeable. The
verses which we find to be unworkable or altogether
repugnant to our moral sense we conveniently ignore.
This very unsatisfactory state of things has to be, some
day or other and somehow, changed if Hindu society is
to become a progressive unit in human evolution. The
British rulers cannot make these changes because of
their different religion and their different ideal. Their
ideal is to sustain their commercial supremacy and to
sacrifice every other interest, moral or otherwise, for
the attainment of that ideal. Unless therefore Hindu
public opinion clearly demands it, and it can be made
without any injury to their ideal, no drastic change in
our customs or so-called laws will be attempted or
countenanced by them. And it is difficult to focus Hindu
public opinion on identical points in a vast territory like
British India covering many schools of thought and law.
And such public opinion as there is is naturally and

necessarily preoccupied with the struggle for political freedom. A State like Mysore however has no such limitations or preoccupations. In my humble opinion, it is its duty to anticipate British India in the matter of removing the anachronisms in the Hindu Law and the like. Mysore State is large and important enough to attempt such changes. It has become a progressively constitutional monarchy. It has a Legislative Assembly representative enough to initiate social changes. It seems already to have passed a resolution asking for the appointment of a committee to consider what changes, if any, are necessary in the Hindu Law. And if a strong committee representing orthodox as well as progressive Hindu opinion is appointed, its recommendations must prove useful and pave the way towards making the necessary changes. I do not know the rules of the Mysore Assembly governing the constitution of such committees, but there is little doubt that they are elastic enough to admit of appointing or co-opting members from outside the Mysore State. Anyway Sjt. Bhashyam Aiyengar has shown that a revision of the Hindu Law is absolutely necessary in several cases. No State is better fitted than Mysore for initiating the belated reform.

*Young India,* 13-10-1927, p. 344

## 61

## THE FEDERAL COURT

[Speech delivered by Gandhiji at the Federal Structure Committee on 23-10-1931 in the course of a discussion on 'Federal Court of India'.]

Lord Chancellor and Fellow Delegates, I feel considerable hesitation in speaking on this subject which has been rendered so highly technical by the course that the discussion has taken; but I feel that I owe a duty to you and a duty to the Congress which I represent. I know that the Congress holds some decided views on the question of the Federal Court, views which, I am afraid, may be very distasteful to a large number of the Delegates here. Whatever they are, seeing that they are held by a responsible body, it is, I suppose, necessary that I should at least present them to you.

I see that the discussions proceed, if not upon utter distrust, upon considerable distrust of ourselves. It is assumed that the National Government will not be able to conduct its affairs in an impartial manner. The communal tangle also is colouring the discussion. The Congress, on the other hand, bases the whole of its policy on trust and on the confidence that when we shall have come into power we shall also come to a sense of our responsibility, and all the communal bias will drop out. But should it prove otherwise, then too the Congress would run the boldest risks, because, without running risks we shall not be able to come to exercise real responsibility. So long as we have the mental reservation that we have to rest upon some foreign power for our guidance and for conducting our affairs at a critical juncture, so long, in my opinion, there is no responsibility.

One feels also embarrassed by the fact that we really are trying to discuss this thing without knowing where we shall be. I should give one opinion if Defence was not under the control of the responsible Government, and another opinion if Defence was under our own control. I proceed upon the assumption that if we are to enjoy responsibility in the real sense of the term, Defence will be under our control, under National control in every sense of the term. I entirely sympathize with Dr. Ambedkar in the difficulty that he raised. It is all very well to have a judgment of the highest tribunal, but if the writ of that tribunal does not run beyond the confines of its own court, that tribunal will be a laughing-stock of the nation and of the whole world. What is then to be done in connection with that writ? What Mr. Jinnah said, of course, came home—that the military would be there—but it will be the Crown that will run the writ. Then I would say, let the High Court also, or the Federal Court, be under the Crown. In my opinion the Supreme Court has to be, if we are responsible, under the responsible Government, and therefore, the process of carrying out the writ has also to be made good by the responsible Government. Personally, I do not share the fears that actuate Dr. Ambedkar, but I think that his objection is a very reasonable objection, and that a Court which gives judgments should also have perfect confidence that its judgments will be respected by those who are affected by its judgments, and hence, I would suggest that the judges should have the power of framing rules in order to regulate matters in connection with those judgments. Naturally the enforcement will not rest with the Courts; the enforcement will rest with the executive authority, but the executive authority would have to conform to the rules that might be framed by the Court.

We fancy that this constitution is going to give us every detail in connection with the composition of this Court. I respectfully differ from that view in its entirety. I think that this constitution will give us the framework of the federal Court, will define the jurisdiction of the Federal Court, but the rest will be left to the Federal Government to evolve. I cannot possibly understand that the Constitution is also going to tell us how many years the judges are to serve,' or whether they are to resign or retire at the age of 70, or 95, or 90, or 65. I think that these will be matters to be taken up by the Federal Government. Of course, we bring in the Crown at the end of almost every sentence. I must confess that, according to the conception of the Congress, there is no question of the Crown. India is to enjoy complete independence, and if India enjoys complete independence, whoever may be the supreme authority there, that supreme authority will be responsible for the appointment of judges and several other matters which today belong to the Crown.

It is a fundamental belief with the Congress that, whatever course the Constitution takes, there should be our own Privy Council in India. The Privy Council's portals, if it is really to give relief to the poor people in matters of the highest importance, should be open to the poorest people in the land and I think that is impossible if the Privy Council in England is to decide our fate in matters of the greatest importance. There, too, I would guide ourselves by implicit trust in the ability of our judges to pronounce wise and absolutely impartial decisions. I know that we run very great risks. The Privy Council here is an ancient institution, and an institution which justly commands very great regard and respect; but in spite of all the respect that I have for the Privy Council I cannot bring myself to believe that we also will not be able to have a Privy Council of our own which will command universal esteem. Because England can boast of very fine institutions, I do not think that therefore we must be tied down to those institutions. If we learn anything whatsoever from England, we should learn to erect those institutions ourselves; otherwise there is poor chance for this nation whose representatives we claim to be. Therefore, I would ask us all to have sufficient trust and confidence in ourselves at the present moment. Our beginning may be very small, but, if we have strong, true and honest hearts to give decisions, it does not matter in the slightest degree that we have not got the legal traditions which the judges in England claim and very properly boast of in the face of the whole world,

## Widest Jurisdiction

That being my view, I feel that this Federal Court should be a court of the widest jurisdiction possible, and not decide only cases that arise from the administration of Federal Laws. Federal Laws of course will be there, but it should have the amplest jurisdiction to try all the cases that may come from the four corners of India.

It is, then, a question where the subjects of the Princes will be and where they will come in. Subject to what the Princes may have to say, I would suggest, with the greatest deference and with equal hesitation, that there will be, I hope at the end of it, if we are going to make something out of this Conference, something which will be common to all India, to all the inhabitants of India, whether they come from the States or whether they come from the rest of India. If there is something in common between all of us, naturally the Supreme Court will be the guardian of the rights that we may consider to be common to all. What those rights should be, I am totally unable to say. It is entirely for the Princes to say what they can be and what they cannot be. In view of the fact that they represent here not only their own Houses but have taken on themselves the tremendous responsibility of representing their subjects also at this Conference, I would certainly make a humble but fervent appeal to them that they would of their own accord come forth with some scheme whereby their subjects also may feel that though they are not directly represented at this table, their voices find adequate expression through these noble Princes themselves.

## Salaries

So far as the salary is concerned, you will laugh, naturally, but the Congress believes that it is an impossible thing for us who, in terms of wealth, are a nation of dwarfs, to vie with the British Government, which represent today giants in wealth. India, whose average income is 3 d. per day, can ill afford to pay the high salaries that are commanded here. I feel that it is a thing which we will have to unlearn if we are going to have voluntary rule in India. It is all very well so long as the British bayonet is there to squeeze out of these poor people taxes to pay these salaries of Rs. 10,000 a month, Rs. 5,000 a month, and Rs. 20,000 a month. I do not consider that my country has sunk so low that it will not be able to produce sufficient men who will live somewhat in correspondence with the lives of the millions and still serve India nobly, truly and well. I do not believe for one moment that legal talent has to be bought if it is to remain honest.

I recall the names of Motilal Nehru, C. R. Das, Manomohan Ghose, Badrudin Tyebji and a host of others, who gave their legal talent absolutely free of charge and served their country faithfully and well. The taunt may be flung in my face that they did so because they were able to charge princely fees in their own professional work. I reject that argument for the simple reason that I have known every one of them with the exception of Manomohan Ghose. It was not that they had plenty of money and therefore gave freely of their talent when India required it. I have seen them living the life of poor people and in perfect contentment. Whatever may be the position at the present moment, I can point out to you several lawyers of distinction who, if they had not come to the national cause, would today be occupying seats of the High Court benches in all parts of India. I have, therefore, absolute confidence that when we come to frame our own rules and so on we will do so in a patriotic spirit and taking account of the miserable state that the millions of India occupy.

One word more and I have finished. Seeing that the Congress holds the view that this Federal Court or Supreme Court—whichever you call it—will occupy the position of the highest tribunal beyond which no man who is an inhabitant of India can go, its jurisdiction, in my opinion, will be limitless. It will have jurisdiction, so far as Federal matters are concerned, to the extent that the Princes are also willing, but I cannot possibly imagine that we shall have two supreme Courts, one in order to deal with merely Federal law and another to deal with all the other matters that are not covered by the Federal administration or the Federal Government.

As things go, the Federal Government may concern itself with the minimum of subjects; and therefore matters of the highest moment will be extra-Federal. Who is to adjudicate upon these extra-Federal matters if not this very Supreme Court? Therefore this Supreme Court or Federal Court will exercise double jurisdiction, if necessary, treble jurisdiction. The greater the power that we give to this Federal Court, I think the greater the confidence we shall be able to inspire in the world and also in the nation itself,

I am sorry to have taken up these precious minutes of the time·of the Conference, but I felt that, in spite of my great reluctance to speak to you on this question of a Federal Court, I must give you the views that many of us in the Congress have been holding for a long time and which, we should, if we could, spread throughout the length and breadth of India. I know the terrible handicap under which I am labouring. All the most distinguished lawyers are arrayed against me; the Princes also are probably arrayed against me so far as the salaries and jurisdiction of this Court are concerned. But I would be guilty of neglect of duty to the Congress and to you if I did not give you the views that the Congress and I hold so strongly on the matter of the Federal Court.

*Young India,*  5-11-1931, pp. 337-38

# 62

# THE FEDERAL COURT

[Speech delivered by Gandhiji at the Federal Structure Committee on 19-11-1931]

I have expressed my own hope in connection with the Federal and Supreme Court. To me the Federal Court is the Supreme Court; it is the final Court of Appeal beyond which there would be no appeal whatsoever; it is my Privy Council and it is the palladium of liberty. It is the Court to which every person who is at all aggrieved can go. A great Jurist in the Transvaal-—and the Transvaal and South Africa generally have undoubtedly produced very great Jurists—once said to me, in regard to a very difficult case, "Though there may be no hope just now, I tell you that I have guided myself by one thing, or else I should not be a lawyer: the law teaches us lawyers that there is absolutely no wrong for which there is no remedy to be found in a court of law; and if judges say there is no remedy, then those judges should be immediately unseated." I say that with all deference to you, Lord Chancellor.

I, therefore, think that our European friends may rest assured that the future Federal Court will not send them away empty-handed, as we expect to go away empty-handed, if we do not have the favour of the Ministers, who are the present advisers of His Majesty. I am still hoping that we shall have their ear and get round their better side and then we may hope to go away with something substantial in our pockets; but whether we go away with anything substantial in our pockets or not, I hope that if the Federal Court of my dreams comes into being, then the Europeans and everybody—all the minorities—may rest assured that that Court will not fail them, though a puny individual like myself may fail them.

*Young India,* 17-12-1931, p. 395

# 63

# THE PLACE OF THE LAWYERS
# IN A NON-VIOLENT SOCIETY

READER: You tell me that when two men quarrel they should not go to a law court. This is astonishing.

EDITOR: Whether you call it astonishing or not, it is the truth. And your question introduces us to the lawyers and the doctors. My firm opinion is that the lawyers have enslaved India, have accentuated Hindu-Mohamedan dissensions and have confirmed English authority.

READER: It is easy enough to bring these charges, but it will be difficult for you to prove them. But for the lawyers, who would have shown us the road to independence? Who would have protected the poor? Who would have secured justice? For instance, the late Manomohan Ghose defended many a poor man free of charge. The Congress, which you have praised so much, is dependent for its existence and activity upon the work of the lawyers. To denounce such an estimable class of men, is to spell injustice, and you are abusing the liberty of the press by decrying lawyers.

EDITOR: At one time I used to think exactly like you. I have no desire to convince you that they have never done a single good thing. I honour Mr. Ghose's memory. It is quite true that he helped the poor. That the Congress owes the lawyers something is believable. Lawyers are also men, and there is something good in every man. Whenever instances of lawyers having done good can be brought forward, it will be found that the good is due to them as men rather than as lawyers. All I am concerned with is to show you that the profession teaches immorality; it is exposed to temptation from which few are saved.

The Hindus and the Mahomedans have quarrelled. An ordinary man will ask them to forget all about it; he will tell them that both must be more or less at fault, and will advise them no longer to quarrel. But they go to lawyers. The latter's duty is to side with their clients and to find out ways and arguments in favour of the clients to which they (the clients) are often strangers. If they do not do so they will be considered to have degraded their profession. The lawyers, therefore, will, as a rule, advance quarrels instead of repressing them. Moreover, men take up that profession not in order to help others out of their miseries, but to enrich themselves. It is one of the avenues of becoming wealthy and their interest exists in multiplying disputes. It is within my knowledge that they are glad when men have disputes. Petty pleaders actually manufacture them. Their touts, like so many leeches, suck the blood of the poor people. Lawyers are men who have little to do. Lazy people, in order to indulge in luxuries, take up such professions. This is a true statement. Any other argument is a mere pretension. It is the lawyers who have discovered that theirs is an honourable profession. They frame laws as they frame their own praises. They decide what fees they will charge and they put on so much side that poor people almost consider them to be heaven-born.

Why do they want more fees than common labourers? Why are their requirements greater? In what way are they more profitable to the country than the labourers? Are those who do good entitled to greater payment? And, if they have done anything for the country for the sake of money, how shall it be counted as good?

Those who know anything of the Hindu-Mahomedan quarrels know that they have been often due to the intervention of lawyers. Some families have been ruined through them; they have made brothers enemies. Principalities, having come under the lawyers' power have become loaded with debt. Many have been robbed of their all. Such instances can be multiplied.

But the greatest injury they have done to the country is that they have tightened the English grip. Do you think that it would be possible for the English to carry on their Government without law-courts? It is wrong to consider that courts are established for the benefit of the people. Those who want to perpetuate their power do so through the courts. If people were to settle their own quarrels, a third party would not be able to exercise any authority over them. Truly, men were less unmanly when they settled their disputes either by fighting or by asking their relatives to decide for them. They became more unmanly and cowardly when they resorted to the courts of law. It was certainly a sign of savagery when they settled their disputes by fighting. Is it any the less so, if I ask a third party to decide, between you and me? Surely, the decision of a third party is not always right. The parlies alone know who is right. We, in our simplicity and ignorance, imagine that a stranger, by taking our money, gives us justice.

The chief thing, however, to be remembered is that without lawyers courts could not have been established or conducted and without the latter the English could not rule. Supposing that there were only English judges, English pleaders and English police, they could only rule over the English. The English could not do without Indian judges and Indian pleaders. How the pleaders were made in the first instance and how they were favoured you should understand well. Then you will have the same abhorrence for the profession that I have. If pleaders were to abandon their profession, and consider it just as degrading as prostitution, English rule would break up in a day. They have been instrumental in having the charge laid against us that we love quarrels and courts as fish love water. What I have said with reference to the pleaders necessarily applies to the judges; they are first cousins; and the one gives strength to the other.

*Indian Home Rule,* 1958, pp. 54-57

# 64

# AN ADVOCATE'S DILEMMA

The following from an advocate has been passed on to me for reply:

"The resolution of Independence means the negation of the King. But by practising in the courts I express my allegiance to the King. It is impossible for me to undergo the sacrifice of giving up my practice, as I have no other source of income, and it would be quite dishonest for me to remain in the Congress after this resolution and continue my practice. My friends in the Congress say that the Congress has not banned the courts. But the question is, that by declaring Independence I am infringing my professional allegiance and conduct. My practice does not of course affect my being a member of the Congress. But I think it is impossible for a practising lawyer to remain in both camps. It may be said, that the Congress has only declared Independence as its immediate objective, but it is not a declaration of Independent Government. It is only intellectual jugglery, I do not see any difference. Please let me know if my view is correct, and if not, why not?"

The dilemma is there. My sympathies and my opinion are with the advocate. But the argument goes deeper than the advocate has carried it. When I use a postage stamp or a coin bearing the King's portrait, I seem to belie my profession of Independence. When I obey a policeman's instructions or pay taxes, I acknowledge the King's authority. And some of these things I should be doing even if we declared an independent parallel Government which we have not as yet. How am I to solve the puzzle? Must I, because I do not or cannot go the 'whole hog', continue to bear allegiance to the King? One escape from the dilemma is to withdraw all such voluntary co-operation as it is possible for me to withdraw and as is calculated to diminish the prestige and the authority of that rule. The Congress could not go further than it did without weaning from it a large number of useful and able workers. Experience has shown that the Congress organisation breaks down where lawyers withdraw their assistance. They have from the very commencement taken the most active and effective part in the Congress. It is unfortunate, that the other classes still feel powerless to run Congress Committees without the assistance of lawyers. They are called officers of the Court. They know what foreign rule means. By training they are the fittest to carry on political agitation when they are honestly and patriotically moved. They have undoubtedly done much for the national movement, but much more is expected from them. And I have no doubt, that when the movement demands from them the last sacrifice, many if not all of them will prove equal to it. Meanwhile since the Congress has not declared boycott of law courts, the matter rests with individual conscience. Where consistently with it, a lawyer cannot both practise and remain in the Congress and cannot give up practice, he may give up Congress, and still help it as effectively as if he was in it, provided of course that he believes in Independence being the right and the duty of every Indian to work for and achieve. I may mention incidentally that many lawyers think that they have a lien on the Congress, and they resent as intrusion the advent of laymen to office; whereas they should deem it a privilege to prepare laymen to take office and make them feel, that if they the laymen have bravery and sacrifice, they can run Congress organisations just as well as lawyers. Indeed there are today several committees that are being efficiently and ably managed by non-professional men. The movement in that direction however needs to receive a much greater impetus. We want a Committee in every one of the seven hundred thousand villages. Thank God we have not got in all India even seventy thousand lawyers. Cobblers, scavengers, tanners, tailors, brick-layers and the like should be found willing and able to work Congress Committees. The educated few can hasten the event, if they will.

*Young India,* 13-2-1930, p. 49

## 65

## 5,000 MILES AWAY

The recent debate in the Assembly over the proposal to appoint two additional judges to the Privy Council for the purpose of hearing Indian appeals has revived the controversy about the location of this final court of appeal. If it were not for the hypnotism under which we are labouring, we would see without effort the futility, the sinfulness, of going five thousand miles away to get (or buy?) justice. It is said that at that delightful distance the judges are able to decide cases with greater detachment and impartiality than they would if they had to hear appeals, say in Delhi. The moment the argument is examined it breaks down. Must the poor Londoners have their Privy Council in Delhi? And what should the French and the Americans do? Must the French by arrangement have their final

Court of appeal in America and the Americans in France? What should we do if India was an independent Country? Or is India an exceptional 'case' requiring special favoured treatment giving the right of appeal in far off London? Let no one quote in support of the seat of the Privy Council in London the case of the Great Colonies. They retain the anachronism out of sentiment. And the movement is on foot in several colonies to have their final Courts of appeal in their own homes. The sentiment in India is the other way. A self-respecting India would never tolerate the location of her final Court of appeal anywhere else but in India.

*Young India,* 18-2-1926, p. 67

## 66

## JUSTICE FROM SIX THOUSAND MILES

No conquest by force of arms is worth treasuring, if it is not followed by cultural conquest, if the conquered do not hug their chains and regard the conqueror as their benefactor. The different forts of India are no doubt a continuous reminder of the British might. But the silent conquest of the mind of educated India is a surer guarantee of British stability than the formidable forts i.e., if the opinion expressed by the distinguished lawyers in *Indian Daily Mail* on the very modest proposal of Sir Hari Singh Gour for the establishment of a Supreme Court at Delhi is an index of that mind. For, these eminent lawyers regard the proposal as premature, in that judgments of the Privy Council sitting six thousand miles away from India would command, in their opinion, greater respect and ensure greater impartiality. This amazing opinion I venture to say has no foundation in fact. But distance lends enchantment to the scene. Members of the Privy Council are after all human beings. They have been found to betray political bias. Their decisions in cases involving questions of custom are often distortions of the reality, not because they are perverse, but because it is not possible for mortals to know everything. A less trained lawyer having a direct knowledge of a local custom is better able to appraise evidence on it than those who, no matter what their attainments are, know nothing of local conditions.

The distinguished lawyers moreover state that expenses will not be less because the final court of appeal is brought down to Delhi. It does not say much for the patriotism of these eminent gentlemen, if they mean that the fees should be on the same scale in poor India as in rich England. A Scotch friend once told me that Englishmen were probably the most extravagant in the world in their tastes and requirements. He told me that hospitals in Scotland were far less expensively fitted than in England though they were in no way inferior in usefulness to those in England. Or does a legal argument increase in weight with an increase in the fees charged ?

The third argument pressed into service in order to oppose the proposed change is that Indian judges will not command the same weight as the wigged ones in White Hall. If this was not an argument advanced by the distinguished lawyers, it would be laughed out. Is respect for judgments commanded by their impartiality, or the location, or the birth, or the colour of the skin, of judges? And if it is the seat or the birth or the pigment that determines the weight to be attached to judges' decisions, is it not high time that the superstition was removed by removing the seat and appointing judges of Indian birth? Or does the argument presuppose partiality on the part of judges of Indian birth? One does sometimes hear of poor people under stress of ignorance desiring an English Collector in the place of an Indian. But greater fearlessness and sanity are surely to be expected of experienced lawyers.

But while in my humble opinion none of the three arguments advanced against the proposal has any force, the deciding reason for having our Supreme Court in India is that our self-respect demands it. Just as we cannot breathe with other lungs, be they ever so much more powerful, so may we not borrow or buy justice from England. We must take pride in being satisfied with the work our own judges may give us. Trials by jury often result, all over the world, in defeating justice. But people everywhere gladly submit to the drawback for the sake of the more important result of the cultivation of an independent spirit among people and the justifiable sentiment of being judged by one's own peers. But sentiment is at a discount in legal circles. And yet it is sentiment that rules the world. Economics and every other consideration is often flung to the winds when sentiment predominates. Sentiment can be and must be regulated. It cannot be, ought never to be, eradicated. If it is not wrong to cherish patriotic feeling, it is surely not wrong to remove the final Court of appeal to Delhi. Just as good government is no substitute for self-government, good justice, if foreign is no substitute for home-made justice.

*Young India,* 12-8-1926, p.281

# 67

## NAVAKAL PROSECUTION
(From "Notes")

The case against Sjt. Khadilkar of *Navakal* I have
headed prosecution. In truth it is persecution. But
under a Government run in the teeth of popular
opposition, especially when as in our case much of
it is suppressed, persecution must be as it is the lot
of every plain-spoken journalist. Sjt. Khadilkar has
always believed in calling a spade a spade. And he
is an effective popular writer. He has paid the price
of popularity based on plain speech. I tender him my
congratulations. I know that he is a philosopher. He
once told me that he often wrote plays to pay the
fines he had at times to pay for his journalistic
adventures. He was content to run this paper and
through it educate public opinion according to his
lights, so long as he could do so without running
into debts for paying fines. The unconcern with which
he was describing his adventures enhanced the respect
I always felt for his ability and constancy of purpose
and sacrifice for the sake of the country. I wish that
he had not thrown away good money in the counsel's
fees. Law courts like every other Government
institution are designed to protect the Government in
time of need. We have had practical experience of
this times without number. They are necessarily so.
Only we do not realize it, when popular liberty and
Government run in the same direction. When however
popular liberty has to be defended in spite of
Government opposition, law courts are poor guardians

thereof. The less we have to do with them the better for us.

*Young India,* 4-4-1929, p. 108 at p. 109

## 68

# AUNDH CONSTITUTION
(From "Notes")

There are several startling things in the Aundh constitution. For the moment I am concerned with only two things — the qualification for the vote and the courts of justice.

I have myself hitherto sworn by simple adult franchise as well for the illiterate as the literate. My observations of the Working of the Congress constitution has altered my opinion. I have come round to the view that a literacy test is necessary for two reasons. The vote should be regarded as a privilege and therefore carry some qualification. The simplest qualification is a literacy test. And if the ministry appointed under the literacy franchise is sincere and solicitous about the disqualified illiterates, the much desired literacy would come in no time. The Aundh constitution has made primary education free and compulsory. I have been assured by Appasaheb that he will see that illiteracy is driven out from Aundh State inside of six months. I hope, therefore, that there will be no opposition in Aundh to the literacy test.

The second important departure from the ordinary practice is the making of justice in the lower court free and incredibly simple. What would, however, displease critics is not the freeness or the simplicity as such but the abolition of intermediate courts and the fate of litigants and persons charged with offences being made to depend on a High Court presided over by one person. In a population of 75,000 a multiplicity of judges would be both unnecessary and impossible. And if the right type of person is chosen as the Chief Judge, he is as likely to deal out unadulterated justice as a bench of highly paid judges. This simplification contemplates abolition of the cumbrous procedure and the use of tomes of law books including hundreds of law reports used in British law courts.

*Harijan,* 14-1-1939, p. 422

## 69

## *CIVIL* v. *CRIMINAL*

When a man wilfully breaks his own laws, the disobedience becomes criminal. For he commits the breach not against himself but against someone else, and not only escapes punishment for the breach for there is none provided against himself by the maker of laws, but he avoids also the inconvenience caused by their observance. What is true of the individual is true of the corporation. At the present moment one observes this criminal breach by the Government of its own laws throughout India. Sections of Penal Code and the Criminal Procedure Code are being freely abused. And because non-co-operators refrain from questioning orders issued by officials, bare-faced illegalities are being committed by them with impunity. We have seen this in Bulandshahr, in Chittagong, all over Sind, and nowhere so systematically and so deliberately as in the Madras Presidency. Mr. Yakub Hassan has pointed out with great justification that his arrest and conviction are contrary to the spirit of the Vicerigal pledge. Indeed it is against not only the spirit of Lord Reading's pledge but it is against the letter even of his predecessor's *communique* in which it was declared in solemn tones that so long as non-cooperation remained non-violent there would be no repression, No one dare accuse Mr. Yakub Hassan of having incited to violence in his Tanjore address before an audience of picked representatives. Nor was any violence done in the Tanjore district as a result of his speech. The Magistrate in the case of Mr. Iyer of the *Deshabhaktan* actually admitted that there was not a trace of violence in the writing that was impeached and that it actually contained exhortations to nonviolence. Mr. Ramaswami Iyenger, leading pleader of Coimbatore, has been arrested for a spirited letter to *The Hindu* though there was no violence in it. And so have Dr. Varadarajulu and Mr. Gopalkrishnayya been arrested for their speeches and writings, although it is known that they not only do not incite to violence but that theirs is actually a restraining influence in the face of provocation. Is it any wonder if one infers from this campaign of repression an intention on the part of the Government to invite violence? In not one of these cases I have mentioned has there been any outbreak of violence as a result of the speeches and writings concerned. And so we see that the Government is guilty of criminal breach of its own laws. And what legal remedy has the afflicted individual against the Government? There is certainly no sanction provided against the Government in law when it prostitutes the law itself to its own base ends. When therefore a Government thus becomes lawless in an organized manner, civil disobedience becomes a sacred duty and is the only remedy open specially to those who had no hand in the making of the Government or its laws. Another remedy there certainly is, and that is armed revolt. Civil disobedience is a complete, effective and bloodless substitute. And it is as well that by exemplary restraint and discipline in the way of submission to unjust and even illegal orders we have created the necessary atmosphere for civil disobedience. For thereby on the one hand the tyrannical nature of the Government has been made more manifest, and on the other by willing obedience we have fitted ourselves for civil disobedience.

It is equally as well that civil disobedience is being confined even now to the smallest area possible. It must be admitted that it is an abnormal state, even as a corrupt and unpopular Government should be in civilized society like disease an abnormal state. Therefore, only when a citizen has disciplined himself in the art of voluntary obedience to the state laws is he justified on rare occasion deliberately but non-violently to disobey them, and expose himself to the penalty of the breach. If then we are to achieve the maximum result in the minimum of time, whilst fiercest disobedience is going on in a limited area, perfect submission to the laws must be yielded in all the other parts so as to test the nation's capacity for voluntary obedience and for understanding the virtue of civil disobedience. Any unauthorized outbreak of disobedience, therefore, in any part of India will most certainly damage the cause and will betray an unpardonable ignorance of the principles of civil disobedience.

*Young India,* 17-11-1921

# 70

## GANDHIJI'S FAMOUS CUSTOMS DECLARATION

[Editor's Note: In the course of history there have been two customs declarations which have become the stuff of legend. The first is that of Oscar Wilde, (1856-1900) the celebrated Irish poet, playwright and man of letters, and the second that of Mahatma Gandhi, (1869-1948) who was the architect of India's freedom through non-violence.

In 1881 Wilde visited America on a lecture tour. When he alighted at the sea port of Boston, the customs officer on duty asked if Wilde had anything to declare. The eccentric poet thereupon came out with his most quoted retort: "I have nothing to declare except my genius."

While Wilde's declaration is well-known and often quoted, much less known but even more witty was Mahatma Gandhi's customs declaration.]

On August 29, 1931 Gandhiji sailed from Bombay by the S. S. Rajputana as the sole delegate of the Indian National Congress to attend the Second Round Table Conference which was being held in London. He disembarked at the French sea port of Marseilles in order to catch the train to London. The French customs officer on duty asked Gandhiji whether he had anything to declare. The Mahatma promptly replied:

"I am a poor mendicant. My kit consists of two spinning wheels, a few jail utensils, a can of goat's milk, four loin clothes, two towels — and my reputation which cannot be worth much."

*Mahatma, Life of Mohandas Karamchand Gandhi,* Vol.3, by D. G. Tendulkar, p. 14

# 71

# VEILED MARTIAL LAW

[BILIMORA,
*April 29, 1930*]

The revival in the form of an ordinance of the Press Act that was supposed to be dead was only to be expected, and I observe that in its new form the Act contains additional provisions making the whole piece more deadly than before. Whether we realize it or not, for some days past we have been living under a veiled form of martial law. After all, what is martial law if it is not the will of the commanding officer for the time being? The Viceroy is that officer, and wherever he considers it desirable he supersedes the whole of the law, both common and statute, and imposes ordinances on a people too submissive to resent or resist him. I hope, however, that the time for tame submission to the dictation from British rulers is gone for ever. I hope that the people will not be frightened by this ordinance. The Press men, if they are worthy representatives of public opinion, will not be frightened by the ordinance. Let us realize the wise dictum of Thoreau that it is difficult under tyrannical rule for honest men to be wealthy. And if we have decided to hand over our bodies without a murmur to the authorities let us also be equally ready to hand over our property to them and not sell our souls. I would, therefore, urge Press men and publishers to refuse to furnish securities, and if they are called upon to do so, either to cease publication or to challenge the authorities to confiscate whatever they like. When freedom is actually knocking at our door and when for the sake of wooing it thousands have suffered tortures, let it not be said of the Press representatives that they were weighed and found wanting. They may confiscate type and machinery, they will not confiscate pen and still less speech, but I recognize that they can succeed in confiscating even these last two. But what they will never succeed in suppressing and what is after all the thing that matters is the thought of the nation and at the present moment there is hardly a man or woman breathing in India who with every breath does not breathe in disaffection, sedition, disloyalty and whatever other term one may use to describe the mentality of the nation which has set its mind on destroying the existing system of Government.

*Young India*, 8-5-1930

# APPENDICES

[The three articles written and published by Gandhiji in his weekly paper *Young India* for which he was tried on the charge of sedition have been reproduced below. The first article "Tampering with Loyalty" was published in *Young India* on September 29, 1921, the second article "The Puzzle and Its Solution" was published in *Young India* on December 15, 1921 and the third article "Shaking the; Manes" was published in *Young India* on February 23, 1922.]

## 1. TAMPERING WITH LOYALTY

His Excellency the Governor of Bombay had warned the public some time ago, that he 'meant business', that he was no longer going to tolerate the speeches that were being made. In his note on the Ali Brothers and others he has made clear his meaning. The Ali Brothers are to be charged with having tampered with the loyalty of the sepoy and with having uttered sedition. I must confess, that I was not prepared for the revelation of such hopeless ignorance on the part of the Governor of Bombay. It is evident that he has not followed the course of Indian history during the past twelve months. He evidently does not know, that the National Congress began to tamper with the loyalty of the sepoy in September last year, that the Central Khilafat Committee began it earlier and that

I began it earlier still, for I must be permitted to take the credit or the odium of suggesting, that India had a right openly to tell the sepoy and everyone - who served the Government in any capacity whatsoever, that he participated in the wrongs done by the Government. The Conference at Karachi merely repeated the Congress declaration in terms of Islam. Only a Musalman divine can speak for Islam, but speaking for Hinduism and speaking for nationalism, I have no hesitation in saying, that it is sinful for any one, either as soldier or civilian, to serve this Government which has proved the treacherous to the Musalmans of India and which has been guilty of the inhumanities of the Punjab. I have said this from many a platform in the presence of sepoys. And if I have not asked individual sepoys to come out, it has not been due to want of will but of ability to support them. I have not hesitated to tell the sepoy, that if he could leave the service and support himself without the Congress or the Khilafat aid, he should leave at once. And I promise, that as soon as the spinning wheel finds an abiding place in every home and Indians begin to feel that weaving gives anybody any day an honourable livelihood, I shall not hesitate, at the peril of being shot, to ask the Indian sepoy individually to leave his service and become a weaver. For, has not the sepoy been used to hold India under subjection, has he not been used to murder innocent people at Jallianwala Bagh, has he not been used to drive away innocent men, women and children during that dreadful night at Chandpur, has he not been used to subjugate the proud Arab of Mesopotamia, has he not been utilised to crush the Egyptian? How can any Indian having a spark of humanity in him and any Musalman having any pride in his religion feel otherwise than as the Ali Brothers have done? The sepoy has been used more often as a hired assassin than as a soldier defending the liberty or the honour of the weak and the helpless. The Governor has pandered to the basest in us by telling us what would have happened in Malabar but for the British soldier or sepoy. I venture to inform His Excellency, that Malabar Hindus would have fared better without the British bayonet, that Hindus and Musalmans would have jointly appeased the Moplahs, that possibly there being no Khilafat question there would have been no Moplah riot at all, that at the worst supposing that Musalmans had made common cause with the Moplahs, Hinduism would have relied upon its creed of non-violence and turned every Musalman into a friend, or Hindu valour would have been tested and tried. The Governor of Bombay has done a disservice to himself and his cause (whatever it might be), by fomenting Hindu-Muslim disunion, and has insulted the Hindus, by letting them infer from his note, that Hindus are helpless creatures unable to die for or defend their hearth, home or religion. If however the Governor is right in his assumptions, the sooner the Hindus die out, the better for humanity. But let me remind His Excellency, that he has pronounced the greatest condemnation upon British rule, in that it finds Indians today devoid of enough manliness to defend themselves against looters, whether they arc Moplah Musalmans or infuriated Hindus of Arrah.

His Excellency's reference to the sedition of the Ali Brothers is only less unpardonable than his reference to the tempering. For he must know, that sedition has become the creed of the Congress. Every non-co-operator is pledged to preach disaffection towards the Government established by law. Non-co-operation, though a religious and strictly moral movement, deliberately aims at the overthrow of the Government, and is therefore legally seditious in terms of the Indian Penal Code. But this is no new discovery. Lord Chelmsford knew it. Lord Reading knows it. It is unthinkable that the Governor of Bombay does not know it. It was common cause that so long as the movement remained non-violent, nothing would be done to interfere with it.

But it may be urged, that the Government has a right to change its policy when it finds, that the movement is really threatening its very existence as a system. I do not deny its right. I object to the Governor's note, because it is so worded as to let the unknowing public think, that tampering with the loyalty of the sepoy and sedition were fresh crimes committed by the Ali Brothers and brought for the first time to His Excellency's notice.

However the duty of the Congress and Khilafat workers is clear. We ask for no quarter; we expect none from the Government. We did not solicit the promise of immunity from prison so long as we remained non-violent. We may not now complain, if we are imprisoned for sedition. Therefore our self-respect and our pledge require us to remain calm, unperturbed and non-violent. We have our appointed course to follow. We must reiterate from a thousand platforms the formula of the Ali Brothers regarding the sepoys, and we must spread disaffection openly and systematically till it please the Government to arrest us. And this we do, not by way of angry retaliation, but because it is our *Dharma*. We must wear *Khadi* even as the brothers have worn it, and spread the Gospel of Swadeshi. The Musalmans must collect for Smyrna relief and the Angora Government. We must spread like the Ali Brothers the Gospel of Hindu-Muslim unity and of non-violence for the purpose of attaining Swaraj and the redress of the Khilafat and the Punjab wrongs.

We have almost reached the crisis. It is well with a patient who survives a crisis. If on the one hand we remain firm as a rock in the presence of danger, and on the other observe the greatest self-restraint, we shall certainly attain our end this very year.

*Young India,* 29-9-1921, pp. 309-10

## 2. A PUZZLE AND ITS SOLUTION

Lord Reading is puzzled and perplexed. Speaking in reply to the addresses from the British Indian Association and the Bengal National Chamber of Commerce at Calcutta, His Excellency said, "I confess that when I contemplate the activities of a section of the community, I find myself still, notwithstanding persistent study ever since I have been in India, puzzled and perplexed. I ask myself what purpose is served by flagrant breaches of the law for the purpose of challenging the Government and in order to compel arrest?" The answer was partly given by Pandit Motilal Nehru when he said on being arrested that he was being taken to the house of freedom. We seek arrest because the so-called freedom is slavery. We are challenging the might of this Government because we consider its activity to be wholly evil. We want to overthrow the Government. We want to *compel* its submission to the people's will. We desire to show that the Government exists to serve the people, not the people the Government. Free life under the Government has become intolerable, for the price exacted for the retention of freedom is unconscionably great. Whether we are one or many, we must refuse to purchase freedom at the cost of our self-respect or our cherished convictions. I have known even little children become unbending when an attempt has been made to cross their declared purpose, be it ever so flimsy in the estimation of their parents.

Lord Reading must clearly understand that the non-co-operators are at war with the Government. They have declared rebellion against it in as much as it has committed a breach of faith with the Musalmans, it has humiliated the Punjab and it insists upon imposing its will upon the people and refuses to repair the breach and repent of the wrong done in the Punjab.

There were two ways open to the people, the way of armed rebellion and the way of peaceful revolt. Non-co-operators have chosen, some out of weakness, some out of strength, the way of peace, i.e. voluntary suffering.

If the people are behind the sufferers, the Government must yield or be overthrown. If the people are not with them they have at least the satisfaction of not having sold their freedom. In an armed conflict the more violent is generally the victor. The way of peace and suffering is the quickest method of cultivating public opinion, and therefore when victory is attained it is for what the world regards as Truth. Bred in the atmosphere of law courts, Lord Reading finds it difficult to appreciate the peaceful resistance to authority. His Excellency will learn by the time the conflict is over that there is a higher court than courts of justice and that is the court of conscience. It supersedes all other courts.

Lord Reading is welcome to treat all the sufferers as lunatics, who do not know their own interest. He is entitled therefore to put them out of harm's way. It is an arrangement that entirely suits the lunatics and it is an ideal situation if it also suits the Government. He will have cause to complain if having courted imprisonment, non-co-operators fret and fume or 'whine for favours' as Lalaji puts it. The strength of a non-co-operator lies in his going to gaol uncomplainingly. He loses his case if having courted imprisonment he begins to grumble immediately his courtship is rewarded.

The threats used by His Excellency are unbecoming. This is a fight to the finish. It is a conflict between the reign of violence and of public opinion. Those who are fighting for the latter are determined to submit to any violence rather than surrender their opinion.

*Young India,* 15-12-1921, p. 418

## 3. SHAKING THE MANES

How can there be any compromise whilst the British Lion continues to shake his gory claws in or faces? Lord Birkenhead reminds us that Britain has lost none of her hard fibre. Mr. Montagu tells us in the plainest language that the British are the most determined nation in the world, who will brook no interference with their purpose. Let me quote the exact words telegraphed by Reuter:—

"If the existence of our Empire were challenged, the discharge of responsibilities of the British Government to India prevented and demands were made in the very mistaken belief that we contemplated retreat from India — then India would not challenge with success the most determined people in the world, who would once again answer the challenge with all the vigour and determination at its command."

Both Lord Birkenhead and Mr. Montagu little know that India is prepared for all 'the hard fibre' that can be transported across the seas and that her challenge was issued in the September of 1920 at Calcutta that India would be satisfied with nothing less than Swaraj and full redress of the Khilafat and the Punjab wrongs. This does involve the existence of the 'Empire', and if the present custodians of the British Empire are not satisfied with its quiet transformation into a true Commonwealth of free nations, each with equal rights and each having the power to secede at will from an honourable and friendly partnership, all the determination and vigour of 'the most determined people in the world' and the 'hard fibre' will have to be spent in India in a vain effort to crush the spirit that has risen and that will neither bend nor break. It is true that we have no 'hard fibre'. The rice-eating, puny millions of India seems to have resolved upon achieving their own destiny without any further tutelage and without arms. In the Lokamanya's language it is their 'birthright', and they will have it in spite of the 'hard fibre' and in spite of the vigour and determination with which it may be administered. India cannot and will not answer this insolence with insolence, but if she remains true to her pledge, her prayer to God to be delivered from such a scourge will certainly not go in vain. No empire intoxicated with the red wine of power and plunder of weaker races has yet lived long in this world, and this 'British Empire', which is based upon organized exploitation of physically weaker races of the earth and upon a continuous exhibition of brute force, cannot live if there is a just God ruling the universe. Little do these so-called representatives of the British nation realise that India has already given many of her best men to be dealt with by the British 'hard fibre'. Had Chauri Chaura not interrupted the even course of the national sacrifice, there would have been still greater and more delectable offerings placed before the Lion, but God had willed it otherwise. There is nothing, however, to prevent all those representatives in Downing Street and White Hall from doing their worst. I am aware that I have written strongly about the insolent threat that has come from across the seas, but it is high time that the British people were made to realise that the fight that was commenced in 1920 is a fight to the finish, whether it lasts one month or one year or many months or many years and whether the representatives of Britain re-enact all the indescribable orgies of the Mutiny days with redoubled force or whether they do not. I shall only hope and pray that God will give India sufficient humility and sufficient strength to remain non-violent to the end. Submission to the insolent challenges that are cabled out on due occasions is now an utter impossibility.

*Young India,*  23-2-1922, p, 119

## APPENDIX II
## GANDHIJI'S THOUGHTS ON
## THE LAW AND THE LAWYERS

1. I had learnt the true practice of law. I had learnt to find out the better side of human nature and to enter men's hearts. I realized that the true function of a lawyer was to unite parties riven asunder. The lesson was so indelibly burnt into me that a large part of my time during the twenty years of my practice as a lawyer was occupied in bringing about private compromises of hundreds of cases. I lost nothing thereby - not even money, certainly not my soul.

*An Autobiography,* (1959), p. 97

2. It was not impossible to practise law without compromising truth. Even truthfulness in the practice of the profession cannot cure it of the fundamental defect that vitiates it.

*An Autobiography,* (1959), p. 269

3. Throughout my career at the bar I never once departed from the strictest truth and honesty. The first thing which you must always bear in mind, if you would spiritualize the practice of law, is not to make your profession subservient to the interests of your purse, as is unfortunately but too often the case at present, but to use your profession for the service of your country. . . . The fees charged by lawyers are unconscionable everywhere. I confess, I myself have charged what I would now call high fees. But even whilst I was engaged in my practice, let me tell you

255

I never let my profession stand in the way of my public service. . . . And there is another thing I would like to warn you against. In England, in South Africa, almost everywhere I have found that in the practice of their profession Lawyers are consciously or unconsciously 'led into untruth for the sake of their clients. An eminent English Lawyer has gone so far as to say that it may even be the duty of a lawyer to defend a client whom he knows to be guilty. There I disagree. The duty of a lawyer is always to place before the judges, and to help them to arrive at, the truth, never to prove the guilty as innocent.

*Young India*, 22-12-1927, pp. 427-28

4. A true lawyer is one who places truth and service in the first place and the emoluments of the profession in the next place only.

*Harijan*, 26-11-1938, p. 351

5. Facts mean truth, and once we adhere to truth, the law comes to our aid naturally.

*An Autobiography*, (1959), p. 96.

6. I recalled the late Mr. Pincutt's advice - facts are three-fourths of the law.

*An Autobiography*, (1959), p. 95

7. Lawyers and English-educated persons do not by any means enjoy a monopoly of hair-splitting.

*Satyagraha in South Africa*, Madras, Ganesan, p. 202

8. Lawyers are also men, and there is something good in every man. Whenever instances of lawyers

having done good can be brought forward, it will be found that the good is due to them as men rather than as lawyers.

*Indian Home Rule,*  1958, p. 55

9. Lawyers will, as a rule, advance quarrels instead of repressing them. Moreover, men take up that profession, not in order to help others out of their miseries, but to enrich themselves. It is one of the avenues of becoming wealthy and their interest exists in multiplying disputes. It is within my knowledge that they are glad when men have disputes.

*Indian Home Rule,*  1958, p. 55

10. I have not a shadow of a doubt that society would be much cleaner and healthier if there was less resort to law courts than there is.

*Young India,*  3-12-1919

11. An unjust law is itself a species of violence. Arrest for its breach is more so.

*Non-violence in Peace and War,*  Vol. 2, p. 150

12. The economic drain that the law courts cause has at no time been considered. And yet it is not a trifle. Every institution founded under the present system is run on a most extravagant scale. Law courts are probably the most extravagantly run. I have some knowledge of the scale in England, a fair knowledge of the Indian and an intimate knowledge of the South African. I have no hesitation in saying that the Indian is comparatively the most extravagant and bears no relation to the general economic condition of the people.

The best South African lawyers - and they are lawyers of great ability - dare not charge the fees the lawyers in India do. Fifteen guineas is almost a top fee for legal opinion. Several thousand rupees have been known to have been charged in India. There is something sinful in a system under which it is possible for a lawyer to earn from fifty thousand to one lakh rupees per month. Legal practice is not - ought not to be — a speculative business. The best legal talent must be available to the poorest at reasonable rates.

*Young India,* 6-10-1920, pp. 2-3

[Ideas derived by Gandhiji from Ruskin's *Unto This Last* in the year 1904:]

13. The teachings of *Unto This Last* I understood to be:

(1) That the good of the individual is contained in the good of all.

(2) That a lawyer's work has the same value as the barber's, inasmuch as all have the same right of earning their livelihood from their work.

(3) That a life of labour, i.e. the life of the tiller of the soil and the handicraftsman is the life worth living.

The first of these I knew. The second I had dimly realized. The third had never occurred to me. *Unto This Last* made it as clear as daylight for me that the second and the third were contained in the first.

*An Autobiography,* (1959), p. 221

14. If all laboured for their bread and no more, then there would be enough food and enough leisure for all.

Then there would be no cry of over-population, no disease and no such misery as we see around. Such labour will be the highest form of sacrifice. Men will no doubt do many other things either through their bodies or through their minds, but all this will be labour of love for the common good. . . . May not men earn their bread by intellectual labour? No. The needs of the body must be supplied by the body. "Render unto Caesar that which is Caesar's", perhaps, applies here as well. Mere mental, that is, intellectual labour is for the soul and is its own satisfaction. It should never demand payment. In the ideal State, doctors, lawyers and the like will work solely for the benefit of society, not for self.

*Harijan,* 29-6-1935, p. 165

15. A medical practitioner from Kenya asks whether medical practitioners can engage in money-lending business or speculation. I have long held the opinion that professional men, whether medical or legal or other, should not seek to add to their income by speculation or other pursuits. It tends to make them careless in their special work. There have been cases in which doctors and lawyers have ruined their reputation by going outside their profession to make money.

*Harijan,* 16-12-1939, p. 379

16. Justice in British courts is an expensive luxury. It is often 'the longest purse that wins'.

17. It is much to be wished that people would avoid litigation. 'Agree with thine adversary quickly' is the soundest legal maxim ever uttered. The author knew what he was saying. But it will be asked, what when we are dragged, as we often are, to the courts?

I would say 'do not defend'. If you are in the wrong, you will deserve the sentence whatever it may be. If you are wrongly brought to the court and yet penalized, let your innocence soothe you in your unmerited suffering. Undefended, you will in every case suffer the least and what is more you will have the satisfaction of sharing the fate of the majority of your fellow-beings who cannot get themselves defended.

*Young India,* 23-7-1919

18. Put your talents in the service of the country instead of converting them into £ s.d. If you are a medical man, there is disease enough in India to need all your medical skill. If you are a lawyer, there are differences and quarrels enough in India. Instead of fomenting more trouble, patch up those quarrels and stop litigation. If you are an engineer, build model houses suited to the means and needs of our people and yet full of health and fresh air. There is nothing that you have learnt which cannot be turned to account.

*Young India,* 5-11-1931, p. 334

[Several Mysore lawyers who had taken part in the Mysore Satyagraha struggle had been disbarred by the Mysore Chief Court. Gandhiji wrote about them :]

19. Let these lawyers be proud of their poverty which will be probably their lot now. Let them remember Thoreau's saying that possession of riches is a crime and poverty a virtue under an unjust administration. This is an eternal maxim for Satyagrahis. The disbarred lawyers have a rare opportunity of so remodelling their lives that they can always be above want. Let them remember that

practice of law ought not to mean taking more daily than, say, a village carpenter's wage.

*Harijan,* 13-7-1940, p. 205

20. If India is to live an exemplary life of independence which will be the envy of the world, all the *bhangis* (sweepers), doctors, lawyers, teachers, merchants and others would get the same wages for an honest day's work. Indian society may never reach the goal, but it is the duty of every Indian to set his sail towards that goal and no other, if India is to be a happy land.

*Harijan,* 16-3-1947, p. 67

21. A wise man deliberately forgets many things, even as a lawyer forgets the cases and their details as soon as they are disposed of.

Letter to Mirabehn, 25-1-1931 in *Bapu's Letters to Mira,* p. 150

22. Only he who has mastered the art of obedience to law knows the art of disobedience to law.

*Young India,* 5-11-1919

23. Once a law is enacted, many difficulties must be encountered before it can be reversed. It is only when public opinion is highly educated that the laws in force in a country can be repealed. A Constitution under which laws are modified or repealed every now and then cannot be said to be stable or well organized.

*Satyagraha in South Africa,* Ch. 10, p. 140

[Editor's Note: In 1927, an American authoress, Miss Catherine Mayo, published under the title *Mother India* a book which was scurrilous and grossly defamatory of India and her people. Reviewing the said book in *Young India* Gandhiji called it a 'Drain Inspector's Report'. In the course of his articles  Gandhiji observed:]

24. "She (Miss Mayo) has done me the honour of quoting me frequently in support of her argument. . . . But in her hurry to see everything Indian in bad light, she has not only taken liberty with my writings, but she has not thought it necessary even to verify through me certain things ascribed by her or others to me. In fact she has combined in her own person what we understand in India the judicial and the executive officer. She is both the prosecutor and the judge.... Having no case, she has followed the method of the pettifogging lawyer who vainly tries to discredit a hostile but unshakable witness by making  him state things  from  memory  which  might  be  found  on verification to be not quite accurate."

*Young India,* 15-9-1927, p. 308 and 2-2-1928, p. 34

25. If everybody lives by the sweat of his brow, the earth will become a paradise. The question of the use of special talents hardly needs separate consideration. If everyone labours physically for his bread it follows that poets, doctors, lawyers, etc. will regard it their duty to use those talents gratis for the service of humanity. Their output will be all the better and richer for their selfless devotion to duty.

*Harijan,*  2-3-1947, p. 47

26. I believe in the division of labour or work. But I do insist on equality of wages. The lawyer, the doctor or the teacher is entitled to no more than the *bhangi*.

Then only will the division of work uplift the nation or the earth. There is no other royal road to true civilization or happiness.

*Harijan,* 23-3-1947, p. 78

27. May not men earn their bread by intellectual labour? No. The needs of the body must be supplied by the body. "Render unto Caesar that which is Caesar's" perhaps applies here as well. Mere mental, that is intellectual, labour is for the soul and is its own satisfaction. It should never demand payment. In the ideal state, doctors, lawyers and the like will work solely for the benefit of society not for self.

*Harijan,* 29-6-1935, p. 156

28. If we were not under the spell of lawyers and law courts and if there were no touts to tempt us into the quagmire of the courts and to appeal to our basest passions we would be leading a much happier life than we do today. Let those who frequent the law courts - the best of them - bear witness to the fact that the atmosphere about them is foetid. Perjured witnesses are ranged on either side ready to sell their very souls for money or for friendship's sake.

*Young India,* 6-10-1920, p. 2

29. I am unconvinced of the advantages of jury trials over those by judges.... At the right moment juries have been found to fail even in England. When passions are roused juries are affected by them and give perverse verdicts. Nor need we assume that they are always on the side of leniency. 1 have known juries finding prisoners guilty in the face of evidence and even judge's summing up to the contrary. We must not

slavishly copy all that is English. In matters where absolute impartiality, calmness and ability to sift evidence and understand human natures are required, we may not replace trained judges by untrained men brought together by chance. What we must aim at is an incorruptible, impartial and able judiciary right from the bottom.

*Young India,* 27-8-1931, p. 240

30. In Independent India of the non-violent type, there will be crime but no criminals. They will not be punished. Crime is disease like any other malady and is a product of the prevalent social system. Therefore, all crime including murder will be treated as a disease. Whether such an India will ever come into being is another question.

*Harijan,* 5-5-1946, p. 124

31. The symbol of a Court of Justice is a pair of scales held evenly by an impartial and blind but sagacious woman. Fate has purposely made her blind, in order that she may not judge a person from his exterior but from his intrinsic worth.

*An Autobiography,* (1959), p. 105

32. All crimes are different kinds of diseases and they should be treated as such by the reformers. That does not mean that the police will suspend their function of regarding such cases as public crimes, but their measures are never intended to deal with causes of these social disturbances. To do so is the special prerogative of the reformer. And unless the moral tone of society is raised such crimes will flourish, if only for the simple reason that the moral sense of these

perverts has become blunt.

*Gandhiji - His Life and Work,* edited by D. G.
Tendulkar and others, p. 381

33. I cannot in all conscience agree to any one being
sent to the gallows.... I would draw the distinction
between killing and detention or even corporal
punishment. I think there is a difference not merely in
quantity but also in quality. I can recall the punishment
of detention. I can make reparation to the man upon
whom I inflict corporal punishment. But once a man is
killed, the punishment is beyond recall or reparation.
God alone can take life, because He alone gives it.

*Gandhiji - His Life and Work,* edited by D. G.
Tendulkar and others, p. 381

34. I do wish as a practised draftsman to warn
writers of petition, whether they be pleaders or
otherwise, to think of the cause they may be espousing
for the time being. I assure them that a bare statement
of facts embellished with adjectives is far more eloquent
and effective than a narrative glowing with exuberant
language. Petition writers must understand that they
address busy men, not necessarily sympathetic,
sometimes prejudiced, and almost invariably prone to
sustain the decisions of their subordinates.

*Young India,* 27-9-1919

35. When there is war, the poet lays down the lyre,
the lawyer his law reports, the school-boy his books.
The poet will sing the true note after the war is over,
the lawyer will have occasion to go to his law books
when people have time to fight among themselves.

*Young India,* 1-9-1921

36. Under the Swaraj Government the law will not tolerate any arrogation of superiority by any person or class whether in the name of custom or religion.

*Young India,* 11-6-1931, p. 143

37. My experience has shown me that we win justice quickest by rendering justice to the other party.

M. K. Gandhi, *An Autobiography,* De Luxe Edition, 1968 Vol. one, p. 270

38. There is a higher court than courts of justice and that is the court of conscience. It supersedes all other courts.

*Quotes of Gandhi,* UBS Publishers, New Delhi (1995) p. 34

39. Justice that love gives is a surrender, justice that law gives is a punishment.

*Quotes of Gandhi,* UBS Publishers, New Delhi (1995) p. 65

40. Legal maxims are not so legal as they are moral. I believe in the eternal truth of 'sic utere tuo ut alienum non laedas' (use thy own property so as not to injure thy neighbour's).

*Young India,* 26-3-1921, p. 50 at p. 51

41. In order to enhance the status and the market-value of the provincial languages, I would have the language of the law courts to be the language of the province where the court is situated.

*Harijan,* 9-7-1938, pp. 177-178

42. The fear of the judge within is more terrible than that of the one without.

*Mahatma,* Vol. 2 by D. G. Tendulkar, p. 63

43. Justice should become cheap and expeditious. Today it is the luxury of the rich and the joy of the gambler.

*Mahatma,* Vol. 4 by D. G, Tendulkar, p. 222

44. Justice does not help the ones who slumber but helps only those who are vigilant. This is not a maxim to be mouthed in courts of law but to be applied in every concern of practical life.

*The Collected Works of Mahatma Gandhi,* Publications Division, Government of India, Vol. XIV, p. 177

45. A Satyagrahi cannot go to law for a personal wrong.

*The Collected Works of Mahatma Gandhi,* Publications Division, Government of India, Vol. XXV, p. 163

46. The recognition of the golden rule of never taking the law into one's own hands has no exceptions.

*Mahatma,* Vol. 8, 2nd Edition (1960) by D. G. Tendulkar, p. 103

47. Where death without resistance or death after resistance is the only way, neither party should think of resorting to law courts or help from government. Even if one of the parties resorts to such aid, the other should refrain. If resort to law courts cannot be avoided, there ought to be at least no resort to false

evidence.

*The Collected Works of Mahatma Gandhii,* Publications Division, Government of India, Vol. XXV; p. 138

48. Independence meant voluntary restraint and discipline, voluntary acceptance of the rule of law.

*Mahatma,* Vol. 8, 2nd Edition (1960) by D. G. Tendulkar, p. 100

49. All taxation to be healthy must return tenfold to the taxpayer in the form of necessary services.

*Mahatma,* Vol. 4, by D. G. Tendulkar, p. 211

50. Legal imposition avoids the necessity of honour or good faith.

*The Collected Works of Mahatma Gandhi,* Publications Division, Government of India, Vol. XXVI, p. 162

51. Whether there is or there is not any law in force, the Government cannot exercise control over us without our cooperation. The existence of a law means that if we refused to accept it, we are liable to punishment, and generally it so happens that the fear of punishment leads men to submit to the restriction. But a Satyagrahi differs from the generality of men in that if he submits to a restriction, he submits voluntarily, not because he is afraid of punishment, but because he thinks such submission is essential to the common weal.

*Satyagraha in South Africa,* De Luxe Edition, 1968, Ch. 22, p. 218

52. It was the function of democracy to make justice cheap and expeditious and to ensure all possible purity in the administration. But, for the ministers to replace or to influence courts of justice was the very negation of democracy and law. No minister has the right to interfere with the course of justice, even for his dearest ones.

*Mahatma,* Vol. 8, by D. G. Tendulkar, p. 193

53. The demands of equity supersede the letter of law. There is a homely maxim of law, which has been in practice for centuries in England, that when common law seems to fail, equity comes to the rescue.

*Mahatma,* Vol. 8, by D. G. Tendulkar, p. 316

54. An oath may be taken in the name of God and yet may not be styled religious. An oath that witness takes in a court of law is a legal not a religious oath, breach of which would carry legal consequences. An oath taken by members of Parliament may be called a constitutional not a religious oath, breach of which may involve mundane consequences. Breach of a religious oath carries no legal consequences, but in the opinion of the taker does carry divine punishment. This does not mean that any of the three varieties of oaths is less binding than the others on a conscientious man. A conscientious witness will tell the truth, not for fear of the legal consequence, but he will do so in every case.

*Harijan,* 22-5-1937, p. 116

55. The poet (Rabindranath Tagore) thinks, for instance, that I want everybody to spin the whole of his time to the exclusion of all other activity, that is to say, that I want the poet to forsake his muse, the farmer

his plough, the lawyer his brief and the doctor his lancet. So far is this from truth that I have asked no one to abandon his calling, but on the contrary to adorn it by giving every day only thirty minutes to spinning as sacrifice for the whole nation.

*Young India,* 5-11-1925

56. It is my confirmed belief that every Government masks its brute-force and maintains its control over the people through civil and criminal courts, for it is cheaper, simpler and more honourable for a ruler that instead of his controlling the people through naked force, they themselves, lured into slavery through courts, etc., submit to him of their own accord. If people settle their civil disputes among themselves and the lawyers, unmindful of self-interest, boycott the courts in the interest of the people, the latter can advance in no time. I have believed for many years that every State tries to perpetuate its power through lawyers.

*The Penguin Gandhi Reader,* Edited by Rudrangshu Mukherjee 1993 p. 135.

57. The master-key to the solution of the problem of Hindu-Muslim Unity is the replacement of the rule of the sword by that of arbitration. Honest public opinion should make it impossible for aggrieved parties to take the law into their own hands and every case must be referred to private arbitration or to law courts if the parties do not believe in non-co-operation.

*Ibid,* p. 262

58. We shall never be able to raise the standard of public life through laws. We are not made that way.

Only if the lives of the leaders, both private and public, are perfect, will they be able to produce any effect on the people. Mere preaching will have no effect.

*The Essential Writings of Mahatma Gandhi,* edited by Raghavan Iyer, Oxford University Press, 1996 p. 411

59. On the political field, the struggle on behalf of the people mostly consists in opposing error in the shape of unjust laws. When you have failed to bring the error home to the law-giver by way of petitions and the like, the only remedy open to you, if you do not wish to submit to it, is to compel him to retrace his steps by suffering in your person, i.e., by inviting the penalty for the breach of the law. Hence, satyagraha largely appears to the public as civil disobedience or civil resistance. It is civil in the sense that it is not criminal.

*Gandhi and Gandhism,* by B. Pattabhi Sitaramayya Vol. 1, Kitabistan, Allahabad p. 104

60. The criminal, i.e., the ordinary lawbreaker breaks the law surreptitiously and tries to avoid the penalty: not so the civil resister. He ever obeys the law of the State to which he belongs, not out of fear of the sanctions, but because he considers them to be good for the welfare of society. But there come occasions, generally rare, when he considers certain laws to be so unjust as to render obedience to them a dishonour, he then openly and civilly breaks them and quietly suffers the penalty for their breach. And in order to register his protest against the action of the law-giver, it is open to him to withdraw his co-operation from the state by disobeying such other laws whose breach does not involve moral turpitude.

*Ibid,* p. 104

61. When the Rowlatt Bills were published, I felt that they were so restrictive of human liberty that they must be resisted to the utmost. I observed, too, that the opposition to them was universal among Indians. I submit that no state, however despotic, has the right to enact laws which are repugnant to the whole body of the people, much less a Government guided by constitutional usage and precedent, such as the Indian Government. I felt, too, that the oncoming agitation needed a definite direction, if it was neither to collapse nor to run into violent channels. I ventured therefore to present satyagraha to the country, emphasising its civil resistance aspect.

*Gandhi and Gandhism,* by P. Pattabhi Sitaramayya Vol. I pp 104-105

62. The councillors want their fares and extras, the ministers their salaries, the lawyers their fees, the suitors their decrees, the parents such education for their boys as would give them status in the present life, the millionaires want facilities for multiplying their millions and the rest their unmanly peace. The whole revolves beautifully round the central corporation. It is a giddy dance from which no one cares to free himself and so, as the speed increases, the exhileration is the greater. But it is a death dance and the exhileration is induced by the rapid heart beat of a patient who is about to expire.

*Young India*, 9-3-1922, p. 148

63. There is no doubt that untouchability is a mental attitude. It cannot be abolished by legislation. Law can touch the body, but not the mind. The mind

can be touched only by love and persuasion.

*The Collected Works of Mahatma Gandhi*, Vol. LIV p. 325

64. People seem to think that when a law is passed against any evil, it will die without any further effort. There never was a grosser self-deception. Legislation is intended to be and is effective against an ignorant or a small evil-minded minority; but no legislation which is opposed by an intelligent and organized public opinion, or under cover of religion by a fanatical minority, can ever succeed.

*Young India*, 7-7-1927, p. 219

65. We must widen the prison gates and we must enter them as a bridegroom enters the bride's chamber. Freedom is to be wooed only inside prison walls and sometimes on gallows, never in the council chamber, courts, or the schoolrooms.

*The Life of Mahatma Gandhi*, by Louis Fischer, Harper & Row Publishers, New York, 1983 p. 204

66. Justice will come when it is deserved by our being and feeling strong.

*Mahatma*, Vol. 2 by D. G. Tendulkar, p. 240

67. The first condition of non-violence is justice all round, in every department of life.

*Mahatma*, Vol. 5 by D. G. Tendulkar, p. 278

68. Peace will not come out of a clash of arms but out of justice, lived and done by unarmed nations in the

face of odds.

*Mahatma*, Vol. 5 by D. G. Tendulkar, p. 193

69. It is open to a war resister to judge between two combatants and wish success to the one who has justice on his side.

*Mahatma*, Vol. 5, by D. G. Tendulkar, p. 197

70. I can certainly imagine a brave and believing weaver or cobbler more effectively leading our struggle than a timid and sceptical lawyer. Success depends upon bravery, sacrifice, truth, love and faith; not on legal acumen, calculation, diplomacy, hate and unbelief.

*Young India*, 25-8-1921 p. 266

71. The removal of untouchability is not to be brought by any legal enactment. It will be brought about only when the Hindu conscience is roused to action and of its own accord removes the shame.

*Young India*, 30-6-1927

72. It is not legislation that will cure a popular evil. It is enlightened public opinion that can do it.

*Young India*, 26-8-1926.

73. We are the makers of our own state. Individuals who realize the fact need not, ought not, to wait for collective action -even as a hungry man does not wait for others to commence a meal before he falls to it. The one necessary condition for action is that like the hungry man, we must hunger after our deliverance. We need the same advice that was given to Martha by Jesus Christ. If we but do "the one thing needful", there

is no occasion for us to be "anxious and troubled" about the many things in the shape of wanting to know what our Governors will do, or who the next Prime Minister is likely to be, or what laws affecting us are likely to be passed.

*Indian Opinion*  14-5-1910

74. For me patriotism is the same as humanity. I am patriotic because I am human and humane. It is not exclusive. I will not hurt England or Germany to serve India. The law of the patriot is not different from that of the patriarch. And a patriot is so much the less a patriot if he is a lukewarm humanitarian. There is no conflict between private and political law. A non-cooperator for instance, would act exactly in the same manner toward his father or brother as he is today acting toward the British Government.

*Young India*, 16-3-1921.

75. The question of reform of the legal profession is a big one. It does not admit of tinkering. I am strongly of opinion that lawyers and doctors should not be able to charge any fees but that they should be paid a certain fixed sum by the state and the public should receive their services free. They will have paid for them through the taxation that they would have paid for such services rendered to citizens automatically. The poor will be untaxed but the rich and the poor will have then the same amount of attention and skill. Today the best legal talents and the best medical advice are unobtainable by the poor.

*The Collected Works of Mahatma Gandhi*, Publications Division, Government of India, Vol. XXXVI, p. 84.

76. The attack against Justice Duleepsingh (Judge of the Punjab High Court who had on appeal acquitted the author of a pamphlet who had been prosecuted and sentenced by the lower courts under Section 153-A of the Indian Penal Code) was uncalled for, undeserved and hysterical. The judiciary is by no means above being influenced by the Government, but it would be wholly unfit to render justice if it was open to popular attacks, threats and insults. So far as the Judge's integrity was concerned, it should have satisfied any Mussalman that he condemned the pamphlet as he did in unmeasured terms. His reading of the section ought not to have been made a cause for virulent attack against him. That other judges have taken a different view from Justice Duleepsingh is irrelevant to the issue. Judges have been often known before now to have given honest and opposite interpretations of the same law.

*The Collected Works of Mahatma Gandhi,* Publications Division, Government of India, Vol. XXXV pp. 15-16.

77. A true Khudai Khidmatgar[1] will not go to a law court. Fighting in a law court is just like physical fighting. Only, you use force by proxy.

*A Pilgrimage for Peace Gandhi and Frontier Gandhi among N.W.F. Pathans,* By Pyarelal p. 61 Navjivan Publishing House, Ahmedabad. 1950

---

1. Literally "servants of God" being the name given by Khan Abdul Ghaffar Khan — the Frontier Gandhi as he came to be known — to his Volunteers when he founded the non-violence movement among the warlike Frontier folk.

# APPENDIX III
## GANDHIJI AS A JURIST

[Editor's Note: In a speech delivered on July 1, 1963 at the Symposium organised by the Bombay Branch of the Gandhi Smarak Nidhi, the late B. N. Gokhale, an ex-Judge of the Bombay High Court has dealt with Gandhiji's legal philosophy. The speech is reproduced below by courtesy Khadi Gramodyog.]

1. We in India have often deplored the lack of jurists in our country and attributed it to our standards of legal education. The University Education Commission presided over by no less a person than Dr. Radhakrishnan had the following observation to make about it :

"In our country, we have eminent practitioners and excellent judges. The law has also given us great leaders and men consecrated to public service. Most conspicuous of these is Gandhiji. We have no internationally known exponents of jurisprudence and legal studies. Our colleges of law do not hold a place of high esteem either at home or abroad, nor has law become an area of profound scholarship and enlightened research."

Since this report was published, undoubtedly our methods of legal training have made some progress but the verdict of the Dr. Radhakrishnan Commission has been confirmed by the Law Commission of India as late as 1958 under the distinguished chairmanship of Shri Motilal Setalvad.

2. I have no doubt that when the sponsors of today's symposium chose the subject of Gandhiji as a Jurist, they did not have in mind the term jurist in its ordinary technical sense. But I do not think that we

shall be doing any injustice to Gandhiji's memory if we do not describe him as a jurist in that sense. It cannot, however, be denied that Gandhiji had a legal philosophy of his own and entertained most refreshing views as to the duties and functions of lawyers as well as of courts of law though they might not have gained acceptance in those days and might not get even today a whole-hearted acceptance. That, however, cannot detract from their value and the fruitfulness of a discussion like that of today's evening.

3. It would be impossible for me to refer in this speech to all the aspects of Gandhiji's legal philosophy. I, therefore, propose to deal only with one or two of the aspects of that philosophy and the question of their general validity.

4. But before I do so, let me pay a tribute to the skilful manner in which Gandhiji analysed and discussed some of the material law cases from the unhappy Punjab of those days in the columns of *Young India*. Gandhiji had then to his credit legal practice of about 20 years mostly in South Africa. As far as is known, he does not seem to have appeared in any case in the Bombay High Court. But as I was saying, the manner in which Gandhiji analysed and discussed these cases arouses one's admiration. His observation about the usual defence of alibi, about the identification parades, about the entries in the police diaries, or the value of approver's evidence or his caution in not accepting extraneous evidence reveal him as a lawyer having a very keen insight into the intricacies of criminal law, and the principles which he touched are valid even today in the light of the rulings of our highest Courts. I would particularly mention in this connection Gandhiji's article on the case of Karamchand, a student of the Dayanand Anglo-Vedic

College. I do not know how far the articles in *Young India* affected the ultimate decision of the Government of India which reviewed some of these cases. But there can be no doubt that those articles aroused and galvanized public opinion in the whole country regarding the enormity of the happenings in the Punjab which otherwise might have been perhaps a closed book.

5. Gandhiji's views regarding the duties and functions of the legal profession must find the first mention in any discussion of his legal philosophy. According to him, though a lawyer must do his very best for his client, he ought not so to identify himself with his client as to transgress the principles of truth and justice. In his very early life, Gandhiji learnt a bitter lesson when he tried to plead with the Political Agent for his elder brother who, as the legal adviser and secretary to the Ranasaheb of Porbunder before he was installed on his Gadi, was said to have tendered wrong advice to the Ranasaheb. The Political Agent was rude to Gandhiji in this matter and Gandhiji was much embittered by the treatment received by him but ultimately accepted the wholesome advice of Sir Pherozeshah Mehta not to do anything rash. Gandhiji has admitted that this incident changed to some extent the course of his life. Gandhiji always regarded that over and above the interests of his clients, he had a prior and perpetual retainer on behalf of truth and justice. That led to his developing certain rules of conduct which he scrupulously followed.

6. Mis anxiety to discover the truth made him attain a good deal of skill in cross-examination and it has been said that he found no difficulty in exposing dishonest witnesses. He always considered that within limits a defence counsel must wield the weapon of

cross-examination to expose the falsity or at least the weakness in the prosecution case. When on one occasion the Chief Justice of the Patna High Court animadverted against what he regarded as the habit of counsel in abusing the privilege of cross-examination, and went to the length of saying that it should be circumstance warranting an enhancement of sentence, Gandhiji publicly protested against this dictum and pointed out that an eminent counsel like Russel could never have succeeded in establishing the Piggot forgeries but for his able and fiery cross-examination. But I have no doubt that Gandhiji would have equally deplored the use of this weapon merely to browbeat witnesses even though the lawyer might be knowing the weakness of his own case.

7. Gandhiji's insistence on truth also enabled him to be strict with his own clients who knowing his views often reserved for him their clean cases entrusting the doubtful ones to other lawyers. In this perhaps Gandhiji was singularly fortunate. It would seem that there were occasions when he would retire from a case even in the midst of the hearing if he realized that his client had deceived him. Other lawyers have done the same. I have known as to how once Shri D. N. Bahadurji, ex-Advocate General and a distinguished lawyer of great integrity, sat down while he was arguing an appeal on the ground that he was misinstructed by the advocate instructing him and had to be cajoled into resuming the argument. How Gandhiji made a merchant-client of his confess to his guilt in smuggling and defrauding the customs authorities is known to every reader of Gandhiji's autobiography. How many lawyers engaged in smuggling cases would be prepared to follow this example ?

8. His adherence to justice and truth also led to another result. Gandhiji was always in favour of setting a case and often advised his clients not to fight to the bitter end. That is illustrated by the very first case in which he was concerned on behalf of his employer one Abdulla Seth, between whom and the opponent Tyeb Seth, he was able to bring about an amicable settlement. This practice often creates a misconception in the clients' mind especially in the case of junior lawyers. But in Gandhiji's case it brought him greater esteem and confidence on the part of his clients. To some extent that was due to the fact that many of his clients were co-workers in his public work in South Africa. Gandhiji has always stressed that it is the glory of the legal profession to bring the two opposing parties together to agree to submitting their disputes to arbitration.

9. Gandhiji, very early in his career as a lawyer, learnt the importance of studying deeply and delving into the facts of a case, because, as he expressed it, if the facts were taken care of, the law would take care of itself. He has mentioned that he learnt this from senior Mr. Leonard, a famous lawyer in South Africa, whom Gandhiji's client had engaged in the very first case to which I have referred above. Gandhiji adhered to and followed this method in his political work also. In some of the martial law cases about which he had occasion to write in the columns of *Young India,* he took meticulous care about his facts and expressed his annoyance if they were not properly handled or the case was spoiled by the improperly worded and angry arguments on the part of the lawyer. Lokmanya Tilak though he had legal training never practised as a lawyer. But he developed the same habit and was known to study law reports to keep himself acquainted

with the legal position in various matters. That enabled him ably to conduct his defence in many of his cases. In writing an article on an important subject for the *Kesari* on the eve of a Congress Session, Tilak is said to have taken 36 hours to gather and collate all the facts. In one of the martial law cases discussed in *Young India,* Gandhiji strongly criticized bad draftsmanship which often spoils good causes. Gandhiji was himself a practised draftsman and has uttered a warning which is as valid today as it was forty-four years ago :

"I do wish as a practised draftsman" he wrote, "to warn writers of petitions, whether they be pleaders or otherwise, to think of the cause they may be espousing for the time being. I assure them that a bare statement of facts unembellished with adjectives is far more eloquent and effective than a narrative flowing with exuberant language."

Gandhiji has fairly admitted that he learnt this lesson from Gopal Krishna Gokhale and Dadabhai Naoroji who always impressed on him that, if he wanted to be heard, he must be brief, must write to the point and adhere to facts, must never travel beyond the cause under notice and that he should be most sparing in his adjectives. Gandhiji has added that if success attended his efforts it was due to his acceptance of what he characterises as 'golden advice' from these illustrious seniors and experienced politicians. The Gold Control Order leaves untouched such 'golden advice', but unfortunately such advice is never sought now nor is it available. The gold streaks in the mines of advice seem to have been completely exhausted.

10. Being a humanist to the core of his being, Gandhiji felt anguish at the sufferings and hardships of the litigants. His protests now and then against high

cost of litigation and exorbitant character of lawyers' fees were symptomatic of this spirit of humanism. A lawyer is undoubtedly entitled to reasonable remuneration for his experience, talents and troubles. It is true, at least in the case of junior lawyers, that dishonest clients often seek to deprive them of even this. At the other extreme are lawyers who are inclined to proceed on the economic principle of the demand for their talents and what they are able to get. This has no reference to dishonest lawyers who can always be brought to book under the disciplinary jurisdiction. Is it consistent with high professional standards to fix fees not compatible with the claim involved in the litigation? It is a difficult question to answer. But I believe it is permissible to say that putting a reasonable ceiling on lawyer's fee deserves to be tackled by lawyers themselves with the creation of a professional council on an all India basis. Gandhiji did not charge fees to his poor clients and I believe many lawyers always have been doing this. But it is for the Gandhi Smarak Nidhi to consider whether among its activities it should not interest itself in the problem of legal aid which has not yet been completely solved considering the interest that Gandhiji took in poor litigants.

11. In his speeches in the Federal Structure Committee of the Round Table Conference in 1931, Gandhiji showed considerable foresight in his demand for the establishment of a Federal or Supreme Court with the widest possible jurisdiction and with no Privy Council to revise its decisions. In the course of 19 years his vision has become a reality with the passage of the Abolition of the Privy Council Jurisdiction Act of 1949 and the creation of the Supreme Court which has established its reputation even outside the borders of India. But even then Gandhiji never thought that such

a court would be able to exercise its jurisdiction over the princely States, and unfortunately he did not live to see the happening of the miracle in 1948 itself when the princes consented to the merger of their States with the rest of India due to the statesmanship of Sardar Vallabhbhai Patel, then in charge of the Home Ministry.

12. One final point and I have done. A reference cannot be avoided to Gandhiji's views on civil resistance which is an important part of his legal philosophy. Some of you might remember how strongly he protested against the dictum of the Bombay High Court that "those who live by the law must keep the law". Commenting on this Gandhiji wrote :

"If it means that no lawyer may ever commit a civil breach without incurring the displeasure of the court, it means utter stagnation. Lawyers are persons most able to appreciate the dangers of bad legislation and it must be with them a sacred duty by committing a civil breach to prevent a criminal breach. Lawyers should be guardians of law and liberty and as such are interested in keeping the statute book of the country 'pure and undefiled'."

It is perhaps true that a situation contemplated by Gandhiji may not arise in an Independent India with a Constitution based on democratic principles. But when a body of lawyers condemns in strong terms legislative measures of Government as unconstitutional and objectionable, as has happened in recent times and may happen in future, it would be an interesting speculation as to what Gandhiji's reaction would have been if he had been alive today and shared the views of these lawyers.

13. As all of you are aware Gandhiji was considerably influenced by the teachings and writings

of Ruskin especially his *Unto This Last*. This is what Ruskin wrote on the function of the five honourable professions to be found in any civilized society.

"Five great intellectual professions relating to daily necessities of life have hitherto been in existence—there exist necessarily in every civilized nation: the soldier's profession to defend it; the pastor's to teach it; the physician's to keep it in health; the lawyer's to enforce justice in it; the merchant's to provide for it. And the duty of all these men is, on due occasions, to die for it. On due occasions, namely, the soldier rather than to leave his post in battle, the physician rather than to leave his post in plague, the pastor rather than to teach falsehood, the lawyer rather than countenance injustice. What is the due occasion for the merchant? It is the main question for the merchant as for all of us. For truly the man who does not know when to die, does not know how to live."

Gandhiji wrote in a similar vein in his *Young India* of November 1931, when he appealed to the professions to put their talents in the service of the country instead of converting them into £. s.d. Gandhiji wrote :

"If you are a medicine man there is disease enough in India to need all your medical skill. If you are a lawyer, there are differences and quarrels enough in India. Instead of fomenting more trouble, patch up those quarrels and stop litigation. If you are an engineer, build more houses suited to the means and needs of our people and yet full of health and fresh air. There is nothing that you have learnt which cannot be turned to account."

In those good old days of 1931, there was no problem of high soaring prices and black-marketeering. Otherwise I have no doubt that Gandhiji would have appealed to the merchants also more effectively perhaps than our public men are able to do now, to restrain their profiteering instincts.

14. It was Gandhiji's claim when he brought two litigants together that he had learnt the true practice of law and that he had learnt the better side of human nature and to enter men's minds. In one of the articles in a volume dedicated to Gandhiji on his 75th birthday in 1944, it is written :

"Many of the world's great figures have entered men's mind only to destroy human fellowship and goodwill. It is Gandhiji's great contribution to the civilization of his day that in entering men's mind he seeks not to destroy but to promote in their hearts a love for their fellowmen."

That was Gandhiji's contribution in the sphere of law also though he gave up the practice of law to serve the country to enable it to attain to the full stature of independent nationhood.

## APPENDIX IV
# GANDHIJI'S APPLICATION FOR ENROLMENT AS AN ADVOCATE OF THE BOMBAY HIGH COURT

Bombay
November 16, 1891

To,
The Prothonotary and Registrar
of the High Court of Judicature
at Bombay.
Sir,

I am desirous of being admitted as an Advocate of the High Court. I was called to the Bar in England on the 10th June last. I have kept twelve terms in the Inner Temple and I intend to practise in the Bombay Presidency.

I produce the certificate of my being called to the Bar. As to the certificate of my character and abilities, I have not been able to obtain any certificate from a judge in England, for I was not aware of the rules in force in the Bombay High Court. I, however, produce a certificate from Mr. W. D. Edwards, a practising Barrister in the Supreme Court of Judicature in England. He is the author of the *Compendium of the Law of Property in Land,* one of the books prescribed for the Bar final Examination.

I beg to remain,
Sir,
Your most obedient servant,
M. K. GANDHI

See *The Collected Works of Mahatma Gandhi,* Vol. I, pp.63-64.

# GANDHIJI'S CERTIFICATE OF BEING CALLED TO THE BAR BY INNER TEMPLE

## INNER TEMPLE

This is to Certify to whom it may concern That Mohandas Karamchand Gandhi of 20 Barons Court Road, West Kensington, the youngest son of Karamchand Uttamchand Gandhi of Porbander, India deceased, was generally admitted of The Honourable Society of the Inner Temple on the sixth day of November One thousand eight hundred and eighty eight and was called to the Bar by the same Society on the tenth day of June One thousand eight hundred and ninety one and has paid all duties to the House and to the Officers thereunto belonging.

In Testimony whereof I have hereunto set my hand and the Seal of the said Society this eleventh day of June in the year of Our Lord One thousand eight hundred and ninety one

Witness          Treasurer

*Mahatma, Life of Mohandas Karamchand Gandhi,* D. G. Tendulkar Vol. I, Times of India Press, Bombay (1951), p. 40

## APPENDIX VI
### CERTIFICATE FROM MR. W. D. EDWARDS, AUTHOR AND PRACTISING BARRISTER IN THE SUPREME COURT OF JUDICATURE IN ENGLAND RECOMMENDING GANDHIJI'S NAME FOR ADMISSION AS AN ADVOCATE OF THE HIGH COURT OF BOMBAY

11, Stone Buildings
Lincoln's Inn
9th June 1891

I beg to recommend Mr. M. K. Gandhi of the Inner Temple, who has been proposed for call to the Bar in England in the present term (Trinity 1891), and who as I understand will be duly called on the 10th instant, as a fit and proper person, upon his admission to the English Bar, to be admitted to practise as an advocate of the High Court of Bombay. Mr. Gandhi has resided in England for a period of about three years during which he has kept terms for the Bar. I believe that his career as a student of the Inns of Court has been in every respect creditable to him, and that he is a gentleman of unexceptionable character.

William Douglas Edwards
11 Stone Buildings
Lincoln's Inn
Barrister at Law
of Lincoln's Inn

*Mahatma, Life of Mohandas Karamchand Gandhi,*
D. G. Tendulkar Vol. I, Times of India Press, Bombay
(1951), p. 40

## APPENDIX VII

## TRUE COPY OF THE ORDER ISSUED BY THE BENCHERS OF INNER TEMPLE ON 10TH NOVEMBER 1922 DISBARRING GANDHIJI AND REMOVING HIS NAME FROM THE ROLL OF BARRISTERS ON HIS CONVICTION AND SENTENCE TO SIX YEARS' IMPRISONMENT ON 18TH MARCH 1922 BY THE COURT OF THE SESSIONS JUDGE, AHMEDABAD

Inner Temple

At a Parliament holden
Friday, 10th day of November 1922

WHEREAS at a Bench Table holden on the 7th day of November 1922 the Treasurer having reported that he had received a certified copy of the conviction and sentence to six years' imprisonment of Mohandas Karamchand Gandhi a Barrister of this Inn at the Court of the Sessions Judge, Ahmedabad, India on the 18th of March 1922 for sedition. It was ordered — That Mohandas Karamchand Gandhi having been convicted by a competent Tribunal of an offence which in the opinion of the Bench disqualifies him from continuing a Member of the Inn should have his name removed from the books. And at the same Bench Table. It was further ordered — That at the Parliament to be holden on Friday the 10th day of November 1922 the said Mohandas Karamchand Gandhi be disbarred and his name removed from the books of this society and that this Order be communicated to the judges of the Supreme Court of Judicature to the other Inns of Court to the General Council of the Bar and by registered letter to the said Mohandas Karamchand Gandhi and be screened in the Hall.

It is at this Parliament ordered — That the said Order be and the same is hereby confirmed and the said Mohandas Karamchand Gandhi is hereby disbarred and his name removed from the books of this society.

Walter G. Wrangham
Sub-Treasurer

*Mahatma, Life of Mohandas Karamchand Gandhi,* by D. G. Tendulkar Vol. 2, Times of India Press, Bombay (1951) p. 136

## APPENDIX VIII
## LETTER TO THE AUTHOR
## FROM THE RT. HON. LORD DENNING

The Lawn,
Whitchurch, Hants.
15 December, 1984

Dear Mr. Kher,

Thank you very much for your letter and especially for *The Law and the Lawyers* by M. K. Gandhi which you compiled and edited.

I have always been interested in Mahatma Gandhi because, as you know, he was a member of the Inner Temple and was called to the Bar here in England in 1891. Very recently, I was present when a special portrait of him was unveiled in the library of the Inner Temple. I have also been much interested in the Great Trial and have seen sketches reproducing it. I am very glad that the book has gone into the 4th edition and been recommended by the universities. This must be most satisfying and encouraging for you.

Thank you for your very kind remarks about my own books. I am very glad that the latest one, *Landmarks in the Law,* has already arrived in Bombay where I have many friends. I do not know whether I shall be able to write any more books because I am getting old now, but I will see if I can think of something.

It is kind of you to send me Christmas greetings, and Lady Denning joins me now in sending you our very best wishes for Christmas and the New Year, and we wish you continued success and happiness in law and in life.

Yours sincerely,
Denning

Mr. Sunit B. Kher,
51 Mahatma Gandhi Road,
Fort, Bombay 400 001

# GLOSSARY

Ahimsa - Non-violence; positively the practice of love.

Ashram - A hermitage; a place for study and discipline of life; a quiet place where people having common ideals lead a community life and follow a particular discipline. The place where Gandhiji resided with his co-workers and disciples was referred to as the Ashram.

Bania - Hindu merchant or trader; member of the third caste among the Hindus, whose traditional occupation is trade and commerce.

Bhai - Brother; comrade. This word is used as an affix and as a term in addressing a gentleman.

Brahman - The first or the highest of the four castes sanctioned by the Hindu religion (literally, one who knows Brahman).

Chaprasis - Peons in uniforms.

Coolie - Term for porter or hired labourer; in South Africa, indiscriminately applied to all Indians.

Crore - Ten millions.

Dayada - Relative; dependent.

Dharma - Religion; moral law or practice; duty. A comprehensive Sanskrit term embracing the concepts of law, justice, duty and virtue rolled into one.

Diwan - Chief minister of a princely state.

Foujdar - The chief constable or sub-inspector of police.

Gadi - A throne; a post of authority.

Hartal - A strike; temporary suspension of business or work as a mark of protest or mourning.

Islam - The religion of the Prophet Muhammad.

Ji - An affix added to names denoting respect, e.g. Gandhiji.

Khaddar or Khadi - Hand-woven cloth from hand-spun yarn.

Khalifa or Caliph - The religious head of Islam.

Khilafat - The office of Caliph.

Khilafat Movement - A movement organized in India by the Indian Muslims under the leadership of Maulana Muhammad Ali, from 1919 to 1924 in order to defend the office of the Caliph of Turkey and to restore his powers as the Head of the Muslim Faith. In 1924, after the proclamation of the Turkish Republic the office of the Caliph in Turkey was abolished by the decision of Mustafa Kemal Pasha. Thus the Indian Khilafat Movement ceased to exist in 1924.

Lakh - One hundred thousand.

Langarkhanas - Community kitchens where food is served free of costs.

Lokmanya - Respected by the people. An honorific title conferred by the people on the late Bal Gangadhar Tilak.

Mahatma - A high-souled man; a noble-minded man; a great soul; a title generally given to Saints. In later years, Gandhi was generally referred to in India as the Mahatma.

Malgujar - A system of land holding (Zamindari) in the former C.P. and Berar Province of which Nagpur was the capital.

Maulana - A learned Muslim divine.

*Mitakshara* - It is a running commentary on the Yajnavalkyasmriti or the Institutes of Yajnavalkya. Yajnavalkyasmriti was compiled by the great sage Yajnavalkya in about the first century after Christ. Mitakshara was written in the latter part of the eleventh century by Vijnaneshwara. In the Mitakshara one finds the quintessence of the Smriti law and its precepts and injunctions. The chief merit of the work consists in its synthesizing of various Smriti texts. It is of supreme authority throughout India except in Bengal where the Dayabhaga of Jimutavahana is given paramount importance. In Bengal the *Mitakshara* is more revered than followed, but its authority is not questioned on points on which there is no conflict between it and the works prevalent there.

Moharrirs - Clerks.

Moplahs - a tribe of Musalmans living in South India in the State of Kerala.

Musalman - Follower of Islam.

Muslim - Belonging to Islam.

Parsi - A follower of Zoroastrianism.

Pugree - Turban.

Ryot - Peasant.

Sabha - An assembly, a meeting.

Sahib - A master; a gentleman; a term of respect; an European.

Samaj - An assembly.

Sanad - A commission, a charter, a giant, a warrant.

Sannyasi - One who has renounced the worldly life; a recluse.

Sapinda - A blood relation or kinsman connected by offering of balls of rice *(pinda)*. The affinity extends to six male descendants in the male line and six male ascendants in the male line. Under the *Mitakshara* the Sapinda relationship arises between two people through their being connected by particles of one body, namely, that of the common ancestor, in other words, from community of blood in contradistinction to the Dayabhaga notion of community in the offering of religious oblation.

Satyagraha - A force which is born of truth and love or non-violence; a tenacious clinging to truth; civil or non-violent resistance; literally, holding on to truth. Name given by Gandhiji to the technique of non-violent resistance as practised by him and under his guidance.

Satyagrahi - One practising Satyagraha.

Shastras - Institutes of religion, law or letters; scriptures.

Shirastedar - Head clerk in a Court of Justice.

Smritis - Social and religious codes of conduct as delivered originally by Manu and other law-givers to their respective pupils and committed by them, from memory, to writing.

Streedhan - Property altogether at the disposal of the wife.

Swadeshi - Manufacture of one's own country; belonging to, or made in one's own country.

Swami - Holy man; master.

Swaraj - Self-government; self-rule.

Tehsildar - The Officer in charge of Tehsil, a subdivision of a district.

# INDEX

297